THE SOCIAL IDEAS
OF THE
NORTHERN EVANGELISTS

NUMBER 580

COLUMBIA STUDIES IN THE SOCIAL SCIENCES

EDITED BY
THE FACULTY OF POLITICAL SCIENCE
OF COLUMBIA UNIVERSITY

THE SOCIAL IDEAS
OF THE
NORTHERN EVANGELISTS

NUMBER 580

COLUMBIA STUDIES IN THE SOCIAL SCIENCES

EDITED BY
THE FACULTY OF POLITICAL SCIENCE
OF COLUMBIA UNIVERSITY

THE SOCIAL IDEAS
OF THE
NORTHERN EVANGELISTS
1826-1860

By CHARLES C. COLE, Jr.

OCTAGON BOOKS

A DIVISION OF FARRAR, STRAUS AND GIROUX

New York   1977

PREFACE

ONE OF the most fascinating and most challenging phases of history is the study of ideas—their evolution, transmission, and influence on the actions of men. While political and economic factors frequently are of primary importance in explaining the past, nevertheless the thoughts men live by, their attitudes, opinions, and prejudices often shape the course of events.

This is a study of the ideas of a group of men who, while holding responsible posts in a profession carrying religious authority, were in a position through their secular pronouncements to influence many in their generation. Although eventually during the expanding industrialization and materialism of the nineteenth century they came to resemble voices crying in the wilderness, the thoughts and writings of American Protestant evangelists were frequently compelling and persuasive in the years before the Civil War.

To Dr. John A. Krout, Vice President of Columbia University, under whose guidance this study was begun, and to Professor Richard B. Morris, whose wise counseling helped to bring it to completion, I owe an immeasurable debt of gratitude. I am also deeply grateful to Professors Dumas Malone, Harry J. Carman, and Henry Steele Commager of Columbia University and Professor Robert T. Handy of Union Theological Seminary for their criticism of the manuscript and for their helpful suggestions. I am indebted to Lawrence H. Chamberlain and Nicholas M. McKnight, Deans of Columbia College, whose constant encouragement was a source of strength. Grateful acknowledgement is due the many librarians whose cheerful co-operation turned the task of research into a fascinating journey of discovery. To my wife, Mary, I am grateful for her ever-present, cheerful support. What errors of fact or interpretation there remain, however, are my own.

CHARLES C. COLE, JR.

CONTENTS

THE SOCIAL IDEAS
OF THE
NORTHERN EVANGELISTS

I. INTRODUCTION

We live Brother Finney in a wonderful age. What mighty overturnings both in the moral and political world! I am expecting some astonishing overturnings in the providence of God, both in church and state, the world over.[1]

Who cannot see and feel that we have entered upon a new era, *that men are loosening their hold upon the things they once held most dear and sacred, and are beginning to enquire what is right irrespective of past usages and opinions.*[2]

The purpose of this work is to study the secular ideas of the Northern evangelists during the years 1826 to 1860 and to evaluate their influence on American social and intellectual development. The nineteenth-century evangelists, in addition to playing colorful roles in religious affairs, engaged in public campaigns of their time and in sermon, book, pamphlet, diary, and letter expressed ideas on political, economic, and social issues which helped mold the opinions and prejudices of a large body of the American public.

This survey embraces the high-water mark of nineteenth-century evangelism, the decade of the 1830's, and covers a crucial period in American religious and social history. The year 1826 marks the start of the major revivals in New York state led by Charles G. Finney, most famous of the nineteenth-century evangelists, and serves appropriately as the beginning of the study. Because of the changes brought about by the Civil War, the year 1860 is a logical terminal point.

The number of evangelists during the period is legion. I have attempted to include a group that would be a cross-section of the profession, comprising as many sects and backgrounds as possible.

---

[1] Dirck C. Lansing to Charles G. Finney, Feb. 25, 1832 (Finney Papers, Oberlin College Library).

[2] Angelina Grimké Weld to Sarah (Grimké), Jan., 1845 (Weld Papers, Library of Congress).

In addition to the major figures, the Finneys and Beechers of the period, I have included some lesser known men where they more accurately reflect the attitudes of their group. Where appropriate I have attempted to relate evangelistic thought to that of the clergy at large. Although I have considered the theological ideas of these men where pertinent, my main concern has been with their secular ideas and with their influence on American life and thought apart from their purely religious contributions. Some biographical material has been included but the work is divided along topical rather than individual lines.

For the most part, I have limited my examination to Northern evangelists and have omitted consideration of the large number active during this period below the Mason and Dixon line. The marked social and cultural differences between the North and South in the ante-bellum era, the difficulties of organization with a large diverse group of individuals, and the inaccessibility to the writer of Southern sources warranted narrowing the focus to the Northern field. Indeed, the study of Southern evangelistic secular thought is a major undertaking in itself and deserves a separate treatment by someone thoroughly familiar with that section's history.

The examination of ideas and the measure of their import is a perilous task. The weighing of the power of a sermon, book, or tract defies the statistician's scales. Ministers especially have a following among the mute millions that written records never can reveal. The student who attempts to gauge a person's hold over his fellow men must recognize his limitations. Although I have attempted wherever possible to interpret the secular ideas of the individuals studied, I have avoided drawing any unfounded inferences. Here will be found no theories about the subconscious minds of the evangelists, no psychoanalytic formulas for explaining the mysteries of religious devotion, no probing beyond the veil of ego and id. Such matters may well be left to those sufficiently trained to undertake the task.

Before proceeding, a number of definitions are necessary. Evangelism, in its strictest sense, means the preaching of the gospel, its proclamation to the unregenerate. It is generally applied to those beliefs held by orthodox Christians which stress the sinfulness of man's nature, the personal relationship of man with his God, his divine salvation through faith, and the need for conversion through preaching and other means. In America in the nineteenth century, evangelism was associated with those Protestant sects—principally Methodist, Baptist, Presbyterian, and Congregational—which were least ritualistic and which most emphasized the personal role of the individual in his search for salvation. Evangelism was closely linked with missionary activities, utilized humanitarian philanthropic operations as a means to its end, and was most characteristically expressed in revivals.[3]

The word "evangelist," originally translated from the Greek to mean the "bringer of good tidings" or the preacher of the gospel, and often used to describe the authors of the Gospels, may be applied to one who engages in and is the agent of evangelism and who in his preaching stresses the conversion of mankind to religion. In modern times the term has been applied to a minister, sometimes an itinerant, who preaches primarily to arouse religious interest at either regular or special religious services. His purpose was the renewal of religious interest, the prevention of spiritual decline, and the wider extension of the gospel, quantitatively through conversions and qualitatively through greater devotion of church members. Albert Barnes, a nineteenth-century evangelist, described his profession in these terms: "The office was distinct from that of the pastor, the teacher and the prophet . . . in which preaching was the main thing." [4] In addition, the evangelist was generally more concerned with religious experience than with theology.

In a broader sense the term can be attached to one who is a spokesman for a cause. We speak of evangelists of democracy, evangelists of education, evangelists of world government. Evangelist, in this respect, denotes one who has an overpowering zeal

---

[3] See Jackson, ed., *The New Schaff-Herzog Encyclopedia of Religious Knowledge*, IV, 225; Mathews and Smith, *A Dictionary of Religion and Ethics*, p. 156; Biederwolf, *Evangelism: Its Justification, Its Operation and Its Value*.

[4] Quoted in Headley, *Evangelists in the Church*, p. 7.

for some issue, whose enthusiasm leads him to advocate its beliefs, and who is willing to sacrifice much in the attainment of his goal.

For the purposes of this study, an evangelist is defined as a minister of an evangelical church who, through his preaching and his pen, sought to advance the cause of Christianity, made special efforts to gain converts, and endeavored to invigorate religion.

The term "revival" is usually applied to a special religious service, or series of services, in which attempts are made to attract the attention of the unconverted and to add to the membership of the church. It presupposes the necessity of conversion, of "getting religion, a change of heart," and involves a public act or commitment indicating this change and eventually meaning the acceptance into full church membership.[5] The aim of those who conducted revivals was to induce members of their audience to make this commitment, to have "a mild, but constant and intense desire of heart for the awakening and conversion of sinners."[6]

Other descriptions of revivalism might make the subject more meaningful. Robert Baird, one of the nineteenth century's religious historians, called revivals "extraordinary seasons of religious interest." Calvin Colton, who took part in a few himself, described them as "great public religious excitements, powerfully affecting the public mind . . . the result of which ordinarily is the apparent and hopeful conversion of many souls unto God, by tens, by fifties, and by hundreds." An English critic was content to call them simply "a species of stimulus, common . . . to almost every sect and creed." One who underwent a religious experience in a revival, however, had a less concise definition: "It is difficult . . . to make those understand whose souls are darkened. A revival means just an elegant kindling of the spirit; it is brought about to the Lord's people by the hands of his saints, and it means salvation in the highest."[7]

---

[5] See Beardsley, *A History of American Revivals*, p. 1; Nichols, *Forty Years of American Life, 1821-1861*, II, 51.

[6] Lyman Beecher to Catherine Beecher, June 30, 1826, in Charles Beecher, ed., *Autobiography, Correspondence . . . of Lyman Beecher*, II, 64.

[7] Baird, *The Progress and Prospects of Christianity in the United States*, p. 443; Colton, *History and Character of American Revivals of Religion*, pp. 1-2; Marryat, *A Diary in America, 1837-1838*, III, 127; Trollope, *Domestic Manners of the Americans*, I, 157-158.

A revival emphasized the emotional rather than the rational elements in religion and centered around the individual rather than on church organization or its government. Revivalism was, as the European theologian Visser T'Hooft has pointed out, the American parallel of Pietism. It produced what Ralph H. Gabriel has called "Romantic Christianity." [8]

During the 1830's a group of ministers devoted much of their energy to fostering revivals and what had once appeared to be special or unusual became commonplace. Generally, it was the more enthusiastic clergy who traveled about the country, preaching for two or three weeks at several services throughout the day in an effort to rouse the inhabitants. Evangelistic methods proved so successful that the reliance placed on this means of enhancing the church membership grew; and in time what had been the exception became the rule, what had been attempted sporadically was resorted to regularly. Calvin Colton noted this new development when he stated, "It is only within a few years, that the promotion of revivals by human instrumentality has, to any considerable extent, been made a subject of study, and an object of systematic effort." [9]

What made evangelism a powerful force in the ante-bellum era was not only its expansion but also its connection with the many efforts to improve society which were then prevalent. Albert Barnes, the Presbyterian minister, may have been too enthusiastic about revivals when he declared, "they are the most remarkable phenomena of our times . . . and have done more than any other single cause to form the public mind in this country," but he was not incorrect when he added, "and society has received some of its most decided directions from these deep and far-pervading revolutions." [10] The rise of these social and moral reform movements

---

[8] Visser T'Hooft, *The Background of the Social Gospel in America*, p. 126; Gabriel, *The Course of American Democratic Thought*, p. 33.

[9] Colton, *History and Character of American Revivals of Religion*, p. 4.

[10] Albert Barnes, "Revivals of Religion in Cities and Large Towns," *The American National Preacher*, XV, No. 1 (Jan. 1841) 1. Gilbert H. Barnes, *The Anti-slavery Impulse*, gives credit to the revivals of Finney for having much to do with the later social crusades of the period. See also Keller, *The Second Great Awakening in Connecticut*, p. 58.

served in turn to intensify subsequent revivals and to enhance the revivalist's influence.   Before turning to the evangelists themselves, we must glance briefly at the American scene as this country stood on the threshold of the Finneyite revivals of 1826.

In July, 1826, the United States was fifty years young.   Emerging out of its infancy into a vigorous adolescence, the expanding nation paused on the brink of a new era.   The twenty-four states now numbered eleven million people who, constantly pushing into the Western lands, had reached the banks of the Missouri River. In spite of the nation's short history, Independence Day and the tradition of flag-waving oratory had already become well rooted. The Fourth of July that year was celebrated "with more than the usual splendor throughout the Union." [11]   Revolutionary War veterans, although declining in numbers, could still recall the exploits of their day, and though memories of the country's struggle for independence were beginning to dim, cannon balls of the Revolution scattered about on the battlefields of Saratoga, Princeton, and Monmouth served as reminders of less secure days.   The sudden deaths of both Jefferson and Adams, eighteenth-century leaders, were symbolic of the old period's passing.

To most Americans, 1826 was just another year.   John Quincy Adams was stubbornly steering the ship of state.   The government, enjoying prosperous times, was flourishing financially, and its energies were directed toward such matters as the commercial interests of its citizens, internal improvements, the organization of a militia, and the establishment of a naval academy.   The Monroe Doctrine was still in its infancy.   Congress was lethargically debating whether or not to send representatives to a Panamanian conference.   Two of the nation's more belligerent politicians, Henry Clay and John Randolph, created a furor by fighting a duel.   By the middle of the year Andrew Jackson had already begun his second campaign for the presidency, and by autumn public interest in the coming election, still two years away, was increasing.   And casting a long shadow before him, C. C. Cam-

---

[11] *Christian Spectator*, VIII, No. 8 (1826), 439.

breling in the halls of Congress chided Edward Everett for his pro-slavery views.[12]

To a few, however, this year marked a milestone. One contemporary journalist described America's growth in these words: "A new era now commenced in its history. Instead of being the relation of fruitless remonstrances against partial commercial regulations, and resistance to colonial oppressions, it became the record of discussions and measures, all having in view the welfare and essential independence of this hemisphere."[13] Almost simultaneously a number of groups organized to further these "discussions and measures" for the benefit of the world. The American Home Missionary Society was organized on May 6, 1826. The American Peace Society and American Temperance Society were started at about this time. The American Tract Society, designed to print and distribute moralistic pamphlets, held its first anniversary meeting in May, 1826. In the same year a society to improve the conditions of sailors was established. On July 4th, 1826, Robert Owen made public his Declaration of Mental Independence and endeavored to save his utopia at New Harmony, Indiana. Acting in a different spirit Josiah Holbrook founded the American Lyceum, while in Massachusetts Horace Mann set about opening coeducational high schools. The winds of intellectual and social ferment were rising.

This year also marked a gain for democracy. In 1826 the New York State constitution was finally amended to abolish tax qualifications for white male voters. The democratic cause gained a champion when young George Bancroft spoke out in favor of "a democracy, a determined uncompromising democracy."[14] Nonetheless, in 1826 large numbers were still disfranchised and the Negro was still enslaved.

The advent of a new epoch in the country's economic growth was heralded at this time. During the year almost twenty thousand craft used the new Erie and Champlain canals, linking the

---

[12] McMaster, *A History of the People of the United States*, V, 442, 502. Schlesinger, *The Age of Jackson*, p. 63.

[13] *American Annual Register*, II, 5.

[14] Bancroft, *An Oration Delivered on the Fourth of July, 1826*, p. 19.

rising East with the expanding West. The following year the
Baltimore and Ohio Railroad received its charter and a new age in
transportation began. From 1825 to 1827 the workers of the
North organized numerous local societies to improve their condition, and this period has traditionally been considered as marking,
weak though it was, the beginning of the labor movement.[15]

The year 1826 was also one of intellectual attainments. James
Fenimore Cooper published *The Last of the Mohicans;* Noah Webster was working on his *American Dictionary;* William Cullen
Bryant, soon to edit the *Evening Post,* arrived in New York; and
Jared Sparks spent the summer traveling through the states searching for George Washington's letters. William Lloyd Garrison,
twenty-one and devoutly orthodox, settled in Boston in that year
and worshipped at the church of Lyman Beecher, another new-
comer to Boston society. Further west the Gerrit Smiths quietly
joined the Presbyterian church in Peterboro, New York. Elsewhere in the Mohawk Valley an unknown itinerant preacher was
"rattling the dry bones" and "reaping a harvest" in a series of
revivals that were soon to make him famous. His name was
Charles Grandison Finney.

What of this age that marked its birth in the 1820's? Historians have given it a variety of names—"the age of moral reform," "the era of social unrest," "the age of the common man,"
"the ante-bellum years," "the middle period"—none of which adequately describes the complex, intricate pattern of events that
took place in the years from 1826 to 1860. More than anything
else this was, in the words of Alice Felt Tyler, a period of "restless
ferment." [16] These were the years when great humanitarian
movements were popular, when temperance and antislavery societies were most vigorous, when missionary societies flourished,
and when education, women's rights, improvement of the condition of the poor, and penal reform were matters of public interest.
Permeating them all was a strong religious force—a moralistic enthusiasm linked, as we shall see, with the many revivals which
were in themselves characteristic of the era.

[15] Commons, *History of Labor in the United States,* I, 169.
[16] Tyler, *Freedom's Ferment,* p. 142.

Difficult though it is to separate the tangled threads of this age, several major traits stand out. First, the years 1820 to 1860 were marked by the rapid physical growth of the nation. The receding frontier, while certainly not the determinant factor the Turner school has claimed, did serve to mold the growth of the American civilization and the pattern of American thought. An expanding society is a dynamic one, and this was an age of expansion.

Second, this was an era of energy. A contemporary traveler caught the spirit well when he wrote, "At present all is energy and enterprise; everything is in a state of transition, but of rapid improvement . . . ten years in America is almost equal to a century in the old continent." [17] Americans themselves were aware of this:

A great spirit of improvement prevails in our country. . . . Never, I suppose, was so much mind at work, and never was matter in such agitation. We are certainly more active than our fathers, if not wiser, and I verily believe we excel them in energy & wisdom. Poor mother earth was never so beat & exercised as now.[18]

Then, too, this age was characterized by an emphasis on organizing, associating, combining for concerted action. As one man put it, "Everything which before had been carried out in scattered, sporadic methods now tended to organization." [19] Indeed, Americans seemed struck with a mania for joining organized movements.

A fourth characteristic of Americans in this age was their boundless optimism, their faith in the future and their assumption, common to the Western world in the nineteenth century, of an inevitable progress. Lewis Tappan, outstanding New York merchant, represented his time when he reflected, "This is a century of inventions. The human mind has received a great impulse, and vast improvements have been made in intellectual, moral, & philosophical matters." [20] Others put it more picturesquely: "Dr. Beecher says 'he would rather live in this day than in the meridian splendor of the millenium.' " [21]

[17] Marryat, A Diary in America, I, 17
[18] Lewis Tappan to Benjamin Tappan, May 14, 1825 (Benjamin Tappan Papers).
[19] Murray, Francis Wayland, pp. 1-2.
[20] Lewis Tappan to Benjamin Tappan, July 9, 1831 (Benjamin Tappan Papers).
[21] Laura F. Judd to Mr. and Mrs. Finney, Oct. 30, 1827 (Finney Papers).

Furthermore, this was a period in our history when religion played a prominent role. While the majority of Americans were, as usual, neither "profane nor pious," an increased fervor manifested itself, especially in the evangelical churches throughout the country, and the result was a coloring of every subject—from the reform of politics to the attack against prostitution—with religious qualities. That master observer of American customs, Tocqueville, summed this up when he remarked, "There is no country in the world where the Christian religion retains a greater influence over the souls of men than in America." [22]

Religious fervor was not the only type of enthusiasm observed in America during this period. Mrs. Trollope quoted a compatriot who found a more sordid spirit in the United States and declared that "in following, in meeting, or in overtaking, in the street, on the roads, or in the fields, at the theatre, the coffee-house, or at home, he had never overheard Americans conversing without the word DOLLAR being pronounced between them." [23] Indeed, another trait of the times might be said to have been an emphasis on extremes, on fanaticism, or "ultraism." "Undoubtedly the great error of the times in which we live," wrote one critic, "is a tendency to ultraism, not only in regard to the concerns of religion, but likewise in respect to most if not all the great principles and objects which are now engrossing the attention of man. We are running into extremes upon almost everything we undertake." [24]

Expansion, energy, organization, optimism, religious zeal, and ultraism stand out as major attributes of this age. The term adolescence is perhaps after all the most appropriate title for these hectic years.

If religion and religious enthusiasm played an important part in American life in the ante-bellum years, the American clergy played an even more dominant role. Ministers were the guardians of morality, the teachers and the revealers of divine truth. They were the spokesmen of truth and right and their word often con-

[22] Tocqueville, *Democracy in America*, p. 285.
[23] Trollope, *Domestic Manners of the Americans*, I, 137.
[24] Stone, *Matthias and His Impostures*, p. 321. For a protest against this ultraism, see Reese, *The Humbugs of New York*.

tained the forcefulness of law. Indeed, considering their following and their respected place in society, almost no other single
class or group exerted as much prolonged and varied influence
upon American thought and society as did the American clergy.
Many foreign observers concluded that the clergy exercised "a
powerful influence on opinion," and even Daniel Webster paid
tribute to the role of the minister in shaping American society.[25]

Before studying the clergy's influence, however, we must consider the condition of the religious denominations in the years
1820 to 1860. Statistically, this period was one of growth for all
religious sects. In 1820 the Presbyterians, for instance, numbered
73,000 communicants and had over 1,200 churches. In one decade they had increased their membership by 100,000 and added
almost a thousand churches. From 1830 to 1833, the period of
widespread revivals, 60,000 more communicants were added.
During the late 1830's, because of controversies within the sect,
reaction from the enthusiasm of the earlier revivals, and the financial panic of 1837, the Presbyterian Church suffered a setback,
but by 1850 that church could count some 487,000 followers.
The Methodists made similar strides. By 1850 their membership
was over one and one quarter million. The Baptists and Congregationalists, though smaller sects numerically, showed equally
strong gains during this period. During the years 1826-1832 it
has been estimated that over 200,000 were added to the evangelical
churches.[26]

The first half of the nineteenth century marked an increase
from 365,000 to some three and one half million members in the
Protestant churches. These years show a relative increase as well
as an absolute one. In 1800, one out of every fifteen was connected with a Protestant church. By 1835, the ratio was one out
of eight, indicating the magnitude of the 1830 revivals. And by

---

[25] Combe, *Notes on the United States of North America*, I, 170; Webster, *Works
of Daniel Webster*, VI, 140-141.

[26] Church statistics are notoriously inaccurate. See, however, Sweet, *The American
Churches*, p. 42; Thompson, *A History of the Presbyterian Churches in the United States*
(American Church History Series, Vol. VI), pp. 93, 126; Gillett, *History of the Pres-
byterian Church in the United States of America*, II, 499 ff.

1850, one out of every seven was a church member.[27]   The influence of an institution such as the church cannot, of course, be
measured by statistics alone.   Other intangible elements—the extent of interest and participation of church members, the regularity with which they come under its control, their dependence
upon it for social or economic reasons—must also be considered.
One is led to conclude that the ante-bellum period was one in
which the American churches thrived and increased their influence
over the thought and habits of the American people.

Although there was great diversity among the various sects during these years, they present a number of common denominators.
First of all, most church members believed that their religion was
the true one, that Christianity was the preserver of all that was
good in their civilization, and that the hand of Providence guided
their own and their nation's destinies.   Most of them held the
same view as that expressed by Lewis Tappan: that "christianity is
the conservator of all that is dear in civil liberty & human happiness; and that infidelity sets loose all the base passions of our nature." [28]

Then, too, church leaders had an almost inflexible belief in the
importance of what they were doing.   We shall see later that
much of the difficulty encountered by evangelists stemmed not
only from their own stubborn dogmatism but also from their un-
shakable assurance that what they said or were about to do was of
vital importance to everyone.   One sermon, one pamphlet, one
conversion was always to them just the thing needed to turn the
tide.   One of their number expressed this certainty in their own
self-importance when he wrote, "I want to see our State evangelized.   Suppose the great State of New York in its physical,
political, moral, commercial and pecuniary resources should come
over to the Lord's side.   Why it would turn the scale and could
convert the world. . . . I shall have no rest till it is done." [29]

---

[27] Loud, *Evangelized America*, p. 195; Grund, *The Americans, in Their Moral, Social,
and Political Relations*, pp. 162-163.   In some sections of the country the figures were
even higher.   In Connecticut, by 1840, church members numbered one out of every
four or five in the population.   Combe, *Notes on the United States of North America*,
II, 146.

[28] Lewis Tappan to Benjamin Tappan, Dec. 12, 1829 (Benjamin Tappan Papers).

[29] M. Hunter to Charles G. Finney, June 7, 1828 (Finney Papers).

A third common denominator was the overwhelming preoccupation of both clergy and laymen with spiritual affairs, with
what Paxton Hibben calls "the absorption in the welfare of the
soul." [30] This emphasis on the spiritual side of one's nature was
nothing new. From Augustine to Bunyan the examples of such a
religious state of mind are legion. For the 1830's, however, the
extent of such introspection seems to have been almost unprece-
dented in modern times. Typical was the following expression of
this at the start of a revival: "How often with wonder and aston-
ishment do I bless the Lord for his goodness in permitting *me un-
worthy me* to live in Rome in the year 1826 and witness such
wonderful displays of his peace, in reviving his own dear children
and the salvation of precious immortal souls." [31] Filling letters
and finishing conversations with such statements became almost a
fad:

How apt am I to be off my guard in time of temptation, and often for
want of resolution shirk from duty under the pretence of inability, instead of placing my confidence in God when feeling my own weakness;
& in every sense my conduct illy becomes a follower of Christ. It is
truly astonishing that the world at best a transient shadow of happiness,
should ever so engross the heart of an expectant if eternal & supreme
felicity, as with so little resistance to carry him along in its shallow
stream. What can be compared with the wicked heart? Who that
knows it can doubt that it is deceitful above all things & desperately
wicked. [32]

Looking at his society, the nineteenth-century religious man
was likely to couple this preoccupation with the future of his soul
with a pessimistic view of the world around him. One minister, a
member of Finney's "holy band," expressed his opinion of the
world about him in this fashion: "From what I know and from
what I hear I do not doubt but there is a spirit of *worldliness—of
covetousness—of temporizing with this ungodly world—of
pride.*" Another living in western New York blamed the Erie

[30] Hibben, *Henry Ward Beecher: an American Portrait*, p. 25. For an example of
this preoccupation with one's soul see Harriet Porter Beecher to Lyman Beecher (n.d.),
Charles Beecher, ed., *Autobiography, Correspondence, . . . of Lyman Beecher*, I, 356-357.
[31] Almira Selden to Mrs. Finney, June 8, 1826 (Finney Papers).
[32] Rhoda Churchill to Mrs. Finney, May 4, 1828 (Finney Papers).

Canal for bringing the "evils rolling through our land and among us" and reported "the people and the church say it cannot be helped—and why do they say this? because the state of religion is so low." The general conclusion seemed to be that the world was "in a dull state" and that "a general apathy seems to brood over the land." [33] Perhaps the worried evangelist was nearer the truth than he realized. To many, there was ample evidence that moral standards in the United States were lower than in Europe and that constant exertions were required to fight the spread of "atheism and infidelity." [34]

Perhaps because of the certainty of their beliefs and a preoccupation with their own spiritual welfare, the nineteenth-century American church members and preachers were endowed with a remarkable amount of intolerance. The dogmatism of evangelists, as expressed in politics, in anti-Catholicism, or in opposition to other sects, will be observed later at length. Suffice to say, Americans gained a reputation early in the century for their bigotry. One observer, comparing Americans with his compatriots, declared, "They differ essentially from the English sectaries in being more solemnly bigoted, more intolerant, and more ignorant of the Scriptures." [35] How better to express this intolerance than in Lewis Tappan's words: "He who scoffs at christianity, or attempts to subvert what are deemed the foundations of the social fabrick, is considered as an enemy to public peace." [36]

With these characteristics, religion and the various accouterments of religion played an important part in affecting the future course of American development. Evangelists, as standard bearers of their sects, had an opportunity to shape the pattern of thought during the ante-bellum years. In political pronouncements, in economic theorizing, in leading various humanitarian movements, and in crusading against slavery, they left their mark on history.

---

[33] H. H. Kellog to Finney, March 26, 1828; Josiah Bissell to Finney, Sept. 15, 1829; Lewis Tappan to Finney, July 10, 1833 (Finney Papers).

[34] Trollope, *Domestic Manners of the Americans*, I, 138; Marryat, *A Diary in America, 1837-1838*, III, 103.

[35] Fearon, *Sketches of America*, p. 47.

[36] Lewis Tappan to Benjamin Tappan, March 8, 1827 (Benjamin Tappan Papers).

Before considering their secular views, however, we must turn our attention to the careers of some of the leading evangelists who stormed across the land during these years.

II. THE NORTHERN EVANGELISTS

One can hardly be in earnest without sometimes using strong language.[1]

*If there is any man on earth who has confidence in you it is the writer.
But you are not infallible and never professed to be. Still I think (I
may be mistaken!) that you have fewer faults than most men. How is
it then that so many people speak ill of you?*[2]

To SPEAK OF EVANGELISTS as though they were all similar is
misleading. They came from different backgrounds, preached
different doctrines, and conducted revivals in a variety of ways.
Their personalities differed; their successes and failures varied. Indeed, their diversity and individuality were their most common
characteristics. But while they differed among themselves, their
lives, careers, and attitudes present, for the most part, a strikingly
homogeneous pattern.

In 1826 some of the leading eighteenth-century evangelistic
figures were still on the scene. The old order was reluctant to yield
to the new, and those men who had lived through the Revolution
and had fought the fight against infidelism shortly thereafter
looked askance at the vigorous, rising generation. Such a man was
Nathaniel Emmons. Born in 1745 of Connecticut parentage,
graduated from Yale in 1767 at a time when its training was poor,
Emmons studied under various ministers, revealing early in his
career an intellectual interest in theology. He was licensed to
preach in 1769, and after several years of itinerant preaching he
settled at a church in Franklin, Massachusetts, near the Rhode
Island border. He remained there from 1773 until the age of
eighty-two, achieving considerable renown.[3]

[1] Colton, *History and Character of American Revivals of Religion*, p. xiii.
[2] Lewis Tappan to Charles Finney, Aug. 12, 1855 (Lewis Tappan Letter Book, Tappan Papers).
[3] Biographies of Emmons emphasize his theological ideas and are singularly mediocre. The most complete is Park, *Memoir of Nathaniel Emmons*. Williams, *A Discourse on the Official Character of the Rev. Nathaniel Emmons*, written at the time of his death is too adulatory. The best study of his theology is found in Foster, *Genetic History of New England Theology*. pp. 340-357. See also *Works of Nathaniel Emmons*.

Emmons, who considered his ideas to have evolved from Hop-kinsianism, was best known for his exposition of the "exercisers" wing in New England theology, as opposed to the "tasters." According to him, human intellectual activity consisted of a series of exercises resulting from divine action. In the religious experience it was the will that was renovated, according to this divine. In his theology he also stressed the concept of a coexistence of the divine and human agency, which was a curious rephrasing of determinism; the assertion of eternal punishment for the slightest breaking of divine law; the acknowledgment of God's sovereignty; and the total depravity of man. Nonetheless, he emphasized the importance of the individual in taking an active role in his salvation. His importance lies chiefly in restating for his time the essential elements of orthodox theology.[4]

A small plump man with a weak, squeaky voice, Emmons was known for his sharp, witty tongue. Although his personality was by no means magnetic he had a strong following among student ministers, many of whom adopted his ideas and preaching techniques. In 1784 his church experienced a revival that lasted about a year and that brought into the church one tenth of the town's population. Revivals followed his preaching at periodic intervals thereafter. A patriot during the Revolution, a Federalist afterward, Emmons opposed Jefferson with a moralistic vigor. At the beginning of Jefferson's administration Emmons preached a powerful sermon against the Virginian denouncing him most bitterly for not being a New England Calvinist. This sermon was welcomed by the Federalists as one of the major political diatribes of the time.[5]

This eighteenth-century divine was a rebel in some things, stubbornly reactionary in others. He clung to the fashions of his youth, wearing a three-cornered hat to his dying day and chewing tobacco with a colonial vigor. Marrying for the third time at the age of eighty-seven, he dressed antiquely, wearing "a cocked hat, silk satin breeches, with large silver knee and shoe buckles, silk vest . . . and a single breasted coat, with straight collar and large

[4] See Emmons, *Works*, III, 79-110.
[5] Dexter, *Biographical Sketches of the Graduates of Yale College*, III, 224.

buttons." [6]   Nathaniel Emmons in 1826 was an old man, on the threshold of retiring. He looked to the past; he was a symbol of a dying era in theology; even his habits had become antiquated.

Emmons represented the old order not so much in what he favored as in what he opposed. He was against the Sunday School because he felt it interfered with the obligations of parents, not to mention the privileges of pastors to give instruction to their flock. He was opposed to the use of musical instruments in church services. He disapproved of revivalists who took an active part in the enlisting of conversions. In many ways he looked askance at the radicalism of the new century. On the other hand, he set the pattern for later evangelists to follow. An outspoken critic and vigilant watchman over the nation's morals, he helped found the Massachusetts Missionary Society, which was a precursor of many of the later benevolent organizations. When Emmons died in 1840, at the ripe old age of ninety-five, the last of the orthodox eighteenth-century preachers in the Puritan pulpit disappeared.

Another representative of the group who bridged the gap between the old age and the new was Asahel Nettleton. Born in North Killingworth on April 21, 1783, Nettleton led a tragic, sickly life. A farmer's son whose early years were not religious, he had been planning a dancing school when he was converted during a revival. He entered Yale in 1805, graduated four years later, was licensed to preach in North Haven in 1811, and was ordained an evangelist by the South Consociation of Litchfield County the summer of 1817.[7]

Initially, Nettleton met with great success. Traveling through Connecticut and New York, he engaged in an almost continual series of revivals. He employed Jonathan Edwards's methods in preaching and avoided excessive bursts of emotion. Indeed, as evangelists go, he was a quiet man. One of his colleagues has given us the best description of his methods in the pulpit. "The

   [6] *Ibid.*, p. 218.
   [7] There is no comprehensive biography of Asahel Nettleton. The most judicious study of him is Birney, *The Life and Letters of Asahel Nettleton, 1783-1844.* Bonar, *Nettleton and His Labours*, which follows with few modifications Tyler, *Memoir of The Life and Character of Rev. A. Nettleton*, besides having the faults of Tyler's work, is marred by a lack of objectivity and perspective.

power of his preaching included many things. It was highly intellectual as opposed to declamation, or oratorical, pathetic appeals to imagination or the emotions. It was discriminatingly doctrinal." [8]

Unlike many in his profession, Nettleton published few articles, books, or sermons. His major venture in the literary field was the publication in 1824 of a hymn book, which he prepared during a two-year convalescence from typhus fever. Nettleton had recognized that the new revival age needed a new hymnology. The *Bay Psalm Book's* "rugged stanzas" were not appropriate to revivals and Nettleton found even Isaac Watts's *Psalms and Hymns* "too formal and lofty for evangelical use." [9] His answer was *Village Hymns, Selected and Original, Designed as a Supplement to the Psalms and Hymns of Dr. Watts,* in which he introduced hundreds of hymns to the American churches. The significance of Nettleton's contribution lies in a book of tunes called *Zion's Harp,* which came out along with the hymnal. Heretofore tunes and words of hymns were not written together. Indeed, most eighteenth-century hymnals gave merely the meter of each hymn. *Village Hymns,* however, went so far as to recommend one or more tunes to fit the words of a particular hymn and all these tunes were to be found in *Zion's Harp.* Thus his work was an important step in the direction of modern hymnology. His book was popular immediately, despite opposition from men such as Emmons, and it quickly sold several editions. Indeed, it was still paying royalties after Nettleton's death.

Nettleton also differed from his fellow evangelists in not seeming to take an interest in secular or political problems. He did take an active part, however, in the early stages of the temperance campaign. His biggest blow for the cause was a long letter he wrote in 1822 to Lyman Beecher on the relation of drinking to revivals which was printed and widely circulated in 1829.[10] Let-

---

[8] Lyman Beecher, *Autobiography,* II, 483. A description of Nettleton's preaching style is found in Davenport, *Primitive Traits in Religious Revivals,* p. 181.
[9] Birney, *The Life and Letters of Asahel Nettleton, 1783-1844,* pp. 92-93.
[10] See Nettleton, *Temperance and Revivals.*

ters were his literary forte. He dispatched long, rambling epistles to both friend and foe, particularly on topics of a doctrinal nature.

Nettleton embraced orthodox opinions with an uncompromising spirit. Clinging to the old conservative ideas of original sin and moral inability, he struggled against Timothy Dwight in 1808 and against Finney in 1827. Originally allied with Beecher against the Western innovators in revivals, he sadly broke with Lyman to join Bennet Tyler in his dispute with the New Haven group. Nettleton never formulated his religious views into a published book, but his numerous letters contain the nucleus of a firmly entrenched conservatism. For fifteen years his quiet revivals in which the old-style approach was employed gave him a well-deserved fame in New England and New York. By 1826, however, the more dramatic revivals of ministers freed from the strict confines of Calvinist thought overshadowed Nettleton's unspectacular work. If anyone symbolized the obsolescence of orthodoxy in the nineteenth century it was Asahel Nettleton.

One of Nettleton's major failings was his inability to gauge the trend of events. In 1823 he wrote, "If I mistake not, the petty differences which for a few years past have been foolishly and wickedly perpetrated between good ministers of the New England and other states are fast subsiding in the growing progress of the spirit of revivals." [11] His defeat at New Lebanon should have indicated the hopelessness of his position, but he carried on the contest against Finneyites long after others had embraced Finney's new measures. Once convinced of man's depravity and of the evils connected with the new revivals, Nettleton stood adamant and the tide of events swept over him.

After 1826 Nettleton was less successful in conducting revivals. His orthodoxy prevented him from adopting the newer techniques. His support of the losing side in the Tyler-Taylor doctrinal dispute ended Nettleton's influence over New England ministers. Even Lyman Beecher, who in 1829 regarded him "as one of the greatest benefactors God has ever given to this nation," changed his opinion in later years.[12]

[11] Asahel Nettleton to Rev. Mark Tucker, April 18, 1823 (Gratz Collection).
[12] Quoted in Nettleton, *Temperance and Revivals*, p. 1.

It was during the latter period of his life that Nettleton was in feeble health and was forced to spend his winters in Virginia and in North and South Carolina. In 1831 he attempted a revival in New York City and Newark but was a "disappointment" to the devout in those cities. A greater star was on the horizon, and after Nettleton had left one of the faithful wrote Finney, "I do not know that anybody regrets his departure." [13]

Nettleton's apparent failure at a time when revivals were increasing in popularity was due to the fact that he was out of step with the times, doctrinally speaking. In the words of one of his opponents, "He wanted to show that there could be as powerful revivals without these 'measures' as they have at the west." His defense of outmoded doctrines "robbed his preaching of its practical edge and of its fruits." [14] He was trying to swim against the stream.

Moreover, his personality acted against him. A frail man who suffered almost continuously from ill health, he was known for his great timidity and sensitiveness. His verbose letters give the picture of a crabby, old man fighting vainly for the status quo. He identified failures as personal assaults against himself and could not tolerate opinions different from his own. A contemporary comparison of Nettleton and Charles G. Finney, the symbol of the new order, reveals much about both men and about the changes in the religious scene which they were witnessing:

He himself was old and broken, Mr. Finney young and robust. The one was reverential, timid, secretive; the other bold, striking, demonstrative. The style of one was subdued, that of the other full of eclat. . . . The one, being crafty, took them with guile; the other, being violent, took them by force. [15]

In spite of the changes taking place around him, Nettleton remained firm in his old-fashioned form of Calvinism. His death in 1844 passed almost unnoticed, obscured as it was by greater, more far-reaching events in the religious world. Perhaps the most char-

[13] W. Brown to Charles Finney, April 3, 1831 (Finney Papers). See also William Hall to Finney, Feb. 4, 1831; O. Smith to Finney, Feb. 17 and March 14, 1831.
[14] Joshua Leavitt to Finney, April 7, 1831; E. W. Clark to Finney, May 23, 1832 (Finney Papers).
[15] Beecher, *Autobiography*, II, 94-95.

acteristic expression of Nettleton's philosophy were his oft-repeated
words, "I think it possible I may get to heaven." [16]

If the old order was represented by Emmons and Nettleton, the
new order was typified by Lyman Beecher and Peter Cartwright.
Lyman Beecher's place in the American scene, although controversial, is nevertheless secure. He may not have been, as Arthur
Hoyt asserts, "the chief human force that turned the tide in New
England, and finally won the day for an evangelical faith," but
in the eyes of his contemporaries Beecher was the champion defender of orthodoxy. In the opinion of his fellow evangelists he
was a bold innovator and exuberant leader; to the twentieth century he may seem to be a quaint old man.[17]

Beecher's life was a succession of struggles. A Connecticut
blacksmith's son, Lyman was born prematurely on October 12,
1775. He spent his boyhood with a stern New England aunt and
uncle, his mother having died two days after his birth. He was
another Yale man who came under the influence of President
Dwight and was affected by the revival witnessed by the college
in 1795. He had originally intended to study law, thinking himself "naturally fitted to be a lawyer," but after his religious awakening in his junior year he had "a sort of purpose to be a
preacher." [18] He was ordained in 1799 and married shortly thereafter Roxanna Foote, who had not been trained to be the wife of
such an energetic man of God. The pace subsequently killed her.

Beecher's first church was at East Hampton, Long Island, where
his salary was $300 a year plus firewood. After five years it was
raised to $400. In 1810 he moved to Litchfield, where he could
be heard by more people and where an increased salary ($800 a
year) enabled him to support the demands of his ever-increasing
family. In 1826 he accepted an invitation from the Hanover
Church in Boston which, at the time, was an orthodox outpost

16 Quoted in Birney, *The Life and Letters of Asahel Nettleton, 1783-1844*, p. 25.
17 Hoyt, *The Pulpit and American Life*, p. 52. Although somewhat inaccurate,
Beecher's *Autobiography* contains much information about him not found elsewhere.
Among modern studies the most useful is Rourke, *Trumpets of Jubilee*.
18 Lyman Beecher, *Autobiography*, I, 45.

surrounded by hostile Unitarian churches. Beecher's chief aim in going to Boston was to fight Unitarianism. He had watched with increasing emotion every step of the controversy from 1805 on and as early as 1819 had taken part in defending the orthodox churches. His preaching at the Park Street Church and elsewhere in Massachusetts in 1823 had gained him an audience and probably had much to do with his call to a Boston pastorate three years later. By the time Beecher arrived in Boston he was ready to engage the foe in battle. As he put it, "It was a fire in my bones; my mind was all the time heating—heating—heating." [19]

As we shall see, the Unitarians were not the only ones to feel Beecher's wrath. He was instrumental in calling the New Lebanon convention in 1827; he joined ranks with Nathaniel Taylor in attempting to restate the traditional doctrines of Calvinism in the 1830's, and he later clashed with the more orthodox in the West where he was put on trial for heresy.

Whether it was heretical or not, Lyman Beecher's theology rested on New School foundations. It was easy to understand—if you were Lyman Beecher. It was easy to misinterpret if you were anyone else! Accepting the essential outlines of orthodox Calvinism, but emphasizing the means by which man received conversion, the flexible Beecher ranged across the spectrum of doctrine, stating his beliefs to fit his needs. Closer to Nathaniel W. Taylor than anyone else, Beecher's sermon "The Government of God Desirable" contained the chief elements of his religious position and gave its author pre-eminence throughout New England.

An indication of Beecher's flexibility is the ease with which he shifted from the Congregational Church to the Presbyterian Church and back. As he put it in 1800, "I didn't care what I was." He could easily adapt himself to local government or to polity of the presbyterian variety. Indeed, he preferred a little bit of both:

The fact is, a Presbytery made up of New England men, raised Congregationalists, is the nearest the Bible of anything there is. But if you go

<hr />

[19] *Ibid.*, II, 53. The best critique of Beecher's battle against Unitarianism is found in Mead, "Lyman Beecher and Connecticut Orthodoxy's Campaign against Unitarianism," *Church History*, IX, No. 3 (1940), 218-234.

to sticking it up, Scotch fashion, with appeals, etc., I wouldn't put myself into the hands of such a power all over the United States.[20]

His preaching was also characterized by this adaptability. If his congregation needed to hear more about man's depravity or regeneration, he would dwell on those topics. If, on the other hand, his audience needed to hear more about man's will or the distinction between moral and natural inability, then he would preach on those themes. Bostonians, for instance, had had their fill of predestination, he believed:

The people did not need high-toned Calvinism on the point of dependence; they had been crammed with it, and were dying with excessive ailment, and needed a long and vigorous prescription of free-agency to produce an alternative and render the truth salutary by administering the proper portions in due season.[21]

This Connecticut firebrand also possessed a remarkable amount of resilience. The ease and audacity with which he sprang to his own defense when tried for heresy is indicative of this quality. He no sooner arrived in Cincinnati when the Old School faction in the West carried on Princeton's fight against him. Letters were written about him, preliminary skirmishes were held at the examination of his son George, and a trial was finally launched against him that dragged on for a year and a half. Although he was victorious, the trial with its upsetting disputes, its petty animosities, its political intrigues, and its interminable publicity helped bring on the death of Lyman's wife. It was also a factor in the shaping of Henry Ward's religious views. Lyman's comment on the trial's unpleasantness was characteristic of his brash optimism: "I knew to a hair's breadth every point between Old School and New School, and knew all their difficulties and how to puzzle them with them." [22]

Beecher's adherence to the fundamentals of orthodox thought must not be overlooked. While he joined Taylor, Barnes, and Finney in modifying the harsher aspects of that orthodoxy, never-

20 Beecher, *Autobiography*, I, 116, 117.
21 *Ibid.*, p. 187.
22 *Ibid.*, II, 352. Details of the trial are found in *ibid.*, pp. 349 ff. See also *Trial of the Rev. Lyman Beecher, D.D., before the Presbytery of Cincinnati on the Charge of Heresy.*

theless he upheld the traditional Christian concept of on all-power-
ful God working with supernatural powers, of fallen man damned
by original sin, of the authority of the Scriptures, and of the essential nature of the trinity.   He never hesitated to uphold traditional
views in the face of heresies more serious than his own appeared
to be.   In doctrinal discussions Lewis Tappan found him "frank,
explicit and sincere." [23]   It was only among more crabbed conservatives that Lyman Beecher was considered a radical.

By 1830 the Beecher family had stayed in Boston long enough
and Lyman began considering a move to the West.   He was attracted to Lane Seminary which had just been established, chiefly
on funds furnished by Lewis Tapan, one of Beecher's Boston converts.   In 1832 Lyman was inducted as president and professor of
theology at Lane Seminary in Cincinnati.   The following year he
took up also duties as pastor of the Second Church in that city.
He kept that post until 1843, resigned his professorship in 1850,
and the following year returned to New England.   He ended his
evangelistic work in Boston and spent the last years of his life in
Brooklyn, basking in the glory of his sons' fame.   He died January
10, 1864, at the age of eighty-eight.

Beecher's versatility was typical of the nineteenth-century evangelist.   Besides conducting many revivals, engaging in theological
controversies, and managing a pioneering Western seminary, he
led in the foundation of the Connecticut Society for the Promotion
of Good Morals and helped in the organization of the American
Bible Society in 1816.   He had a hand in the establishment of the
Christian Observer in 1824 and periodically gave advice on articles
and editorial policy to the editors of other religious journals.   His
polemics in 1806 against dueling brought him nation-wide renown,
while his six sermons on *The Nature, Occasions, Signs, Evils and
Remedy of Intemperance*, first published in 1827, marked a new
chapter in the history of that crusade.   Moreover, although a reluctant one, he was an antislavery reformer.[24]

[23] Lewis Tappan Diary, Aug. 12, 1827, p. 92 (Lewis Tappan Papers)
[24] See Keller, *The Second Great Awakening in Connecticut*, p. 221, for Beecher's
role in the temperance campaign.   For his influence on religious periodicals, see his
Autobiography, I, 268; II, 13.

Beecher cut a striking figure as he battled for the Lord. Perhaps the best description of him comes from his own pen. Writing to his wife, he recounts:

My dear Friend,—

. . . . I have rather a thin, spare face, a great nose, and blue eyes; just above my nose, in my forehead, is the cavity of wisdom, and just above that my hair, which is now getting to be long, and stands out in all directions, giving me an appearance of fierceness which might alarm, were it not apparent every time I speak or laugh that my teeth are gone so that I can not bite, and did not the cross in my forehead appear as the token of a religious, placable disposition.[25]

A later description of him while he was in Boston fills in some of the details. Constance Rourke describes him as "quiet and quizzical and silvery, his head gently turned, though his mouth was still ironic and shoulders ruggedly squared." [26]

But he was far from quiet! "Papa loves to laugh as well as any of us," Catherine Beecher reported, "and is quite as much tickled at nonsense as we are!" [27] Indeed those evenings after services with his children when he would take up his fiddle and let off steam must have been wondrous to behold! And Lyman Beecher had a lot of steam to let off. Another of his daughters, Harriet Beecher Stowe, recalled that he used to work off nervous excitement by shoveling sand or sawing wood:

He had also in the back yard, parallel bars, a single bar, ladder, and other gymnastic apparatus, where he would sometimes astonish his ministerial visitors by climbing ropes hand over hand, whirling over the single bar, lifting weights, and performing other athletic feats in which he took for the time as much apparent delight and pride as in any of his intellectual exertions.[28]

Others gave witness of his physical prowess while in the pulpit. Only Lyman Beecher could have thrown a tree trunk over the

[25] Lyman Beecher to Roxanna Beecher, March 5, 1810, in Lyman Beecher, *Autobiography*, I, 190.

[26] Rourke, *Trumpets of Jubilee*, p. 36.

[27] Catherine Beecher to Edward Beecher, Nov. 29, 1819, in Lyman Beecher, *Autobiography*, I, 424.

[28] *Ibid.*, II, 113.

heads of his congregation while preaching in Boston.[29]   He was an
exhibitionist with a careless untidiness about his dress.   Although
he vowed never to return to East Hampton, Long Island, when he
left for greener pastures, he retained many of the village parson's
characteristics.   There was a roughness, a lack of polish, a loud
domineering manner upon which he knew how to capitalize.
There was also a sternness in his crudity which made Henry Ward,
for one, look back on his childhood with unhappy regret.[30]

Beecher's preaching, although there are differences of opinion
regarding it, was doubtless effective.   Contrary to the Puritan tradition of long, closely reasoned, written sermons, Lyman preferred
to speak as the spirit moved him.   "They like my extempore discourses more than the written," he reported to Roxanna.   "I fully
believe they do more good." [31]   Characteristic of his style was a
colloquialism that some found "truculent" and offensive.   He enjoyed to "hew down" theological antagonists, to "wring their
necks off" and "hang them on their own gallows." [32]   Lewis
Tappan, recording in his diary the details of one of Beecher's sermons, wrote: "It was partly extempore, and was delivered quite
powerfully.   He was very strong and decided against neutrality
. . . or a compromising spirit." [33]   Catherine Beecher may be ex-
cused for some filial pride when she remarked, "The fact is, I
never hear anybody preach that makes me feel as father does;
perhaps it may be because he is father.   But I can not hear him
without its making my face burn and my heart beat." [34]   Lyman
himself had an explanation for the effectiveness of his preaching.

[29] "He seized the trunk of a gnarled oak and lifted it high . . . whirled it around
and around till its own motion had given it a headlong momentum and then away it
whizzed far over the heads of all who heard him and fell very harmlessly without the
camp."   Milton Brayton to Finney, May 18, 1827 (Finney Papers).
[30] Hibben, Henry Ward Beecher: an American Portrait, pp. 26-31.   For a less critical
picture of Lyman, see Bacon, Sermon at the Funeral of Rev. Lyman Beecher, D.D.
[31] Lyman Beecher to Roxanna Foote, March 26 (1799), in Lyman Beecher, Autobiography, I, 106-107.
[32] Ibid., II, 11.
[33] Lewis Tappan Diary, Oct. 14, 1827, p. 109 (Tappan Papers).
[34] Catherine Beecher to Edward Beecher, July 18, 1824, in Lyman Beecher, Autobiography, II, 15.

"I did it by instinct," he recorded. "I was made for action. The Lord drove me, but I was ready. I have always been going at full speed." [35]

Dogmatically domineering, full of restless energy, and always ready for a theological battle, Beecher never quite knew what he wanted. Many of his ideas were inconsistent, many of his actions contradictory. He considered novels as trash yet urged his children to read Sir Walter Scott. He lamented "the wasted life" of Byron but had an intense admiration for that "glorious fellow" Napoleon Bonaparte. He dedicated books to the working men of his country but confessed an occasional preference for tyranny rather than democracy. Irrational and inconsistent, he nevertheless threw his entire energies behind those crusades in which he believed. He even rode to Boston on horseback through a blizzard to joust with Unitarians there when the roads were so blocked with snow the stages could not get through. Such a man was Lyman Beecher. [36]

Peter Cartwright's career was equally colorful. Born in 1785 in Amherst County, Virginia, Peter was eight when his family moved to Kentucky, eventually settling at Red River, called the "Rogues' Harbor" of Logan County. [37] He was an impressionable adolescent when the famous Awakening of 1799-1800 hit the back country, and the emotional lad was finally converted, though not without some difficulty. [38] In 1806 he became a deacon in the Methodist Church, and thereafter he devoted some sixty-five years to the active ministry. He became an elder in 1808 and a presiding elder in 1812, and he was elected some thirteen times as a delegate to the Methodist General Conference which met once every four years.

[35] *Ibid.*, p. 70.
[36] *Ibid.*, I, 517, 520, 531.
[37] Loud, *Evangelized America*, p. 129.
[38] The details of his conversion are told in his *Autobiography*, pp. 34-38. Few works deal adequately with his career. The most enthusiastic account is Waters, *Peter Cartwright*. More judicious treatments are found in Seitz, *Uncommon Americans*, and Macartney, *Sons of Thunder*.

Cartwright's work took him from circuit to circuit through Kentucky, Tennessee, Ohio, Indiana, and Illinois, so that he became thoroughly identified with the expanding frontier during the 1820's and 1830's. His forty-five years in Illinois marked the most fruitful part of his life. In spite of his peripatetic career, he found time to marry Frances Gaines in 1811 and to raise a family of nine children. It has been estimated that this roving revivalist preached some 14,600 sermons during his lifetime, averaging 400 a year for the first twenty years.

Cartwright had not the time nor the opportunity to obtain much education during his youth. While he felt this lack in his own case and contributed what he could to the dissemination of learning in the back country, nevertheless, he discounted the need for education when it came to saving souls.[39] As he put it, "It is true we could not, many of us, conjugate a verb or parse a sentence, and murdered the king's English almost every lick. But there was a Divine unction attended the word preached." [40] Indeed, Cartwright felt that theological education sometimes hindered the work of an evangelist. He attributed the gains made by Methodism to ignorant preachers like himself and minimized the work done by the "sapient, velvet-mouthed, downy D. D.'s" of the period.[41]

Cartwright may have been ignorant in terms of formal education or theological training but he was shrewdly wise in matters of ministering and saving souls. He knew how to handle men—and women. He stalked through Tennessee and Kentucky, playing upon the emotional stops of his audience and defying the opposition that was raised against him. Those that he could not win by prayer and persuasion he could defeat by physical force. Many a mob was repelled by his fearlessness; many an individual felt

[39] The claim has been made that during his career he distributed some $10,000 worth of literature along the sparsely settled frontier. See Waters, *Peter Cartwright*, p. 27. For his support of schools, see Pratt, "Peter Cartwright and the Cause of Education," *Illinois State Historical Journal* (1936), pp. 271-278.

[40] Cartwright, *Autobiography*, pp. 6-7.

[41] *Ibid.*, p. 408.

the full force of his fist. He was a man of God but he always enjoyed a good old-fashioned fight.[42]

Physically he was nearly six feet in height with a large head
("It seems as large as half a bushel") and long, brawny arms and
hands that had a "bearlike" grasp. His bronzed complexion gave
evidence of his outdoor life. His voice, compared at times to "the
clangor of an alarm bell," could make the forests tremble. He
had thick black hair that flowed back over his ears in unruly curl-
ing ringlets. His eyes attracted particular attention. "His eyes are
intensely deep in color, and shine like dark fires beneath his shaggy
eyebrows." He seemed a human dynamo, full of exhaustless
energy. "He could sing, exhort, and pray day and night the whole
week through, and not grow weary."[43]

No one could excite audiences more by the power of his oratory
than Peter Cartwright. Preaching with an emotional eloquence,
he spoke in a colloquial manner which was a language his hearers
understood. His tongue was sharp; he did not spare his audiences.
Some of his sermons have been called "as keen as whip lashes."
Edward Eggleston, whose *The Circuit Rider* is a fictional account
of some of Cartwright's exploits, described his style in this fashion:
"His speech was full of dialectic forms and ungrammatical phrases.
His illustrations were exceedingly uncouth."[44]

Cartwright knew how to make the most of an incident. At
every opportunity he struck a blow for the Lord. Outside the
pulpit, even while traveling, he was ever eager to battle for religion
and his stern moral code. He boasted in his *Autobiography* of several parties and dances which he broke up by attempting to start
a revival on the dance floor.[45]

This Methodist marvel did not limit himself to riding circuits.
He was intensely patriotic and never hesitated to speak his mind

[42] For an enthusiastic description of some of his tussels with mobs, see *ibid.*, pp. 131-
132, 228-231, 236-237, 321-324.

[43] Loud, *Evangelized America*, pp. 126-128; Waters, *Peter Cartwright*, pp. 30, 80-81;
Chamberlin, "Rev. Peter Cartwright, D.D.," *Transactions of the Illinois State Historical
Society for the Year 1902*, p. 53.

[44] Eggleston, *The Circuit Rider*, p. 72.

[45] For one such incident, see Cartwright, *Autobiography*, p. 207 ff.

regarding the public issues of his day. During the War of 1812 he was a chaplain in the army under Andrew Jackson and climaxed his military career by taking part in the Battle of New Orleans. He was a lifelong Democrat and was elected twice to the Illinois state legislature from Sangamon County. He ran for Congress in 1846, and it took Abraham Lincoln to defeat him.[46] Although he tended to be conservative in most matters, he took part in moral reform movements with a gusto, suporting the temperance and antislavery causes with particular enthusiasm. He fought against slavery in the pulpit and on the floor of the General Conference. He tried to prevent the separation of Northern and Southern Methodism in 1844, but the tide against him from his more extreme colleagues was too strong.[47]

Although he had his limitations, Cartwright's role in the religious scene cannot be minimized. He was no theologian, and his contribution to the shaping of religious thought when compared with that of Beecher or Finney was slight. His frontier background was a handicap as well as a blessing, and his prejudice against non-Methodists was hardly commendable. Nevertheless, by his influence and popularity he left his mark throughout the West.[48]

The Baptists in America provided equally colorful evangelists. Philadelphia had its Henry Holcombe, New York its David Benedict, and the entire country knew the name of Jabez Swan. But the most influential Baptist standard bearer in the 1830's was Jacob

[46] For an account of this interesting campaign, see Ross, *Lincoln's First Years in Illinois*, p. 37.

[47] For an account of his role in the Methodist schism of 1844, see Cartwright, *Autobiography*, pp. 425-438.

[48] Another Methodist evangelist whose career paralleled that of Cartwright was James Finley. Born in 1781 in North Carolina, he spent his boyhood in Virginia and Kentucky, was converted during the Cane Ridge revival of 1800, and after seven unsuccessful years farming and hunting he became a Methodist and joined the ranks of the circuit riders. His most important work was done at the Wyandott mission, a school established for Indians in Ohio. See Finley, *Autobiography*, *History of the Wyandott Mission*, and *Life among the Indians*. His other works include *Memorials of Prison Life*, and *Sketches of Western Methodism*, ed. by Strickland.

Knapp who, it has been claimed, converted one hundred thousand in his career.[49]

Knapp was born in Otsego County, New York, in 1799 and was raised an Episcopalian. Like many another minister he had a deeply moving religious experience in the woods when he was seventeen but, as he recounts it, soon reverted to his worldly ways. The following year his family moved to the headwaters of the Ohio River, but he was sent back East to attend school in Delaware County, New York. It was not long before he underwent another religious experience, and his conversion started a revival. In 1825 he received his diploma from the Hamilton Literary and Theological Institute and almost immediately was ordained, married, and installed as pastor of a Springfield church. The year 1830 found him in Watertown, and from 1832 until 1834 he was preaching in the major towns of Jefferson, Oswego, Lewis, and Cayuga counties. Two thousand conversions were counted in eighteen months as a result of his endeavors.[50]

Knapp first hit New York City in the spring of 1835. By that time the metropolis had had its share of revivals, but Knapp took over the Broome Street Baptist Church and added fresh fuel to the flames of urban religious zeal. During the rest of the 1830's he divided his energies between the Mohawk Valley and such cities as Brooklyn and Baltimore. In 1840 the Baptist Tabernacle in New York was turned over to him.

In 1841 he was ready to invade New England. His first stop, New Haven, was almost disastrous. Yale students broke up his meetings; mobs threatened his life and attempted to kidnap him. As he recalled it, all such plans were foiled. He converted seventy sons of Eli and even got the college to postpone "the annual ball of the Junior Class!" [51]

[49] The most complete account of Knapp's life is in his own *Autobiography of Elder Jacob Knapp*. There are uncritical studies of his career in Beardsley, *A History of American Revivals*, Loud, *Evangelized America*, and Miller, *God's Great Soul Winners*.
[50] See Loud, *Evangelized America*, p. 184; Knapp, *Autobiography*, p. 29.
[51] Knapp, *Autobiography*, p. 119. The story has a sequel. Shortly after he left New Haven, arrangements were made by the unconverted and a new date was set for the dance. "But one of the managers was taken sick suddenly, and died."

Providence, Rhode Island, gave Knapp an equally warm wel-
come and he was served with a summons for disturbing the peace
as he left church. Mobs opposed him in Boston as well. He was
more successful, however, in the less populous districts of New
England. He tried to convert Washington in 1843, Chicago in
1849 and 1857, and St. Louis in 1858. In 1860 he was back in
Boston, while Wilmington, Philadelphia, and New York were his
stamping grounds during the Civil War. He went West thereafter
but stayed in the pulpit until he died in 1874.

What seems to have roused so much opposition to Knapp as he
ranged the country was not so much what he said but the way he
said it. He was not a man of great tact. Blunt, outspoken, easily
provoked himself, he had a facility for provoking others. In spite
of his size—James Gordon Bennett distastefully called him "a
short little fat fellow"—he was a born fighter. His tongue was
sharp and he lashed his congregations unmercifully. "He was a
man of uncommon powers, and skilled in all the tricks of popular
oratory," wrote the English divine Edward Waylen. "His sermons, though . . . were sometimes marred by the grossest vul-
garisms which even bordered on profanity." [52]

Knapp had a different impression of his peculiarities of speech:

I was not punctilious as to my modes of speech, and more anxious to
reach the consciences of men, than to please their fancies or their love of
display. . . . Much complaint in those days was made because I ventured
to cross the ancient landmarks, and got betimes out of the old ruts. I
sometimes made remarks which did not always accord with every person's notion of propriety.[53]

He was not one to flinch in the face of criticism. His reply to
a fellow minister who admonished him not to use new measures in
New York City because the prejudices of the people would not
permit it was characteristic of his temperament: "I am not going
to be crowded into the gutters by the prejudices of the people," he
replied. "I am going straight through, let the consequences be
what they may." [54]

[52] Waylen, *Ecclesiastical Reminiscences of the United States*, pp. 238, 239.
[53] Knapp, *Autobiography*, pp. 80, 91.
[54] *Ibid.*, p. 43.

The oposition he brought down upon his head almost pleased his fellow evangelists. As Edward N. Kirk put it, "I delighted to follow Mr. Knapp. . . . They were too mad to hear him, they were under too deep conviction to rest content; so, many gladly came to listen to me who might have gone, unmoved, to perdition, had it not been for the sledgehammer style of Mr. Knapp." [55]

Knapp's religious activities represent but one side of his career. Any movement aimed at the improvement of man's condition had his support. He was sympathetic to all philanthropic causes. He pioneered in the temperance crusade, aided missionary enterprises, and joined in schemes for the education of ministers. Moreover, he spoke out against slavery, even preaching against the institution in Louisville, Kentucky, in 1858. He saw fit to pass judgment on economic matters as well, and the New York *Herald* even circulated his views on the tariff.[56]

But Jacob Knapp reflects the transient quality of much of an evangelist's influence. Except for a sentence here, a paragraph there, he is well-nigh forgotten in the twentieth century. It is indicative of the sublime optimism and religious zeal of his age that the nineteenth century said of him, "Perhaps there is no minister of the gospel who has toiled harder, has been opposed more, has complained less, and has accomplished so much." [57] Twentieth-century opinion is likely to be less sweeping and less kind!

One could not find a man more different from Elder Jacob Knapp than Francis Wayland, Baptist minister and educator, considered by Arthur S. Hoyt as "second only to Timothy Dwight as a preacher to college men." [58] Wayland was born in 1796 in New York City to middle-class parents of English descent and died in

[55] Quoted in *ibid.*, p. 137.
[56] *Ibid.*, p. 109.
[57] Jeffery, "Knapp and His Ministry," Knapp, *Autobiography*, p. xi.
[58] Hoyt, *The Pulpit and American Life*, p. 189. The two men had almost opposite opinions of each other. Wayland "was not very favorably impressed" with Jacob Knapp. Knapp, on the other hand, asserted, "I have rarely come across the writings of any man from which I have derived more pleasure and profit." Knapp, *Autobiography*, p. 122.

1865.[59]   When Francis was eleven, the family moved to Pough-
keepsie and later to Albany.   In 1811 he entered Union College,
joining the sophomore class at the age of fifteen and graduating
two years later.   The following winter he attended medical lectures in New York City but soon abandoned that career in favor
of the ministry.   In the autumn of 1816 he entered the theological seminary at Andover.

From 1818 to 1821 he worked as a tutor at Union College, but
this employment convinced him all the more that he wanted to
enter the ministry.   It is interesting to note that instrumental in
his decision was the influence of Asahel Nettleton, who was conducting, at that time, a revival in the vicinity which spread to
the college.   At first Wayland considered the West as his field for
service but finally decided to accept the invitation proffered by the
First Baptist Church of Boston.   It was while he was stationed in
that city that he married Lucy L. Lincoln in 1825.

In the spring of 1826 Eliphalet Nott, president of Union College, led Wayland back to the academic walk of life.   At that time
he accepted the chair of professor of moral philosophy.   He was
also given the professorships of mathematics and natural philosophy.   He had no sooner begun his duties, however, when he was
unanimously chosen president of Brown University.

The rest of Wayland's life was, in a sense, a dedication to Brown
University.   As its president for almost thirty years, he became
one of the leaders in American education, inaugurating many educational reforms.   His writings on the subject of education, notably the *Report on the Condition of the University*, *Report to the
Corporation of Brown University on the Changes in the System of
Collegiate Education* (1850), and his *Thoughts on the Present Collegiate System in the United States* (1842) are outstanding landmarks that compare favorably with the works of Barnard and
Horace Mann.[60]

---

[59] The most detailed work on Wayland is the memoir written by his sons, Francis
and H. L. Wayland, *A Memoir of the Life and Labours of Francis Wayland*.   A more
judicious account of his career will be found in Murray, *Francis Wayland*.   See also
Mueller, *The Life of Trust*.

[60] For a detailed study of Wayland's work at Brown, see Roelker, "Francis Wayland,
a Neglected Pioneer of Higher Education," *Proceedings of the American Antiquarian
Society*, LIII, 27-28.

Wayland did not limit himself to educational topics in his writings. He defended his political views in such works as *The Duties of an American Citizen* (1825) and *The Affairs of Rhode Island* (1842). His *Elements of Political Economy* (1837) was for many years a standard textbook. He wrote on slavery, the missionary enterprise, the Kansas-Nebraska bill, and the role of science. Religious topics also received a fair share of his attention. Although he did not consider himself a theologian, his denominational views are stated fully in a work entitled *Notes on the Principles and Practices of Baptist Churches.* In 1835 he published a textbook, *Elements of Moral Science,* which was blessed with praise from James Kent and which was quickly republished in England and Scotland. Another text, *Intellectual Philosophy,* was also a best seller among religious circles.

Wayland worked for prison reform and gradual emancipation. For awhile he taught a Sunday School class of colored boys, which he considered was one method of fighting against slavery. He was a trustee and frequent visitor of the Butler Asylum for the Insane near Brown University and for a number of years served as an inspector of the state prison. He was also associated in an editorial capacity with the *American Baptist Magazine* during the 1820's.

There is divided opinion as to his pulpit personality. One of his contemporaries thought his manner in the pulpit was "unattractive," adding that "he was tall, lean, angular" and that he "spoke with but little action, rarely withdrawing his hands from his pockets, save to turn a leaf." [61] An admirer, on the other hand, spoke glowingly of his "massive and stalwart form . . . his strongly marked features . . . his piercing eye sending from beneath that olympian brow its lordly or its penetrating glances" and hailed him as "the incarnation of majesty and power." [62]

Evaluating the extent of his influence would be difficult. Suffice to say, he helped mold the course of higher eduction in America, he gave to the ranks of evangelism an intellectual atmosphere that otherwise was lacking, and he shaped the ideas of indi-

[61] Quoted in Murray, *Francis Wayland*, p. 45.
[62] Chace, *The Virtues and Services of Francis Wayland*, p. 22.

viduals in much the same way as Beecher's pamphlets or Finney's sermons. The classic example is perhaps Andrew White, president of Cornell, who as a youth in 1856 heard Wayland speak of the need for evangelizing and educating the West. According to White, "It changed my whole life. I gave up law, literature, and politics, and thenceforward my strongest desire was to work anywhere and anyhow at the West on education." [63] An English traveler summed up Wayland's role succinctly when he remarked, "He is one of those men who have a great share in the work of directing the public mind." [64]

One of the more active Congregational evangelists was Joshua Leavitt (1794-1873).[65] Unlike many of his fellow ministers, Leavitt's fame rests not in his preaching but in what he wrote. He was considered by Theodore Weld to have "revolutionized the character of the religious periodical press" and to have had in the 1830's "more actual influence over the giving, doing, daring, praying and accomplishing part of the Church than any other man." [66] He was better known in his own day than he is now and at one time was considered by abolitionists as one of their ablest leaders.

A good scholar, Leavitt graduated from Yale in 1814 in the same class with Theodore Dwight, Samuel B. Ruggles, and Henry D. Chapin.[67] He studied law and was admitted to the bar in 1819. Turning to religion in 1823, he completed the divinity course at Yale two years later, was ordained the same year, and began his preaching career at Stratford, Connecticut.

[63] Quoted in Murray, *Francis Wayland*, p. 120.

[64] Waylen, *Ecclesiastical Reminiscences of the United States*, p. 148.

[65] There is no satisfactory biography of Joshua Leavitt. The richest source of information is found in the Leavitt Papers in the Library of Congress. Autobiographical material may also be found in the periodicals Leavitt edited. See also Dexter, *Biographical Sketches of the Graduates of Yale College*, VI, 673-678, and Wright, "The Father of the Liberty Party," *The Independent*, Jan. 30, 1873. Finney, *Memoirs*, contains useful information on Leavitt's career.

[66] Theodore Weld to James G. Birney, June 26, 1837, in Dwight L. Dumond, *Letters of James Gillespie Birney, 1831-1857*, I, 390.

[67] See Joshua Leavitt to the Class of 1814, June 20, 1859 (Leavitt Papers).

Early in his life he revealed an interest in reforming others. While an undergraduate he organized the Yale College Benevolent Society which from 1813 on attracted pious youths anxious to aid their fellow man. After 1826 he entered upon a strenuous round of missionary and reforming activities, becoming Secretary of the Seaman's Friend Society in New York City, founding sailors' missions in seacoast towns and becoming one of the first lecturers for the American Temperance Society. He also interested himself in the American Seventh Commandment Society, helping edit for awhile their *Journal of Public Morals*.

It was in editing religious and quasi-religious periodicals that Leavitt made his mark. In 1831 he brought out the *Evangelist*, an important journal that fostered religious revivals, and antislavery, temperance, and other reforms. The *Evangelist*, which was associated with the New School faction doctrinally, had a circulation that once approached ten thousand. But its bellicose editor brought considerable criticism upon it, and it was never without its difficulties. Asahel Nettleton blamed the *Evangelist* for giving the British Isles an inaccurate picture of American revivals and others denounced it for its "absolute falsehoods." [68]

After selling this paper in 1837 Leavitt took up the editorship of the *Emancipator,* moving it in 1842 to Boston, where he carried on the antislavery cause as well as the campaign for cheap postage, free trade, and temperance. He also undertook the editorship of the *Ballot Box*, which supported James G. Birney in the 1840 election. The year 1841 found him editing the *Free American*, a short-lived abolitionist paper. By 1848 the *Emancipator* had outlived its usefulness and was having financial difficulty. Whereupon, on Lewis Tappan's advice,[69] Leavitt returned to New York City to become assistant editor of the *Independent*. In 1858 he became its editor, which was done, as he put it, echoing Whittier's

---

[68] See Asahel Nettleton to William B. Sprague, March 16, 1833. Quoted in Birney, *The Life and Letters of Asahel Nettleton, 1783-1844*, p. 358; Waylen, *Ecclesiastical Reminiscences of the United States*, p. 414.

[69] "You have performed a great service for the slave and for your country . . . Perhaps, if your feelings are right, a religious newspaper would be the most useful thing you could attend to." Lewis Tappan to Leavitt, Dec. 9, 1846, Lewis Tappan Letter Book (Tappan Papers).

words of advice, "to give me a permanent support in my old age." [70]   For some twenty-five years he devoted the bulk of his energies to this organ.   In time he was outshined on the *Independent* by such men as Theodore Tilton and Henry Ward Beecher, and by 1866 he was dividing his labors between that journal and the *Evening Post* and writing articles for other papers as well.   It made for more steady work and increased his meager salary.[71]

Leavitt had a life-long interest in politics.   His contributions to the Liberty party are well known.   In December, 1841, with financial assistance from Lewis Tappan, he traveled to Washington to work in the antislavery petition fight then raging in Congress.   In 1847 he was involved in the Massachusetts fight over railroad charters and the following year found him attending the Free Soil party convention.   It was here that he moved Van Buren's unanimous nomination and rejoiced at the "translation" of the old Liberty party.   During 1852-1853 and in 1855 he interested himself again in Massachusetts politics.   In 1852 he predicted in eight years the victory of what became the Republican party.   He took an active part in Lincoln's campaign and counted the hours until his inauguration.   He supported the Civil War with gusto, asserting that it was "not only a duty but a privilege" to do so.[72]

Leavitt was an ardent free trader and wrote a number of pamphlets in its support.   Indeed, after the Civil War he devoted his chief energies toward tariff reform in Washington and seeing "if any thing can be done in favor of Free Trade." [73]   He had little influence, however, among the Radical Republicans and he was something of an anachronism in the Gilded Age.

Like Nettleton, Leavitt also brought out a collection of revival hymns which he called the *Christian Lyre*.   It included the favorite tunes of various denominations and was intended to "aid in re-

[70] Joshua Leavitt to Hooker Leavitt, Oct. 15, 1858 (Leavitt Papers).

[71] Joshua Leavitt to Hooker Leavitt, July 29, 1866 (Leavitt Papers).

[72] See Joshua Leavitt to Hooker Leavitt, March 2, 1861 (Leavitt Papers).

[73] Joshua Leavitt to Hooker Leavitt, Feb. 11, 1868 (Leavitt Papers).   Leavitt's chief articles on the subject include *An Essay on the Best Way of Developing Improved Political and Commercial Relations between Great Britain and the United States, Memorial on the Tariff Laws,* and *England and America.*

vivals of religion." [74] Leavitt even asked Finney to help in getting it circulated. It was designed primarily to increase the editor's income, but in this respect it was a dismal failure.

Leavitt was a versatile, if not completely successful, author. He published texts for elementary schools, wrote political tracts against Henry Clay, penned pamphlets favoring cheap postage, and gave the world his views on such other matters as the Monroe Doctrine, the history of Poland, and the position of Denmark in world affairs. In spite of his active career he periodically felt discouraged and considered returning to the pastorate of a church. Writing his brother at the time the *Emancipator* was about to collapse he confided, "I may receive a call and settle in the ministry somewhere in the country. . . . I am now preaching at South Weymouth where the people are Hopkinsians of the deepest dye, so that it is uncertain whether I shall pass for orthodox enough to suit them." [75]

Poor all his life, Leavitt seems to have developed a poverty complex. After his attack of cholera in 1835 he wrote his mother, "I felt as if there was a storm coming, and did not know what to do. Nothing afforded me encouragement, nothing excited me to action. I felt as if I had lost my labor, and lost my property, and lost my character, and lost my friends, and lost my hope." [76] The financial panic of 1837 was particularly disastrous to him. The *Evangelist* faced bankruptcy and only through a hasty sale was he saved from ruin. Four years later his antislavery society failed him. It could no longer pay his salary. Indeed, all his life he found it "very difficult to obtain the means of support in my present position." [77] But if reform movements and religious journals could not support him there was always the ministry: "What will be the next move I cannot tell. It may be I shall be driven back to the old hive, with all my helpless brood, but not if I can help it, I will work harder than I have yet, i.e., if I can find any thing to do." [78] At the end

[74] Joshua Leavitt to Charles Finney, Nov. 15, 1830 (Finney Papers).
[75] Joshua Leavitt to Hooker Leavitt, Dec. 7, 1847 (Leavitt Papers).
[76] Joshua Leavitt to Mrs. Leavitt, Jan. 17, 1835 (Leavitt Papers).
[77] Joshua Leavitt to Hooker Leavitt, Nov. 21, 1840 (Leavitt Papers).
[78] Joshua Leavitt to Hooker Leavitt, Nov. 9, 1841 (Leavitt Papers).

of his life he was still worrying about his poverty and considering himself a failure.

The New School Presbyterians contributed more than their share of vocal evangelists, of whom none was more prolific than Albert Barnes.[79] Barnes was born in Rome, New York, in 1798 into a family of Methodists. He worked with his father as a tanner until the age of seventeen, at which time he left home to study law. After attending an academy in Fairfield, Connecticut, he was enrolled in Hamilton College. It was here that the youth changed his vocational plans and during a revival decided to enter the ministry. He graduated from Hamilton in 1820, went through Princeton Theological Seminary, was licensed to preach in 1823, and subsequently became the pastor of the Presbyterian church at Morristown, New Jersey.

It did not take Barnes long to become well known. Although he was a quiet man lacking the bellicose manner of a Beecher, he was an outspoken advocate of what were then considered radical doctrines within the church. In 1829, in a sermon entitled *The Way of Salvation,* Barnes took the position that the sin of Adam was not charged against his descendants, thus seeming to deny the old Westminster Confession and the teachings of Jonathan Edwards. As he put it in his conclusion,

It is not part of this scheme . . . that God made men on purpose to damn them. . . . God made men to glorify himself in their holiness and felicity; and has made provision for their salvation, and if they do not choose to be saved . . . and HE does not choose to save them against their will, they cannot blame him for their self-chosen condemnation. . . . This scheme [Calvinism] if I understand it, contains nothing more than an enlargement of the principles which I have stated in this discourse. It neither asserts that God made men to damn them,—nor that infants will be damned nor that sinners will be lost, do what they can,—nor that God is unwilling to save them,—nor that a poor penitent may not be saved.[80]

---

[79] Autobiographical material may be gleaned from Albert Barnes, *Life at Three-Score,* and *Life at Three-Score and Ten.* See also David Magill, "Albert Barnes," *The Evangelical Witness and Presbyterian Review,* VII, No. 9 (1868), 233-237.

[80] Albert Barnes, *The Way of Salvation,* pp. 20, 27-28.

When Barnes moved to the First Presbyterian Church in Philadelphia, his position became more precarious. The more conservative of his colleagues opposed his installation and appealed to the Synod which in turn ordered the Presbytery to examine the sermon. The Rev. Ashbel Green, orthodox Philadelphian, was instrumental in leading this attack on Barnes's theology, and Barnes, put in a position similar to that of an accused Communist in the 1950's, had to prove the orthodoxy of his views. The outcome was a draw. Barnes's sermon was criticized; he refused to retract; and the General Assembly in 1831 condemned the position taken by his sermon but upheld his defense of his Philadelphia pastorate.[81]

His theological career was stormy. With every new work from his pen he was under the close scrutiny of the conservative elements in the Presbyterian Church. In 1835 there appeared his *Notes, Explanatory and Practical on the Epistle to the Romans* which touched off new charges against him which he in turn denied. This was followed by other commentaries on portions of the Old and New Testament in the same series, all of which constituted a New School interpretation of the Scriptures. That same year George Junkin, Old School Presbyterian minister, charged him with heresy on ten specifications but he was acquitted by his presbytery. An appeal was made to the Synod and Barnes was suspended from the ministry. The following year, when the New School faction had the majority in the General Assembly, the Synod's decision was reversed. Although Barnes's trial and the undercurrent of opposition to his theological teaching were not the only factors contributing to the disruption of the Presbyterian Church in 1837, they nevertheless played a very important part in the development of this schism.[82]

Barnes was also noted for his secular contributions. He played an essential role in the abolition and prohibition movements. His *An Inquiry into the Scriptural Views of Slavery* (1846) and *The*

---

[81] See Thompson, *History of the Presbyterian Church in the United States*, pp. 105-107.

[82] For a detailed description of this trial, see Gillett, *History of the Presbyterian Church*, II, 473 ff.; *Trial of the Rev. Albert Barnes*. See also *A True and Complete Narrative of all the Proceedings of the Philadelphia Presbytery, and of the Philadelphia Synod, in Relation to the Case of the Rev. Albert Barnes*, and *A Report of the Debates in the Presbytery of Philadelphia*.

Church and Slavery (1857) expounded forcefully the religious opposition to the "peculiar institution." He joined his colleagues in lashing out against Catholics, Unitarians, and Episcopalians with vigorous impartiality. Concerning his attack upon the latter, one critic remarked that it was "full of ignorance, and misapprehension, and misrepresentation of facts." [83]

But unlike many of his contemporaries, Barnes was more vitriolic in his pen than in his person. He was a quiet, gentle man, "tall and slender, of refined face and manner, without the physical elements of the orator." [84] He was considered an introvert by many of his associates. "He is not a social man," one wrote, "perhaps too much of the reserved temperament, nurtured, no doubt, by long and wearied contests with men, and by his habits of seclusion in his study." [85] It was alone in his study, in which he wrote from four until nine each morning, that he was most happy.[86]

Barnes helped instigate a great schism which for thirty-three years split one of the foremost sects in America. In his literary endeavors he contributed more than his share to the bulk of American religious literature. His eleven volumes of *Notes, Explanatory and Practical*, published between 1832 and 1853, sold over a million copies, attesting somewhat to his influence in the nineteenth century. Except for a few occasions when he failed to rouse a protracted meeting to the pitch of a revival, he was successful in the pulpit. By and large, in spite of the opposition raised against him during the seventy-two years of his life, his career was a series of well-enjoyed victorious engagements.

Horace Bushnell was an evangelist in spite of himself. Born in Litchfield in 1802, he graduated from Yale in 1827, tutored and taught school, worked on the editorial staff of the *New York Journal of Commerce,* and studied law before he turned to the

---

[83] *Remarks on Barnes' Inquiry,* p. 1. His attack was entitled *The Position of the Evangelical Party in the Episcopal Church.*
[84] Hoyt, *The Pulpit and American Life,* p. 220.
[85] Magill, "Albert Barnes," *The Evangelical Witness and Presbyterian Review,* p. 237.
[86] Albert Barnes, *Life at Three-Score,* pp. 54-55.

ministry.[87]   His editorials in the *Journal of Commerce* attracted
favorable attention, and the affairs of the office were left in his
hands the ten months that he was associated with the paper.   But
Bushnell found life in New York "terrible" and resigned to enter
law school at New Haven.   His brief teaching experience made
him equally miserable.[88]   In 1833 he became pastor of the North
Church of Hartford, Connecticut, which he served for the next
twenty-one years.

Although he did not devote his career to conducting revivals and
although he remained at one pastorate for most of his ministerial
days, nevertheless he may be considered a spokesman for evangelism.   In his personality, in his activities, and in many of his ideas
he resembled the Beechers and Finneys of American Protestantism.
His modification of determinism was similar to that of other evangelists.   His emphasis on the individual in Christian experience, his
magnetic qualities of religious leadership, his ability to weld public
sentiment, and his tendency to antagonize less cautious clerical
colleagues justify including him among the representative evangelists.

Symbolic of Bushnell's connection with evangelism was his reply
to a fellow minister who objected to the arrival of a special revivalist in Hartford.   "However we may differ about the desira-
bleness of revivals," he declared, "we can certainly agree that we
all need reviving." [89]   Although he is noted for his contributions
to New England theology his primary emphasis was on religious
experience rather than on the fine points of doctrine and only re-
luctantly did he enter the lists to battle with the theological hair-
splitters.   He summed up his opinion of doctrinal wrangling when
he wrote, "May God in his mercy deliver me . . . from all this

[87] There is no satisfactory biography of Bushnell. Cheney, *Life and Letters of
Horace Bushnell*, while detailed in every respect, is handicapped by a daughter's uncritical admiration. Munger, *Horace Bushnell, Preacher and Theologian*, is a more
critical study of his theological views. See also Brastow, *Representative Modern
Preachers*, and Foster, *A Genetic History of New England Theology*.

[88] "I don't make a good pedagogue . . . . It requires too much patience and forebearance for my composition." Horace Bushnell to Cortlandt Van Rensaelaer, Dec.
23, 1827, in Cheney, *Life and Letters of Horace Bushnell*, p. 49.

[89] Quoted in Trumbull, *My Four Religious Teachers*, p. 105.

ecclesiastical brewing of scandals and heresies, the wire-pulling, the schemes to get power or to keep it, the factions got up to ventilate wounded pride and get compensation for the chagrin of defeat." [90]

Bushnell's biographers, by emphasizing his opposition to the excesses of revivals and by narrowly interpreting his comments on Christian nurture, have placed him outside the evangelistic camp.[91] His "Spiritual Economy of Revivals of Religion," widely hailed as a rebuke to revivals, contained praise for evangelism as well as criticism. This work, first published in the *Quarterly Christian Spectator* in 1838, was republished in Bushnell's *Views of Christian Nurture* in 1847 and included in an 1881 posthumous volume entitled, *Building Eras in Religion*.

The purpose of this essay was, in Bushnell's words, "to establish a higher and more solid confidence in revivals, and at the same time, to secure to the cause of evangelical religion a more natural, satisfactory, and happy, as well as a more constant movement." He believed there were good and bad elements in revivals and following the approach of Jonathan Edwards, he desired to improve the former and remove the latter. "They are grounded . . . both in honor and dishonor. They belong in part to the original appointment and plan of God's moral administration, in which part, they are only modes or varieties of divine action, necessary to our renewal and culture in the faith." The deleterious part, he believed, rested on the instability of man. Revivals were useful as a dramatization of divine action, but he opposed, as did many ministers, the separation of "the divine agency in men, from the general system in which it belongs." [92]

The Hartford divine found ample justification for revivals in the omnipresence of God, in the change inherent in the universe, and in the changing moods, fluctuations, or "mental tides" that rolled around the earth:

[90] Horace Bushnell to Rev. A. S. Chesebrough, Jan. 23, 1854, in Cheney, *Life and Letters of Horace Bushnell*, p. 324.

[91] See, for instance, Myers, *Horace Bushnell and Religious Education*, pp. 8-9.

[92] Horace Bushnell, "Spiritual Economy of Revivals of Religion," *Quarterly Christian Spectator*, I, No. 1 (1838), 132.

We only know that God is present to these fluctuations, whatever their real nature, and that they are all inhabited by the divine power. Is it incredible, then, that this same divine power should produce periodic influences in the matter of religion, times of peculiar, various and periodical interest? For ourselves we are obliged to confess, that we strongly suspect that sort of religion which boasts of no excitements, no temporary and changing states; for we observe that it is only towards nothing, or about nothing, that we have always the same feeling.[93]

Revivals of religion, therefore, resemble the spring of the year. Both are periods of excitation, new feeling, a rousing of spiritual lethargy. He declared there was nothing derogatory in concluding that "the spiritual spring cannot remain perpetual; for there is progress in God's works." [94]

Bushnell's plea for diversity in religion, for attention to the more tranquil aspects of religion, did not prevent him from underscoring the significant role he believed evangelism should play. He affirmed, "there is no doubt that changes and seasons of various exercise, like these called revivals, add to the real power of the faith." Continuing his praise of "periodic exaltations" he maintained:

Nature would make no manifestation of him who dwells in her forms, if all stood motionless; if the sun stood fast and clear in everlasting noon; if there were no births, decays, explosions, surprises . . . . So the Spirit will reveal his divine presence through the church, by times of holy excitement, times of reflection, times of solitary communion, times of patient hope.[95]

Bushnell found particular satisfaction in the "participation" revivals afforded to churchgoers:

What a community, what a crowded assembly feels, is powerfully felt. Hence it is an article of the divine economy in revivals, that whole communities shall be moved together, as it were by common gales of the Spirit. The hold thus taken of men is powerful, often to a degree even tremendous, and many a covenant with death is disannulled which no uniform or unvaried tenor of divine agency, no mere personal and private dealing of the Spirit, would ever have shaken.[96]

93 *Ibid.*, p. 137.
94 *Ibid.*
95 *Ibid.*, p. 139.
96 *Ibid.*, p. 140.

What perplexed Bushnell about revivals bothered Beecher and Finney as well. He deplored, first, the "backslidings, or declensions of religious principle" which came in their wake and, second, the feeling among some evangelists that a high pitch of excitement had to be kept at all times. There were intervals when the church should not expect many conversions, protracted meetings, and the other accouterments of a revival. "The Christian warfare is not all battle. There are times in it for polishing the armor, forming the tactics, and feeding the vigor of the host." [97]

Bushnell's criticism of the excesses of revivals was shared by others. Nettleton and later Finney echoed the Hartford minister's attack on the extremists who were doing more harm than good. Most evangelists agreed with his statement, "Where too much is made of conversions, or where they are taken as the measure of all good, it has a very injurious influence. . . . The great business of the gospel is to form men to God. Conversion . . . is the beginning of the work." [98]

Critical though he was, Bushnell's essay defended the grounds on which revivalism rested and parts of his essay were an eloquent rationale for evangelistic activity. His conclusion illustrates Bushnell's middle position:

Nothing was ever achieved, in the way of a great and radical change in men or communities, without some degree of excitement; and if anyone expects to carry on the cause of salvation by a steady rolling on the same dead level, and fears continually lest the axles wax hot and kindle into a flame, he is too timorous to hold the reins in the Lord's chariot. What we complain of and resist is, the artificial fireworks, the extraordinary jump and stir, supposed to be requisite when anything is to be done.[99]

Attempts to classify Bushnell and his theology in one or another of the discordant groups which divided the Congregationalists and Presbyterians in the early nineteenth century and which split within themselves over fine points of doctrine are fruitless. He was, like Erasmus before him, his own party, an uncompromising individualist. Indeed, he has been called the man "who finally re-

97 *Ibid.*, pp. 141, 142.
98 *Ibid.*, p. 144.
99 *Ibid.*, pp. 143-144.

leased Congregational theological thought . . . from the confining bonds of a Calvinism which had lost its creative significance." [100] In constructing his theology he drew from all groups and all ages. [101] In his own words, his main aim in preaching was never "to overthrow one school and set up the other; neither was it to find a position of neutrality midway between them; but as far as theology is concerned, it was to comprehend, if possible, the truth contended for in both." [102] Nevertheless, William Warren Sweet has put it well in remarking that because of the logic and coldness in it, Bushnell "threw Calvinism overboard." [103]

Unwilling to take sides, reluctant to give battle, Bushnell nevertheless became entangled in a number of doctrinal disputes. He was sufficiently free of orthodox restraints to incur the wrath of more consistent Calvinists. He was sufficiently conservative to prevent a widespread acceptance of his views. His argument with Hawes of Hartford who helped form the "Pastoral Union" and the attacks upon him made by the Fairfield West Association prevented him from enjoying a more placid life as pastor of the North Church in Hartford. [104]

Each new work from his pen drew barbs of criticism. His *Views of Christian Nurture* (1848), with its thesis that a child was able to grow up a Christian and never be anything else, drew scorn from those who saw in it a break with the Edwardean tradition. His *God in Christ* (1849) was attacked by enthusiasts of revivals for its criticism of that mode of conversion. It was also condemned in the major religious journals as a pantheistic work. The New York *Evangelist* devoted three articles to it; the *Biblical Repository and Princeton Review* denounced it soundly; and the Boston *Christian Observatory* gave sixty pages of one issue over to a severe attack. *Christ in Theology* (1851) had a similar recep-

---

[100] Atkins and Fagley, *History of American Congregationalism*, pp. 173-174.

[101] The best expressions of Bushnell's theology are to be found in *Views of Christian Nurture, God in Christ*, and *Christ in Theology*.

[102] Bushnell, *Twentieth Anniversary, a Commemorative Discourse*, p. 14.

[103] Sweet, *The American Churches*, p. 128.

[104] For an account of Bushnell's theological disputes, see Cheney, *Life and Letters of Horace Bushnell*, pp. 234 ff.

tion. His later works, *Nature and the Supernatural, The Vicarious Sacrifice* and *Forgiveness and Law* brought their share of criticism.

Bushnell's reaction to this almost ceaseless round of controversy was typical. "I begin to find that I am looked upon hereabout as a mortally dangerous person," he exclaimed in 1848. "I think I have never seemed to be quite so much isolated as now." [105] "Have you read the long review in the Princeton?" he wrote one friend. "You have seen me a pantheist in the Evangelist. Why not an atheist as well, with a special incarnation and a plan of supernatural redemption? This would enlighten the Germans!" And to his wife he confided, "I am looked at here by the mass as a kind of horned animal." [106]

Bushnell struck back forcefully at his critics and at the hair-splitting doctrinal disputants. In caustic tones he declared in the Preface to his *Christ in Theology*:

To see brought up, in distinct array before us, the multitudes of leaders and schools and theologic wars of only the century past,—the Supralapsarians and Sublapsarians; the Arminianizers and the true Calvinists; the Pelagians and the Augustinians the Tasters and the Exercisers . . . nothing I think would more certainly disenchant us of our confidence in systematic orthodoxy, and the possibility in human language of an exact theologic science, than an exposition so practical and serious, and withal so indisputably mournful—so mournfully indisputable.[107]

Bushnell's chief contribution to New England theology was in making it more flexible, broader in its scope, and more inspiring to the individual. In redefining the basic beliefs of his church he was able to avoid the pitfalls of an austere incomprehensibility on the one hand and heresy on the other. Nowhere is this contribution better illustrated than in his chapter on "Preliminary Dissertation on the Nature of Language" as related to thought and spirit which was included in *God in Christ*. His thesis in this chapter was that our language is insufficient for the uses of dogma and that much of the difficulty involved in theological study arises from the

---

[105] Horace Bushnell to Dr. Bartol, Oct. 11, 1848, quoted in *ibid.*, p. 211.

[106] Bushnell to Rev. Henry Goodwin, April 12, 1849, Bushnell to Mrs. Bushnell, May 30, 1849, in *ibid.*, p. 221.

[107] Bushnell, *Christ in Theology*, pp. v-vi.

multiplicity of meaning and interpretation possible in our tongue. "In algebra and geometry," he pointed out, "the ideas themselves being absolute, the terms or names also may be; but in mental science and religion, no such exactness is possible, because our apprehensions of truth are here only proximate and relative." [108] Mere human language then cannot produce a complete Christian theology nor can truth be made to fit into the molds of any particular statement. The Hartford divine expressed only pity for those who blindly tried to explain with frail words the immensity of religious thought. Equally shocking, in his opinion, was the action of those who warred with words against what they considered the heresies of others. Creeds and catechisms, he reminded his readers, have not the certainty they are commonly supposed to have. Truth is dynamic; civilizations change. Words give us the meaning of an author only at a precise moment in time and they are true only at that time. A decade or century later the truth must be rephrased, redefined.

Words, therefore, are inexact representations of thought symbols, "proximate expressions." Is there any hope that they will be anything else, that religious truth will ever be more understandable to man? Bushnell believed so:

It is, that physical science, leading the way, setting outward things in their true proportions . . . will so perfect our knowledge and conceptions of them, that we can use them in the second department of language with more exactness. . . . Therefore, as nature becomes more truly a universe only through science revealing its universal laws, the true universe of thought and spirit cannot sooner be conceived.[109]

If anyone desired unity and piety within the church it was Horace Bushnell. Wearily he chided his contemporaries for their divisiveness: "Opinions, deductions of mere logic, dogmas impotent and dry, discussed, debated, stood for by some, rejected by others, yielding to none the true food of life—these, with such intermixtures of strife and fire as are naturally to be expected, constitute the history of religion." [110] Again, "We cannot, therefore, spend

[108] Bushnell, *God in Christ*, p. 72.
[109] *Ibid.*, pp. 78-79.
[110] *Ibid.*, p. 338.

our strength now upon exclusive and distinctive dogmas, but we must proceed in a catholic and comprehensive spirit. Otherwise we shall be at war with each other, and shall only spend our forces, in demolishing all the force we have." [111]

But while Bushnell was one of the most influential theologians in New England, his activities were not by any means limited to doctrinal disputes and complicated points of theology. His interests embraced most of the major reform movements of the day; he was an energetic proponent of missionary activities, an outspoken critic of Catholicism, and an enthusiastic crusader in educational circles.[112] Early in his career he declined the presidency of Middlebury College and later, in 1856, while in California for his health, he was instrumental in picking a site for and founding the University of California, the presidency of which was later offered him. He has been credited with deciding the best route for a transcontinental railroad across the Sierra Nevada Mountains, and his views on the slavery issue were original and important. Strongly nationalistic, few issues escaped his comment, and in later life he went so far as to declaim vigorously against the women's suffrage movement.[113] He was actively vocal on matters ranging from presidential elections to the fate of the Hartford water works.

Bushnell's appearance changed with the years. One biographer describes him as "strong of physique, tall, muscular, with a head of unusual size covered with black hair; and a ruddy complexion, with deepset gray eyes." Another speaks of him as "of medium stature, without bulk of figure, rather delicate in organization, yet lithe and full of nerve force." His daughter pictures "the spare, sinewy figure, tense yet easy in its motions . . . the high broad forehead . . . the kindling gray eyes, deep-set under beetling black eyebrows." And a Yale student used these words: "Gaunt was he, gray, ashen of skin, thin-voiced till he got under way,

---

111 Bushnell, *Barbarism the First Danger*, p. 31.

112 For the most blatant example of Bushnell's anti-Catholicism see *Barbarism, the First Danger*. Another anti-Catholic work, *Common Schools*, best expresses his educational views. For his antislavery position, see "Horace Bushnell and the Slavery Question," *New England Quarterly*, XXIII, No. 1 (1950), 19-30.

113 See Bushnell, *Women's Suffrage, the Reform against Nature*.

stopping time and again to cough." Many spoke of his "chronic cough" and of his eyes "so piercing and benign." One biographer has written, "The one supremely masterful thing about his physical manhood was the eagle eye. There was a singular fascination about it. It held one as a spell." [114]

Well in advance for his age, this quietly eloquent divine did for nineteenth-century theology what Jonathan Edwards accomplished for the eighteenth. His influence among religious thinkers was revealed in the 1840's when several prominent religious periodicals attacked his major work, *God in Christ,* but were unable to silence him or prove their charges of heresy against him. He pioneered in the field of religious education with his book, *Views of Christian Nurture.* Many preachers of the Social Gospel later in the century acknowledged their debt to him.[115]

If he was versatile enough to have been an artist or an architect, a surveyor or a scholar, the contributions Bushnell made to his own field were sufficient on which to base his fame. In religious matters he came along at the precise moment to bring about the final overthrow of Calvinism's tyranny over the minds of American divines and his writings were among the first signs of a new theology for which his generation was not yet ready. The opinion of George B. Stevens that Bushnell was "one of the greatest religious geniuses which Christianity has hitherto produced," while a bit too adulatory is nevertheless understandable in the light of all his achievements.[116] Bushnell was a man to be reckoned with.

Henry Ward Beecher was, by far, the most famous of Lyman's sons. He was a man of robust vitality, of medium height, endowed with a rich voice, "a lionesque head," a ruddy face, bushy eyebrows, and long flowing hair that fell over his ears and coat collar. Lyman Abbott, who knew him well, described him as "slightly under six feet; powerfully built; not corpulent, but

---

[114] Addison, *The Clergy in American Life and Letters,* p. 271; Brastow, *Representative Modern Preachers,* pp. 155, 158-159; Cheney, *Life and Letters of Horace Bushnell,* p. 171; Munger, *Horace Bushnell, Preacher and Theologian,* pp. 290, 361.
[115] Gladden, *Pioneers of Religious Liberty in America,* pp. 227-263.
[116] Quoted in Buckham, *Progressive Religious Thought in America,* p. 6.

stocky. His general appearance suggested great strength." To others it suggested something else, and not everyone was as kind as Abbott in overlooking his excess weight. Fowler, the phrenologist, summed it all up by calling him a "splendid animal." [117]

Henry Ward's major activities occurred after the Civil War, and it is only with the first portion of his career that this study is concerned. He was born in Litchfield in 1813 and died in Brooklyn in 1887. Much about his later unusual personality can be explained in terms of his early lonely, suppressed life. His father squelched his boyhood plans for a life at sea, and after a religious experience resulting from a revival he turned toward the ministry much to Lyman's great delight. He graduated from Amherst in 1834 and studied theology at Lane under his father's tutelage. That his theological views in later life should have been so far from those of Lyman Beecher's is partly owing to this intensive grounding in the fundamentals of Calvinist thought.

Henry Ward's first pastorate was at the Presbyterian church in Lawrenceburgh, Indiana, where he was installed in 1837. Partly because of his father's reputation, he encountered difficulty in getting ordained. It was not until 1838 that he was finally made a full minister by a New School Synod in Cincinnati. His religious views were too radically inclined for him long to remain within the Presbyterian fold. In 1847 he became a Congregationalist because of the greater freedom that sect afforded him in terms of theology and polity. And while his older brother was championing the antislavery cause Henry Ward chose a less controversial subject and attacked drunkenness with all his vigor.

In 1839 he moved to Indianapolis, where he stayed until 1847. It was not until that year, however, that at the age of thirty-four he came East to the Plymouth Church in Brooklyn and began attracting public attention. People flocked to hear him in increasing numbers. His unconventional personality, his colorful mode of delivery, emphasizing a picturesque and dramatic speech, his

[117] Abbott, *Henry Ward Beecher*, p. 100. The latest and most complete biography is Hibben, *Henry Ward Beecher: an American Portrait*, which is distinguished for its detailed, critical account. Useful earlier works, such as Barrows, *Henry Ward Beecher*, and Howard, *Life of Henry Ward Beecher*, are hampered by their uncritical praise.

wit and natural friendliness made him the idol of many. His Sunday congregations, made up of all classes of persons, averaged twenty-five hundred. Visitors from all parts of the country made it a point to hear him preach. His church was an important stop on any sightseeing tour of the metropolis. His sermons were printed in pamphlet form and widely circulated. He was a regular contributor to the *Independent* and from 1861 until 1864 was its editor. From 1870 until 1881 he was editor of the *Christian Union* and also contributed to the New York *Ledger*. His writings for these papers have been called the "strongest editorials in the American press." [118]

Soon after arriving in Brooklyn he was forced to take a stand on the slavery issue. He also felt called upon to air his views on other public questions. Often inconsistent, he opposed the compromise of 1850 and advocated disobedience of the fugitive slave law. His antislavery activity was brought to a climax in the Kansas-Nebraska dispute. He campaigned strenuously for Frémont and in 1860 for Lincoln, although his contribution to his party's victory was undoubtedly less than he imagined. His visit to England in 1863 was controversial but of little significance. In spite of Oliver Wendell Holmes's assertion, Henry Ward's activity in the British Isles had little or no effect upon the course of the Civil War.[119]

In addition to his antislavery activities he supported other moral reform movements, notably the temperance crusade. He spoke in favor of women's suffrage, was an advocate of free trade, and after the Civil War was enthusiastic, although somewhat inconsistent, in his acceptance of evolution. In whatever movement he espoused, he was always the showman. His auctioning of Negro slave girls was but one example of his fondness for publicity. He

---

[118] William P. Trent, John Erskine, Stuart P. Sherman, Carl Van Doren, *Cambridge History of American Literature*, III, 325.

[119] See Oliver Wendell Holmes, "The Minister Plenipotentiary" in Henry Ward Beecher, *Patriotic Addresses*, pp. 422-434. See also Hibben, *Henry Ward Beecher: an American Portrait*, p. 191. Of interest is the following letter from one of Finney's English friends: "Your paper and your great preacher the Rev. Beecher have sadly maligned our country and view us altogether in the same sense [sic] as though we were to say there is no difference between the north and the south." Potto Brown to Charles Finney, Dec. 6, 1863 (Finney Papers).

made an appeal for temperance on the same platform with P. T. Barnum and went out of his way to visit the frigate Niagara that was to lay the cable across the Atlantic Ocean. He put Plymouth Church at the disposal of Louis Kossuth and in his introduction of the revolutionist flamboyantly asked his congregation to "bear witness . . . how often from this place prayers have been offered and tears shed when we have heard of the struggles of Hungary." [120]

In true evangelistic tradition he published *The Plymouth Collection of Hymns and Tunes* (1855), which he claimed were "wide enough in range to be used by any evangelical church." [121] Compared with what Nettleton and Leavitt turned out, Henry Ward's hymnal was unusual to say the least. One of the tunes used was the same as that of "Tippecanoe and Tyler Too!" At a time when Edward and Catherine Beecher and Harriet Beecher Stowe were making their literary marks, *The Plymouth Collection* was hardly a masterpiece. But Henry Ward was proud of it nonetheless and preferred to ignore the caustic comments of the *Independent* which called the collection "better suited for Christy's Minstrels than for a church." [122]

Beecher's private life and amorous peccadillos are of little significance as far as this study is concerned. The Tilton affair merely brought to a climax the series of personal difficulties of a private nature in which the nineteenth-century evangelist became embroiled. Its inconclusive outcome was typical of such cases. It is interesting to note, however, that at the time of Henry Ward's trial, Charles G. Finney for seventeen cogent reasons could not help but conclude that Lyman's son was guilty. [123]

Henry Ward was not an original thinker but rather a popularizer who was able to judge keenly the course of public opinion. He reached his conclusions as the result of emotional outbursts rather than dispassionate thought. He thundered from the crowd

---

[120] Quoted in Abbott, *Henry Ward Beecher*, p. 214.

[121] Henry Ward Beecher, *The Plymouth Collection of Hymns and Tunes*,

[122] Quoted in Hibben, *Henry Ward Beecher: an American Portrait*, p. 156. See *The Independent*, Nov. 22, 29, Dec. 13, 1855.

[123] See "Why I Cannot Believe Mr. Beecher Innocent" (undated MS, Finney Papers).

but was rarely in its front ranks. He may have been a "born belligerent" but he was also a cautious one.[124]

Henry Ward Beecher was the last of the mid-century men of God. In a sense, he stands as the bridge between the Finneys of the 1830's and the Moodys of the 1880's. He belonged to both ages although he reached the culmination of his powers after the Civil War. When he died in 1887 some forty thousand persons paid tribute to him before his burial. Some measure of his influence can be seen in Lyman Abbott's confession: "His exuberant life, his startling audacity, his dramatic oratory, his passionate fire, his flashes of humor, his native boyishness, all combined to fascinate me." Even the judicious Ernest T. Thompson has been led to conclude that Henry Ward Beecher "was the most popular preacher of his day; the most powerful preacher, many think, ever to appear in America; the greatest pulpit orator, some have even dared to claim, in the whole history of the Christian Church." Paxton Hibben has appropriately summarized the theme of his life in words that could well apply to all evangelists as a "hunger for love . . . hunger for power." [125]

The greatest evangelist of all was Charles Grandison Finney.[126] Born in 1792 in Warren, Litchfield County, Connecticut, Finney spent his boyhood along the frontier in Oneida County, New York. The War of 1812 led him to seek enlistment in the Navy and he went to Sackett's Harbor with that intention, but his services were not accepted. The town at the time has been described as "a scene of confusion and disorder"; Finney was accosted by an "abandoned woman" in it. He retreated home after these ex-

[124] John R. Howard, "Review of Mr. Beecher's Personality and Political Influence," in Beecher, *Patriotic Addresses*, p. 19.

[125] Abbott, *Henry Ward Beecher*, p. 7; Thompson, *Changing Emphases in American Preaching*, p. 53; Hibben, *Henry Ward Beecher: an American Portrait*, p. 324.

[126] The most complete biography of Finney is Wright, *Charles Grandison Finney*. Beardsley, *A Mighty Winner of Souls, Charles Grandison Finney*, is a more recent work which focuses on the revivalist's evangelistic talents. Much illuminating information is contained in Fletcher, *A History of Oberlin College*. Typical of the eulogistic, uncritical religious biographies is Miller, *Charles G. Finney, He Prayed Down Revivals*. Essential biographical material is also contained in the Finney Papers, Oberlin College Library.

periences to spend the rest of his youth in more peaceful pursuits.[127]
He taught school and worked in a law office before entering the
ministry in 1822.

It was in 1821 that Finney had the religious experience that directed him toward evangelism. He went off into the woods and
came out a new man. This conversion molded his methods as well
as his life, and the emotional struggle through which he went influenced his later techniques at conversion.[128] Instead of going to
Princeton as he was advised, Finney pursued his theological studies
under George W. Gale, the local pastor, and was licensed to preach
in March, 1824.[129] So advanced were some of his religious views
that after his first sermon Gale exclaimed, "Mr. Finney, I shall be
very much ashamed to have it known, wherever you go, that you
studied theology with me!"[130] That same month he received a
commission from a women's missionary society to labor for six
months in the northern part of Jefferson County.[131] It was a
lowly start. The next year he was employed by the Oneida Evangelical Association at a salary of $600 "to labor in such places as
your best judgment shall direct."[132]

Finney first attracted national prominence during his phenome-
nally successful revivals through the Mohawk Valley in 1826.
These, called at the time the "Western Revivals" carried Finney
through Western, Rome, Utica, and Troy, leaving in his wake
religiously reinvigorated communities. Scores of converts were
added to the church. As he later put it, "The sword of the Lord
slew them on the right hand and on the left."[133] It was during
this revival that the vigorous neophyte first came to the attention
of the older, more experienced members of his profession, such as

[127] Beardsley, A Mighty Winner of Souls, Charles G. Finney, p. 13.

[128] A vivid account of his conversion is contained in his Memoirs, pp. 14-21.

[129] According to his occasionally inaccurate Memoirs the date is 1824, but according
to the minutes of the presbytery he was licensed Dec. 30, 1823. See Fowler, Historical
Sketch of Presbyterianism within the Bounds of the Synod of Central New York, p. 258.

[130] Finney, Memoirs, p. 52.

[131] Utica Female Missionary Society to Finney, March 17, 1824 (Finney Papers).

[132] Oneida Evangelical Association, Utica to Finney, Jan. 1, 1827 (Finney Papers).

[133] Finney, Memoirs, p. 74.

Nettleton and Lyman Beecher, leading to a meeting which had profound repercussions for the revival movement.[134]

During the rest of his career Finney conducted revivals in many parts of the country, preaching first in Philadelphia in 1827, in New York in 1829, and in Boston in 1831. He was instrumental in the free church movement in New York and was named first pastor of the Broadway Tabernacle Church when it was organized in that city in 1834. In 1835 he helped establish a theological department at Oberlin and for a number of years combined college teaching with the conducting of revivals in the East. He also took on the pastorate of the First Congregational Church in Oberlin. From 1851 until 1866 he served as president of Oberlin. He made two trips to England during his career, married three times, and had five children. He finally died in 1875 at the age of eighty-three.

Finney played a varied, active role in early nineteenth-century American history. Although he was noted principally for his work in conducting religious revivals throughout the country, he also threw himself into the antislavery and temperance movements as well as other reform activities. While a member of the Oberlin faculty he became interested in the cause of education in the West. He engaged at frequent intervals in animated theological controversies with his ministerial colleagues, and with Asa Mahan of Oberlin he elaborated the religious theories of perfectionism. After the Civil War, still looking for new worlds to conquer, he joined his last great crusade, the drive against secret societies.

This remarkable revivalist had a great facility for precipitating disputes, causing crises, and contributing to controversies. Early in his career, he and Lyman Beecher crossed verbal swords over the heads of converts while both men were engaged in carrying on a revival in Boston. At other times Finney disputed with Asahel Nettleton, with Horace Bushnell, and with other religious notables of the time. Even in his travels to England he left controversy and dissension behind him. One of his English correspondents, in commenting on Finney's style of preaching, expressed the views

---

[134] For a study of this conference and its results, see "The New Lebanon Convention," *New York History*, XXI, No. 4 (1950), 385-397.

of his compatriots when he declared that "the system is not adapted to England. My own opinion is that it is not adapted to any place." [135]

Nonetheless, much of Finney's success was attributed to the methods he employed in his preaching—using colloquial speech, appealing to the emotions of his audience, praying for individuals by name, permitting women to pray in his services, using assistants who formed "a holy band" to help him win converts. In time this preaching style became synonymous with what were called "new measures." To Finney, these were not theatrical tricks. Desperate occasions demanded desperate devices.

Finney's physical features, his tall massive figure, his thick eyebrows which hung over fiery expressive eyes which were often called "hypnotic" suggested the restless, forceful character. As his biographer has indicated, Finney had "a fine physical frame, exceptional grace of movement, and a commanding appearance. He had a voice of rare clearness, compass, and flexibility, and he was passionately fond of music." [136] In the pulpit such a man radiated energy. He was vigorous in his delivery, dramatic in his method of attack, magnetic in his appeal. In the words of one of his contemporaries, "He threw his whole self into his work." [137] His awe-inspiring figure underscored the impact of his message. To one admirer, "The glance of his full sharp eye and the tones of his commanding voice were in keeping with the sterner aspects of truth, which he never failed to present with searching discrimination and powerful effect." [138]

The impressions of Finney's pulpit style are varied. Lewis Tappan recorded in 1828 the reactions of the typical stranger upon first encountering Finney:

Went to Dr. Spring's to hear the celebrated Mr. Phinney [sic] He preached extemporaneously. . . . His discourse was perhaps an hour long. . . . His prayer was fervent, and his sermon pungent. He appears to be a

---

[135] M. Robinson to Finney, Feb. 4, 1859 (Finney Papers).
[136] Wright, *Charles Grandison Finney*, pp. 18-19.
[137] Fowler, *Historical Sketch of Presbyterianism within the Bounds of the Synod of Central New York*, p. 259.
[138] Hawley, *The History of the First Presbyterian Church, Auburn, N.Y.*, p. 50.

man of good natural powers; is often effective, solemn, and tender; is fearless and plain; and at the same time has too many common place phrases. He did not displease me as much as I expected—preached better —but did not so affect the audience or leave so great an impression as I had expected. He is a spiritual harrow.[139]

A year later Tappan knew his hero better; his record of Finney's sermons was briefer: "Heard Mr. Finney on Mercy. Matter good. Manner faulty—and effect not solemn." [140]

Much of the criticism of his style in the early days stemmed from his extemporaneous, coarse, colloquial expressions. As he himself put it, "They used to complain that I let down the dignity of the pulpit; that I was a disgrace to the ministerial profession; that I talked like a lawyer at the bar; that I talked to the people in a colloquial manner." [141] One contemporary described his preaching as "a rude and vulgar dialect, ornamented with a selection of slang expressions, enforced with grimaces, and theatrical gestures." [142]

Later in his career, after an acquaintance with city congregations, complaints came from the opposite direction. He became in the minds of many too refined. Even brother Tappan noticed the change: "Mr. F. is less effective than formerly I think," he confided to his diary, and later he wrote the evangelist warning him against his more cultured trend: "*Confidential*—I am afraid but few of your audience understood your first Lecture, and some of those who did understand it thot [sic] it too *bookish* and unpopular." [143] But whether he was being coarse or cultured, Finney "corralled his audience; he drove them before him, penned them in, coerced them by his logic . . . compelled them to accept his conclusions despite their resistance."[144]

[139] Lewis Tappan Diary, July 20, 1828, p. 39 (Lewis Tappan Papers).
[140] *Ibid.*, Oct. 18, 1829, p. 90.
[141] Finney, *Memoirs*, p. 83.
[142] Baird, *A History of the New School*, p. 266.
[143] Lewis Tappan Diary, Mar. 13, 1836, p. 14; Lewis Tappan to Finney, Dec. 2, 1842 (Lewis Tappan Papers).
[144] Abbott, *Henry Ward Beecher*, p. 401.

In the early 1830's Charles Finney was close to Lyman Beecher in many of the fine points of theology. Their followers tended to think of them as cut from the same cloth; their names were linked by opponents of the New School. Indeed, the Rev. J. L. Wilson pinned much of his heresy arguments against Beecher on the grounds that there was a close affinity between them. In 1831 the ministers of New Haven wrote Finney that his views were theirs with minor exceptions. Finney himself recorded that Beecher had told him "he had never seen a man with whose theological views he so entirely accorded, as he did with mine." [145]

Finney's theology went through a number of phases. First, there were the early formative years from his conversion until 1826 when the conservative doctrines of his theological teacher, George W. Gale, conflicted with his youthful individualism and exuberant impatience. During these years he was "but a child in theology." [146] The second stage from 1826 until 1835 marked the years when Finney experimented with new measures and moved into the orbit of the New Haven group. During this period he had no well-defined set of theological principles. His move to Oberlin marked the beginning of the third phase which contained the bulk of his published work and in which he moved steadily toward what was then termed "sanctification" or perfectionism.

As Finney began preaching he discovered that much of the Old School thought was foreign to his methods. The old ideas stood in his way. The assumption of the impotence of man and the all-powerfulness of God had brought about a certain passivity which he deplored. The feeling among churchgoers was that if they were elect, in time the Spirit would move them and they would become converted. If they were not of the elect, nothing they could do for themselves or that anyone else tried to do could possibly save them. Finney believed that moral depravity was a voluntary attitude of the mind and consequently something which sinful man

---

[145] See *Trial of the Rev. Lyman Beecher, D.D., before the Presbytery of Cincinnati on the Charge of Heresy*, p. 21; Ministers of New Haven to Finney, April 12, 1831 (Finney Papers); Finney, *Memoirs*, pp. 316-317.

[146] Finney, *Memoirs*, p. 42. For his description of his clashes with Gale, see pp. 42-58 and 153-158.

could help change. He believed also that the influence of the Spirit of God on man was moral, persuasive, that man could be led to recognize how he in his limited way could come upon conversion. As Finney put it, "I held also that there are means of regeneration, and that the truths of the Bible are, in their nature, calculated to lead the sinner to abandon his wickedness and turn to God." [147] Furthermore, Finney held that the preacher fulfilled a function in bringing about this conversion in that the Holy Spirit operated in him, clearly revealing those truths which when eloquently set before an audience were calculated to bring about their conversion. His use of the anxious seat in revivals was symbolic of his break with the old orthodoxy, for it was an invitation to the individual who was ready to repent of his sins to come forward for spiritual guidance. He was the first to admit, "I was regarded by many as teaching new and strange doctrines." [148]

Another notable deviation in his theology was his insistence that conversion was merely the beginning of one's religious experience. The new convert must apply his religion to daily life, carrying on from where his conversion left off. The tendency therefore was to make religion more practical for the individual participant.

Then too, the Oberlin divine was noted for his dislike of ecclesiastical machinery. He lacked the patience to weather annual assemblies and ministerial discussions. He had no time for synods and for the presbyterian hierarchy. As he once put it, "there was a jubilee in hell whenever the Presbyterian General Assembly met." [149] It was surprising that he waited until the Broadway Tabernacle was built in 1836 to withdraw from the Presbyterian Church. Earlier his good friend Luther Myrick had told him, "I believe you mistaken as to the course that ought to be pursued to bring about a reform—I predict you never will do it by remaining in the presbytery. . . . Congregationalism is far preferable." [150]

[147] *Ibid.*, p. 154.
[148] *Ibid.*, pp. 157-158.
[149] Quoted in Wright, *Charles Grandison Finney*, p. 266.
[150] Luther Myrick to Finney, Sept. 19, 1833 (Finney Papers).

It was in an effort to clear up misunderstanding that Finney brought out his major theological work, *Sermons on Important Subjects*, in 1836. In this hastily written work the evangelist best clarified his modification of the orthodox concept of predestination. "There is a sense in which conversion is the work of God. There is a sense in which it is the effect of truths. There is a sense in which the preacher does it. And it is also the appropriate work of the sinner himself," he explained.[151] The actual turning, he pointed out, is the work of the individual. The agent responsible for the action is the Spirit of God, assisted by the preacher. The truth, or message, is the inducement used by the agent to get the sinner to turn toward conversion. He used the analogy of a man saved from stepping over the brink of Niagara by the shout of someone nearby who ascribes his rescue first to the man nearby, then to the word of warning, next to his own action, and finally to the mercy of God.

Finney stressed that the voluntary part of the act of conversion was not only justified but also necessary. The sinner is doing what God requires in turning to salvation and what God requires of an individual He cannot do for him. "It must be your own voluntary act. It is not the appropriate work of God to do what he requires of you." [152]

Throughout this work Finney criticized other sects and other religious solutions. He castigated Antimonians, Universalists, and Unitarians. He contradicted those who, in his view, overemphasized man's physical depravity, inability of the individual to accept the gospel, and constitutional regeneration—a term which he described as "another death-dealing tradition of the elders." According to the Oberlin revivalist, to demand of an individual that he hold on to the pessimistic dogma of the past and hope for his conversion was expecting too much. "To suspend salvation upon impossible conditions," he declared, "at once insults his understanding and mocks his hopes. Is this the gospel of the blessed God? Impossible! It is a libel upon Almighty God!" [153]

---

[151] Finney, *Sermons on Important Subjects*, pp. 19-20.
[152] *Ibid.*, pp. 28-29.
[153] *Ibid.*, pp. 81-82.

Preceding his *Sermons on Important Subjects,* Finney brought out a volume entitled *Lectures on Revivals of Religion* (1835), which was a blueprint giving his formula for conducting revivals and insuring their success.   Originally delivered to his own congregation and printed in the New York *Evangelist* to help his friend Joshua Leavitt bolster circulation, Finney in twenty-two lectures went into great detail on some controversial subjects connected with revivals.   Although he admitted the book's imperfection, he was greatly pleased when the *Lectures* received the enthusiastic response of his followers.   Charles Hodge, spokesman for the Old School at Princeton, reviewed the volume for the *Biblical Repertory and Princeton Review,* however, and caustically called it "composed of exploded errors and condemned heresies." [154] Finney's *Lectures to Professing Christians* in 1837 indicated that Hodge's criticism had been unheeded.

Having gone so far at a time in his career when he was not systematically studying theology, it is perhaps understandable that, once he established himself at Oberlin, Finney should continue his journey across the theological spectrum away from the old orthodoxy.   In the company of Asa Mahan, Cowles, and Morgan of the Oberlin faculty, Finney evolved the idea of sanctification, the third stage of his religious development.

That Finney had anticipated some higher phase in his religious thought is evident in his autobiography.   As the evangelist put it, "I was led earnestly to inquire whether there was not something higher and more enduring than the Christian church was aware of, whether there were not promises, and means provided in the Gospel, for the establishment of Christians in altogether a higher form of Christian life." [155]   This led him to study the Scriptures until he was satisfied that a higher type of Christian life, bordering on perfect consecration to one's God was attainable.[156]

In 1840 Finney finished his *Views of Sanctification,* adding little that his colleagues, Mahan, Cowles, and Morgan had not already

---

[154] *Biblical Repertory and Princeton Review,* VI, No. 3 (1835), 482.

[155] Finney, *Memoirs,* p. 340.

[156] An excellent critique of the Oberlin theology is found in Foster, *A Genetic History of The New England Theology,* pp. 453-470.

written. In 1846 he published his work, *Lectures on Systematic Theology*, in which he discussed the subject of entire sanctification at great length. An English edition was circulated in 1851, and in 1878 President Fairchild of Oberlin brought out an abridgment.

Finney's study began with a repudiation of orthodoxy that was far-reaching:

The truths of the blessed gospel have been hidden under a false philosophy. Of this I have been long convinced. Nearly all the practical doctrines of Christianity have been embarrassed and perverted by assuming as true the dogma of a Necessitated Will. This has been a leaven of error that, as we shall see, has "leavened nearly the whole lump" of gospel truth. In the present work I have in brief attempted to prove and have every where assumed the freedom of the Will.[157]

The bulk of the work dealt with Finney's theories and their application to moral government but in the chapter on "Moral Depravity and Regeneration" he went farthest afield. The main theme of the *Lectures* was that perfection was attainable, that it was within the reach of everyone, and that there was nothing unusual about sanctification. According to the Oberlin divine, it did not differ much from the experiences of ordinary Christians. In a sense, sanctification rested on a dualistic view of the universe. Man was either good or bad; perfectionism recognized no in between, no imperfect holiness. Regeneration meant "an instantaneous change from entire sinfulness to entire holiness."[158]

This work touched off considerable controversy. Stinging reviews, led by Hodge's long criticism in the *Biblical Repertory and Princeton Review*, attacked Finney and his group for their deviations from orthodoxy. Hodge's kindest words were, "It is as hard to read as Euclid."[159] He echoed the comment written earlier when Finney's first sermons on the subject appeared in print: "One great conclusion may be drawn from the history of this heresy, that departures from the standard of truth, however specious or apparently trivial, are like the fabled dragon's teeth,

---

[157] Finney, *Lectures on Systematic Theology*, p. 3.
[158] *Ibid.*, p. 500.
[159] *Biblical Repertory and Princeton Review*, XIX, No. 2 (1847), 237.

inert and harmless as they are cast into the earth, but presently producing a harvest of armed men."[160]

Earlier, before sanctification had been completely developed and defended, the lines of battle were beginning to form. As one of his friends warned Finney, "If I see straight, the doctrine of perfection will shake the church yet, as much as abolition."[161] When Joshua Leavitt opened the columns of his *Evangelist* to Finney's perfectionist ideas, old Asahel Nettleton shook his head and the letters started flying once more.[162] Conventions were called to check Oberlin's influence, and even Lyman Beecher in Cincinnati aimed the thunder of his denunciation against his old friend.[163]

Some of Finney's followers were concerned at the extremes to which he went. "Some of the *friends* of the Oberlin Evangelist here are of the opinion that the subject of 'Christian perfection' occupies too large a space in that paper," Josiah Chapin complained, adding that he thought the whole thing was "a hobby at Oberlin."[164] Those who had condemned Oberlin for its radical antislavery and educational views pointed to the new fad as corroborating their claims. Others, however, flocked to Finney's support, decrying the "spirit of heresy hunting."[165] Still others described their conversion to perfectionism and sought theological advice from the master. Perfectionism drew a sharp line in the Western Reserve between those who backed Oberlin and those who opposed it. For many it was a continuation of the old struggle against conformity and the status quo. For Oberlin it was a

---

[160] *Ibid.*, VII, No. 2 (1841), 250. For Finney's response, see Finney, *Memoirs*, pp. 347 ff; "An Examination of the Review of Finney's Systematic Theology published in the Biblical Repertory," *Oberlin Quarterly Review*, III, No. 1 (1847), 23-81; "A Reply to the Warning against Error Written by the Rev. Dr. Duffield, *ibid.*, III, No. 4 (1848), 373-417.

[161] William Green, Jr. to Finney, June 21, 1837 (Finney Papers).

[162] See Asahel Nettleton to Leonard Woods, March 8, 1837, in Birney, *The Life and Letters of Asahel Nettleton, 1783-1844*, p. 394.

[163] See Finney, *Memoirs*, pp. 343-345; Catherine Beecher to Finney, Nov. 4, 1839 (Finney Papers).

[164] Josiah Chapin to Finney, Nov. 9, 1840 (Finney Papers).

[165] Mrs. C. C. Copeland to Mrs. Finney, Aug. 13, 1846 (Finney Papers).

storm that it managed to weather successfully.[166] For Finney it was the climax of his theological career.

Finney was probably the most famous evangelist of the nineteenth century. His travels were reported by the religious press, and the progress of his revivals was followed by the religious community. Invitations to visit churches and religious societies poured in upon him from all directions. He was continuously in great demand. As he put it, "Am pulled many ways." [167] One of his major works, his *Lectures on Revivals,* ran into six editions and sold twelve thousand copies in the United States. It was reprinted in England and France and translated into Welsh, French, and German. If we are to believe him, copies of it "were very extensively circulated throughout Europe, and the colonies of Great Britain," and were instrumental "in promoting revivals in England, and Scotland, and Wales, on the continent in various places, in Canada East and West, in Nova Scotia, and in some of the islands of the sea." [168] But then, Finney was not a modest man.

His correspondence, however, was not conducive to modesty. Letters expressing gratitude or recognition of his influence arrived with comfortable regularity. From Wales came the report, "Although we are on another continent far apart your name is familiar to us. With your christian labours we are also acquainted." [169] After his two visits to the British Isles Finney's fame there was even greater. Ministers of all faiths asked him for help; pious persons who had seen or heard him expressed, sometimes in faltering language, their dependence on his guidance. Women especially confessed that they felt somehow drawn to him.

Some of this influence stemmed from his magnetic hold over people. Davenport in his *Primitive Traits in Religious Revivals* analyzed Finney's power over the wills of his audiences and con-

---

[166] For the role of Oberlin in the religious history of the Western Reserve, see Atkins and Fagley, *History of American Congregationalism,* pp. 153 ff.; Fletcher, *A History of Oberlin College from Its Foundation through The Civil War.*

[167] Charles Finney to George W. Gale, Feb. 16, 1831 (Finney Papers).

[168] Finney, *Memoirs,* pp. 330-331.

[169] Congregational Ministers of North Wales to Charles Finney, Feb. 27, 1840 (Finney Papers).

cluded that it was stronger than in any other evangelist.[170] His ability to compel people to do his bidding was almost psychic. His autobiography is loaded with examples—staring down disbelievers, winning over Universalists, silencing angry mobs. He helped mold the development of whole towns like Rochester and Utica. He upset scheduled meetings in his vicinity by attracting crowds to his revivals. Even Theodore Dwight Weld was forced to yield to his will. A would-be assassin expressed it in these words, "But when I saw you, my heart began to burn and grow hot within me, and instead of feeling as if I wanted to avoid you, I felt so drawn that I came across the street to see you." [171] General William Booth expressed a debt to the Oberlin divine when he declared that but for his influence the work of the Salvation Army might never have taken place.[172] It has been estimated that some 500,000 persons were converted as a result of his preaching. He was indeed a powerful figure stalking across the American religious stage and scorching the consciences of countless in his generation.

These then were the men destined to have a profound effect on the social and intellectual development of the young nation. In the ensuing chapters their secular ideas and the extent of their influence will be examined. We must first, however, consider the revivals in which they took so active a part.

---

[170] Davenport, *Primitive Traits in Religious Revivals*, pp. 194-195.

[171] Quoted in Finney, *Memoirs*, pp. 151-152. For a similar incident, see *ibid.*, p. 183. For an account of Finney's disruption of the anniversary exercises at Andover Theological Seminary in 1831, see Wright, *Charles Grandison Finney*, pp. 71-72.

[172] See Beardsley, *A Mighty Winner of Souls, Charles G. Finney*, p. 118.

III. REVIVALS—" THE GRAND ABSORBING THEME "

But it is now getting to be more generally understood, that to wait God's time, in this matter, is not to wait at all. . . . . Revivals of Religion now . . . are made matters of human calculation, by the arithmetic of faith in God's arrangements.[1]

If there be any true religion in the world, I have not the slightest doubt it is found in its most unequivocal form as the fruits of our great revivals in America.[2]

WRITING in 1830, Calvin Colton, Presbyterian and Episcopalian minister, pamphleteer, journalist, and political economist, announced that revivals "have become the grand absorbing theme and aim of the American religious world—of all that part of it, which can claim to participate in the more active spirit of the age." [3] His conclusion aptly described the religious scene. For two hundred years successive waves of revivals marked the course of this country's religious history and had become, by the 1830's, a dominant characteristic of American Christianity.[4]

In listing the revival periods in American history, one generally starts with the Great Awakening, made famous by Theodorus

[1] Colton, *History and Character of American Revivals of Religion,* pp. 5-6.
[2] Charles Finney to Robinson, Feb. 5, 1859 (Finney Papers).
[3] Colton, *History and Character of American Revivals of Religion,* p. 59. Calvin Colton (1789-1857) graduated from Yale and Andover and engaged in evangelistic work in New York State until 1826 when his wife died and his voice failed. After ten years as a journalist he joined the Episcopalian Church, was rector of the Church of Messiah in New York in 1837-1838 until poor health forced him to return to journalism, presumably a less exacting occupation than the ministry. He became active in politics aiding the Whigs and is best known for his *Junius Tracts* and biographies of Henry Clay. It is ironical that Clay's first biographer should have been a man twice blessed in the ministerial orders. For biographical details, see Dexter, *Biographical Sketches of the Graduates of Yale College,* vol. VI; George W. Colton, *A Genealogical Record of the Descendants of Quartermaster George Colton,* and Hotchkiss, *History of Western New York*
[4] For a picture of the place of revivals in the American scene, see Mode, *Frontier Spirit in American Christianity,* and William W. Sweet, *Revivalism in America,* Beardsley, *A History of American Revivals,* Davenport, *Primitive Traits in Religious Revivals.*

Frelinghuysen in the early 1720's in the Raritan Valley of New
Jersey, by Gilbert Tennant near Philadelphia, and by Jonathan
Edwards in 1734 in his rural Northampton parish.   There had
been revivals, however, earlier in colonial history.   The Rev.
Solomon Stoddard had what he called "harvests" among his flock
at Northampton in 1679, 1683, 1696, 1705, and 1712.[5]

By 1739 evidences of a general revival were exhibited not only
in New England but also by Presbyterian churches as far south
as New Jersey.   It was at this moment that George Whitefield, an
Anglican clergyman with a voice like "all the pipes of a great
organ," arrived in this country to become "the first great footloose
Protestant evangelist." [6]   He traveled the length of the colonies,
preaching as he went, and a revival was started that lasted eighteen
months.   By the end of 1742 almost every parish had in some
way experienced the fruits of this revival, and by 1743 even the
South was undergoing a Great Awakening.   There were, it is true,
some excesses encountered in the revival.   Gilbert Tennant of New
Jersey and James Davenport represented the most hysterical element.   When the phenomenom was over some 150 new Congregational churches had been formed and, it is estimated, between
25,000 and 50,000 added to New England churches alone.   If
we take the figure 340,000 for the population of New England in
1750, we can estimate that about one seventh of the population
of that area came into the church as a result of the Great Awakening.[7]

After 1760 other matters attracted the attention of the colonists
and there was a general slump in religion which was accentuated
by the outbreak of hostilities in 1775.   Revivals were practically
unknown during the Revolutionary War and, with a few exceptions, during the 1780's.   What few there were in the "critical
period " were, for the most part, under the leadership of "new
divinity" men whose doctrinal ideas linked them with Edwards.

---

[5] Beardsley, *A History of American Revivals*, p. 20.
[6] Atkins and Fagley, *History of American Congregationalism*, p. 109.
[7] See *ibid.*, p. 110; Beardsley, *A History of American Revivals*, p. 64.

After 1790 signs of renewed religious vigor appeared throughout the country. A number of revivals occurred in Virginia and Georgia in 1787. One hit Boston in 1790, and after 1792 they extended throughout New England, reaching western New York in 1798 and spreading to western Pennsylvania and northeastern Ohio after 1802. The center of the revival was in Connecticut, although Vermont and even Maine had what were at the time called great "outpourings of the Holy Spirit."[8] The Awakening of 1800 in New England, as this wave has been called, had not the same sort of excitement about it that had marked the earlier period. It had no great names connected with it, no itinerant evangelist whose fame could match Edwards's or Whitefields's. Its most spectacular aspect was probably the work done by Timothy Dwight at Yale in 1802.

The Awakening of 1800 had important results for the course of religious thought. The revival invigorated the churches, which since the Revolutionary War had been in a weakened condition, their members surrounded by the general laxness of morals characteristic of a war period. It checked the spread of what was considered infidelity—the Americanization of the Enlightenment as expressed in the philosophy of Paine and Jefferson—and it also contributed to the crisis that was developing within Congregationalism between the liberal and evangelical parties which resulted in the Unitarian schism.

While New England and the Middle Atlantic states were experiencing this second wave of religious enthusiasm, the frontier was also engaged in a revival of a different sort. Prior to 1796 religion in the back country was at ebb tide. The Methodists, for instance, had lost an average of four thousand members annually prior to 1796.[9] Other denominations were in a similar state.

In Logan County, Kentucky, in 1797, however, a great event occurred that shook the foundations of religious society. The first camp meeting in this country was conducted by Presbyterians,

[8] The best accounts of this revival are found in Beardsley, *A History of American Revivals,* Keller, *The Second Great Awakening in Connecticut,* and Ludlum, *Social Ferment in Vermont.*

[9] Beardsley, *A History of American Revivals,* pp. 81-82.

and a revival was soon in progress.[10]   In this area because there were few church buildings, meetings lasting several days were held in groves or in a clearing in the forest.   Settlers from miles around would converge, set up tents, and camp in one place while services were conducted.   A number of revivalists would take part, assisting each other in the meetings and often holding several services at once.   The primary object was, of course, the conversion of souls, but socially the camp meeting provided a necessary bit of variety to the otherwise rugged, routine life of the early Southwest.   It is no wonder that their popularity grew and their effectiveness in corraling church members increased.   In 1811 there were more than four hundred of them while by 1820 almost a thousand had been held.[11]   The most spectacular of these early camp meetings was probably the one held at Cane-Ridge in 1801. It was at this one that Peter Cartwright was converted and also here that many of the peculiar physical exertions to which the more excitable members of the congregation were addicted were widely exhibited.

In the Southwest the Methodists were in the most advantageous position to benefit from this wave of revivals.   Their system of church government permitted Methodist evangelists to make the most effective use of the camp meeting and the most notable aspect of frontier religion was the rise and growth of Methodism. Methodist revivalists, such as Peter Cartwright, James Caughey, and William Taylor, reaped the harvest sowed at Cane-Ridge and elsewhere.

One of the most colorful evangelists taking part in the Logan County revival was James McGready.   McGready, who preached a modified form of Calvinism, came to Kentucky from North Carolina in 1796 and was immediately successful.   A contemporary in describing him said that "he would so array hell before the wicked that they would tremble and quake, imagining a lake of

---

[10] Although 1799 is the usually accepted date for the first campmeeting there had been earlier ones in 1791 and 1794 in Lincoln County, North Carolina, which were attended by both Presbyterians and Methodists.

[11] Sweet, *American Churches*, p. 54.

fire and brimstone yawning to overwhelm them and the hand of the Almighty thrusting them down the horrible abyss." [12]

As the nineteenth century opened, revivals increased. In Vermont during the first decade there were almost continual ones which were by no means limited to Congregational societies. The Baptists profited from them as well. Indeed, practically every community in the state had at least one revival during these years. [13] Even the students of Middlebury College had a succession of revivals in 1805-1806, 1809, 1811, and 1814. [14]

The same pattern could be found elsewhere. Rhode Island and western Massachusetts exhibited increased religious activity in 1807-1808. [15] In Connecticut, soon to be called for the strength of its religious fervor, "the dullest, most disagreeable state in the Union," [16] a graph of the incidence of revivals would indicate peaks in 1807-1808, 1812, 1815-1816, 1820-1821, and 1825-1826. There were fifteen different periods of revivals at Yale during the years 1800-1840. Indeed, there was no complete interruption of revivals in the state during the first four decades of the century. [17]

The third major period of revivals, however, may be dated from the beginning of Charles G. Finney's preaching in western New York. His Western Revival in 1826 touched off a spark that ignited the entire religious community. The following year revivals occurred in all the presbyteries of New York state and from there they spread in all directions. At the same time sections of Georgia and South Carolina in 1826-27 were also under the influence of a revival which was centered at Athens. [18] By 1827 one religious periodical in the habit of listing them reported, "Revivals, we re-

12 Quoted in Davenport, *Primitive Traits in Religious Revivals*, p. 67.
13 Ludlum, *Social Ferment in Vermont*, pp. 47-48.
14 *American Quarterly Register*, XII, No. 1 (1839), 57.
15 Walker, *A History of the Congregational Churches in the United States*, p. 320.
16 Marryat, *A Diary in America, 1837-1838*, I, 241.
17 Keller, *The Second Great Awakening in Connecticut*, p. 42; Tyler, *Freedom's Ferment*, p. 30. For a history of revivals in Yale College see the *American Quarterly Register* for Feb., 1030.
18 Gillett, *History of the Presbyterian Church in the United States of America*, p. 356; Lacy, *Revivals in the Midst of the Years*, p. 96.

joice to say, are becoming too numerous in our country to admit of being generally mentioned in our Record." Later it announced with obvious satisfaction, "Revivals seem to be increasing in number and power throughout our country. They exist at the present time in more than two hundred towns in the New England and Middle States." [19]

One hundred years of schooling finally bore fruit. Wherever one turned in the 1830's there were evidences of increased revivalistic vigor. New York City and Philadelphia played host to Finney and members of his "holy band." "There is considerable attention to religion in this city," Lewis Tappan wrote his brother from New York, "and christians are praying for a revival that will shake the city to its foundations." [20] As the decade began Albert Barnes was shaking Philadelphia's foundations. The Great Boston Revival saw that city the target of Knapp, Finney, and Edward N. Kirk.[21] In 1831 a religious hurricane fostered by Charles Finney in Rochester swept through more than fifteen hundred towns and the burnt-over district of western New York was on fire once more.[22]

Estimates vary on the intensity of religious interest in the 1830's. Church statistics, never reliable, become less accurate during revivals. Nonetheless some nine hundred conversions were reported for the city of New Haven in 1831 alone. One hundred persons joined the First Presbyterian Church in Rochester at one time in January, 1831, at the peak of Finney's revival. During the first five months of that year it is claimed some fifty thousand persons were

[19] *Christian Spectator*, N.S., I, No. 1 (1827), 50, and I, No. 5 (1827), 296.

[20] Lewis Tappan to Benjamin Tappan, Feb. 5, 1831 (Benjamin Tappan Papers).

[21] Edward N. Kirk (1802-1874) was a second-rate evangelist who was most successful following in the wake of one or another of his more famous colleagues. He graduated from Princeton at the age of eighteen and after a brief term in a law office was dramatically converted in 1822. He was licensed for the ministry in 1826 and traveled as a missionary agent through the Middle Atlantic and Southern states before taking a pastorate in Albany. Active in revivals, temperance and abolition, he subsequently became interested in the Evangelical Alliance and was a chaplain during the Civil War. Although he wrote widely, his articles and pamphlets reveal little originality and almost no intellectual depth. For biographical details, see David O. Mears, *Life of Edward Norris Kirk*.

[22] Beardsley, *A History of American Revivals*, pp. 161-162; Fletcher, *A History of Oberlin College*, pp. 17-23. For an analytic study of the impact of Finneyite revivals on western New York, see Whitney R. Cross, *The Burned-over District*.

converted while some statistics put the addition to the churches as a result of this revival at one hundred thousand. During the first thirty years of the nineteenth century membership in the Presbyterian Church increased fourfold, that of the Baptist Church threefold, while the Congregationalist membership doubled. In 1830 the Methodist Episcopal Church had seven times as many members than in 1800.[23] While attention is usually focused on increases in Northern churches, those in the South also reported widespread religious interest at this time. By 1832 some 700 congregations in sixty-eight presbyteries had experienced revivals.[24] This resurgence of religion in 1830 was so extensive that a great interest in accounts of revivals was taken even in England.[25]

The 1830 revivals differed markedly from those of the 1740's and 1800's in that previously salvation of the unconverted was the end in view, whereas in the 1830's the objective became the saving of the world through organized movements. Consequently, the converts of the 1830's were led to concern themselves with the great social questions of the day and to bring about a better world. Finney himself indicated what were to be the major reforms in which his believers should take part. They were "abolition of slavery, temperance, moral reform, politics, business principles, physiological and dietetic reform."[26] On this bridge between religion and secular topics of national concern rested the influence of the nineteenth-century evangelist.

If the 1830's were blessed with revivals, in the 1840's the pendulum swung in the opposite direction. Indeed, from the panic of 1837 on the churches encountered lean times. One minister's wife grasped the situation well in 1839 when she wrote from Rome, New York, "There is no particular seriousness here. I have been truly astonished at the change since 1827-1828."[27] Even the

[23] Dorchester, *Christianity in the United States*, p. 375; Fletcher, *A History of Oberlin College*, p. 21; Beardsley, *A History of American Revivals*, pp. 161-162; Loud, *Evangelized America*, p. 7; Stevenson, *The Growth of the Nation, 1809-1837*, p. 412.
[24] Lacy, *Revivals in the Midst of the Years*, p. 104.
[25] Anson G. Phelps to Finney, Aug. 29, 1833 (Finney Papers).
[26] Charles G. Finney, "A Seared Conscience," *Oberlin Evangelist*, III, No. 9 (1841), 65.
[27] Mrs. Amelia Norton to Mrs. Finney, March 11, 1839 (Finney Papers).

popular, reliable Maternal Association meetings were poorly attended.

The decline in revivals can be explained partly by the shift that took place from moral to economic reform after the 1840's, but the decline in religious vitality was absolute as well as relative. There were a few successful revivals here and there, especially in 1841-1842 but even Finney found Boston less receptive by 1843. Edward N. Kirk, Lyman Beecher, Horace Bushnell, and later Finney found occasion to visit Europe, finding home soil "barren." Later that decade the Mexican War detracted public attention from religious affairs.   Merchants who normally were pillars of church support had other pressing matters.   One of Boston's outstanding laymen explained the situation to Finney: "The war has made the money market hard, my time much taken up . . . the churches are ded [sic]." [28] Some church memberships even decreased.

Things remained at a low level until 1857, when the fourth and last great wave of revivals spread across the country.[29]   Once again the evangelists went to work and converted souls by the scores. Finney returned East from Oberlin; Knapp held forth in Boston once more; and Henry Ward Beecher comforted penitents in Brooklyn.   The 1857-1858 revival marked the end of a religious era.   Although such evangelists as Moody and Sankey continued the tradition and although evangelism continued to thrive until the Civil War, industrialism and the new science spelled the eventual doom of Finneylike revivals.

One historian has attempted to work out what he calls an evangelistic index to measure the statistical effect of revivals on church membership.   Taking the index to represent the figure of new members in any one year divided by the total membership and expressing the result in terms of a percentage, he has found that the evangelistic index for Protestantism as a whole has been 5.6 per

---

[28] Willard Sears to Finney, April 9, 1846 (Finney Papers).

[29] For a detailed survey of this revival see Beardsley, A History of American Revivals, p. 213: Greenblatt, Some Social Aspects of the Panic of 1857, chap. iv; Spicer, The Great Awakening of 1857 and 1858; Francis, "The Religious Revival of 1858 in Philadelphia," Pennsylvania Magazine of History and Biography, LXX, No. 1 (1946), 52-77.

cent. The Methodist Church has over the years achieved the highest evangelistic index, attaining 6.3 per cent. Weber estimated the Presbyterian index at 6.29 per cent, the Baptist at 5.6 per cent, and the Congregational at 4.8 per cent. The peak year for any sect was 1832, when Finney's revival produced an index of 15.7 for the Presbyterians.[30]

It is interesting to note the effects of wars, business activity, and depressions on evangelism. Peace and prosperity are the most satisfactory periods for revivalists, who generally are hard put to secure financial support during wartime. The Revolution, the War of 1812, the Mexican War, and the Civil War, except for the revival among soldiers of the Confederate army, were lean times for evangelism.[31] The years immediately following a war, however, are more productive for revivals. Although hard times send persons flocking to the churches, in the ante-bellum period depressions, in withdrawing the economic support of the business group, spell defeat for revivalistic efforts. The years 1819 and 1837 brought a decline in the numbers of revivals, and the 1857 enthusiasm, somewhat different in make-up and character, while it proceeded through the panic, might possibly have been even more successful had prosperous times continued. While some converts were drawn from the lower classes, it would appear that revivals were a middle-class phenomena, subject to all the trials and tribulations of that economic group.[32]

Most revivals have been strongly emotional in character, but the 1830 religious outpourings rivaled even the Cane-Ridge camp-meetings in their irrational approach to religion. Francis Lieber observed that one of the most important aspects of religious excitement was the dislike of reasoning on the part of the evangelists. Appealing to reason was more difficult, less likely to succeed. Evangelists were certain they were right "because God is within

[30] Weber, *Evangelism, a Graphic Survey*, pp. 40-41, 45.

[31] See Bennett, *Narrative of the Great Revival Which Prevailed in the Southern Armies during the Late Civil War.*

[32] For other interpretations of this relationship see Keller, *The Second Great Awakening in Connecticut*, p. 55; Ludlum, *Social Ferment in Vermont*, pp. 61-62; Robert E. Thompson, *A History of the Presbyterian Church in the United States*, p. 126; Herman C. Weber, *Evangelism, a Graphic Survey*, pp. 95, 106.

them—they have the light." [33]   Revivalists themselves recognized that their chances of success were greater among the emotional, less educated portion of the population.   As one group put it, "It is more difficult to labour with educated men, with cultivated minds and moreover predisposed to skepticism, than with the un-educated." [34]   Indeed, it was the "nervously unstable" that first responded to the plea of a revivalist, and the appeal made to them was an emotional rather than a rational one.[35]

Perhaps it is for that reason primarily that the majority of re-vivals occurred in the country and small town rather than in the city.   While great waves of religious feeling did roll over the metropolises from time to time, the strength of the movement was to be found in the smaller community where education was not as widespread, where fewer social attractions competed with the church, and where religion had a stronger hold.   The evangelists themselves noted this.   "It is certain that in our own land they have occurred much more frequently in the comparatively quiet retreats of the country," wrote Albert Barnes, "and that such scenes as are characteristically known as revivals of religion are scarcely known in large cities like the one where we dwell." [36] There was too much distraction in the city:

I am still of the belief that cities are poor places to promote Revivals, at least such as we have in the country.   The business, the bustle, the dis-sipation, the etiquette and a countless number and variety of things seem to stand in the way of good.   There is a kind of moral atmosphere so to speak even in the religious world in such places which seems to taint and transform everything about them.[37]

Another distinctive feature of the 1830 revivals was the differ-ence in the methods used to gain converts.   These methods were known as new measures and were described by Finney as "simply

[33] Lieber, *The Stranger in America*, II, 221.

[34] Committee in behalf of pious students of Union College to Finney, Feb. 7, 1831 (Finney Papers).

[35] See Davenport, *Primitive Traits in Religious Revivals*, pp. 3, 4, 10, 28; McComas, *The Psychology of Religious Sects*, pp. 153-154.

[36] Albert Barnes, *Revivals of Religion in Cities and Large Towns*, p. 3.

[37] George W. Gale to Finney, Jan. 21, 1830 (Finney Papers).

preaching, prayer and conference meetings, much private prayer, much personal conversation, and meetings for the instruction of earnest inquirers." [38]   Most evangelists were colloquial in their preaching.   In the pulpit they radiated energy, were earnest and vigorous in their delivery, emotional and dramatic in their methods of attack.   Finney, for instance, selected words and illustrations that would be understood by his audience.   Other new measures included the "breaking down" of the audience by prolonged addresses, the praying for individuals by name, permitting women to pray in the services, holding inquiry meetings (after the regular service had concluded), and employing the "anxious seat," a row of seats at the front of the church reserved for those who felt themselves "convicted" of sin.   According to Beardsley, the Methodists were the first to make use of it but it was Finney's employment of it that publicized it so well.   The anxious seat was objected to at first, but even Timothy Dwight finally acceded to its use.   Inviting Finney to help out in a revival in New Haven, he wrote, "For fear there may be some misapprehension on the subject of measures to be adopted, I would state, that no objection will be made to calling the anxious forward to be prayed for; but I do suppose, if females were called upon to pray in promiscuous assemblies, it would be objected to." [39]

Another new measure was the protracted meeting, a succession of religious services scheduled to be held on successive days.   Usually protracted meetings were held for a three- or four-day period, although one such gathering lasted thirty-three days. [40]   The usual

---

38 Finney, *Memoirs*, p. 77.

39 Timothy Dwight to Finney (March, 1831) (Finney Papers).

40 J. Hopkins to Finney, March 4, 1833 (Finney Papers).   The evangelist Burchard engaged in another marathon protracted meeting that lasted twenty-seven days.   See Henry S. Hutchinson to Mrs. Finney, April 7, 1835 (Finney Papers).   One meeting held in a private house started in the morning, lasted all day, into the night, and was going strong at eleven the following day!   See Samuel Moss to Finney, Feb. 6, 1827 (Finney Papers).   In some areas the schedule was even more crowded.   Following Finney's visit to Rome, New York the following regimen was adhered to: "We have three sermons every Sabbath, . . . Monday and Tuesday evenings we have preaching and morning prayer meeting every day from house to house and prayer meetings Tuesday and Friday evenings at the school house generally well attended."   A. Bullock to Mrs. Finney, Jan. 9, 1829 (Finney Papers).

procedure was to hold several a day, followed by smaller inquiry meetings and interspersed with individual visits. Their effect was similar to that of a prolonged artillery barrage on an enemy position. A person hearing a revivalist three or four days in a row was more susceptible to conversion than after only one session. Calvin Colton justified them by declaring, "extra efforts and extra measures, in some form, are indispensable to a revival . . . the world, the Church itself continually requires some fresh and rousing impulse. It needs to be waked up." [41] The Baptist evangelist Knapp claimed that protracted meetings were one of the most important means of "breaking up this apathetic state in the churches, in bringing into the ranks of the ministry men earnest in winning souls, and into the ranks of the laymen men zealous in supporting all our benevolent enterprise." [42] And while it was not a new measure, all evangelists were in the habit of rebuking those who opposed revivals. The choicest epithet used to describe those lukewarm to revivals was one employed by Finney who called such people, "cold, stupid or dead." [43]

Although the use of new measures indicated a certain loose interpretation of the role of the minister in the act of conversion and although most revivalists came from the ranks of those considered most unorthodox doctrinally speaking, there were a number of theologically conservative evangelists who employed them as well. The most notable example was Daniel Baker, Old School Presbyterian, who often utilized the anxious seat and the protracted meeting.[44] Writing in 1831 he announced, "We are at this time seriously thinking of the propriety of having a four days' meeting in

[41] Colton, *History and Character of American Revivals of Religion*, pp. 106-107.
[42] Knapp, *Autobiography*, p. 40.
[43] "Minutes of the New Lebanon Convention," New York *Observer*, Aug. 4, 1827.
[44] Daniel Baker (1791-1857) preached in every state below the Mason and Dixon line. From 1839 until 1842 he traveled through Texas and boasted that he was the first Protestant minister to set foot in some sections of the Lone Star State. He was later instrumental in helping establish Austin College and as general agent made six fund raising trips on its behalf. The most complete account of his career is Baker, *The Life and Labors of the Rev. Daniel Baker*. See also Henry A. White, *Southern Presbyterian Leaders*; Henry S. Little, *Home Missions Heroes*, chap. iv; and Wells, *Southern Presbyterian Worthies*.

my church. It will certainly be a new thing here; and some may think it carrying the matter rather too far; but I hope we shall have it, nevertheless." [45]

Evangelists went about their task with a businesslike approach. Explaining the secret of their success, Calvin Colton related, "They endeavor to ascertain, generally and particularly, as far as possible, the character and temper of the community," and, he pointed out, they adopted their system of preaching to "the exigencies of the public mind." [46] Lyman Beecher has given us his prescription for beginning a successful revival:

I always took it by word of mouth first, talking with single cases, and praying with them. Went on so till I found twelve, by watching and picking them out. I visited them, and explained what an inquiry meeting was, and engaged them, if one was appointed, to agree to come. I never would risk a blank attempt.[47]

There were no shrewder opportunists than the Northern evangelists. Part of their success was also due to the efforts of church members themselves to gain converts. The pressure exerted on unwilling and unconverted neighbors and relatives sometimes reached extremes. Almost every mail carried the hopes of Lewis Tappan that his unconverted brother would see the light. "There are indications that a revival of religion will prevail over the United States," he once wrote. "God grant it may include all my beloved friends." [48]

Naturally there was a great deal of opposition to revivals and revivalists, both from within and without the church. In the 1830's this took a number of forms. First, there was physical violence usually perpetrated by groups against an evangelist or a congregation engaged in a worship service. This was reminiscent of the 1800 camp meetings when mobs attacked the religious assemblies, often to be met by the physical might of the evangelist himself or his followers. Peter Cartwright, perfect example of the backwoods preacher, liberally interspersed his preaching with

---

[45] Quoted in Baker, *The Life and Labors of the Rev. Daniel Baker*, pp. 146-147.
[46] Colton, *History and Character of American Revivals of Religion*, pp. 273-274.
[47] Beecher, *Autobiography*, II, 76.
[48] Lewis Tappan to Benjamin Tappan, April 11, 1831 (Benjamin Tappan Papers).

fights against gangs or individual hecklers. Black eyes and broken ribs were the occupational hazards of an itinerant operating in New York state at the time of the Western Revivals. From Little Falls, the Rev. G. W. Burrett could write the following:

Yesterday we were forcibly thrown out of doors in one house and threatened in another and vilified in another and scoffed at and sneared at in the streets. . . . This morning the whole village is boiling hot with rage and infuriated madness. You might see them standing at the corners of the streets five or six together swinging their fists or telling what they would do and christians are together two or three in a place praying for them.[49]

Similarly, Father Nash, one of Finney's revivalist colleagues, reported in 1826, "Mr. Finney and I have been burned in effigy. We have frequently been disturbed in our religious meetings. . . . There is almost as much writing, intrigue, lying and reporting of lies as there would be if we were on the eve of a presidential election."[50]

Some ministers seemed to encourage and revel in the violence they incited. Jacob Knapp enjoyed telling about the mobs that attacked him in Rochester, New Haven, and Boston. Nor were evangelists the only targets for violence. In Albany, for instance, a Bible class had been started "when it was obliged to be given up on account of the mob that raised to oppose it."[51] Not all the acts of violence were committed by the unchurched. A Pennsylvania evangelist recorded the following: "The hostility of the wicked here is sometimes vengeful. During the revival a universalist shot at me with a rifle—the ball whizzed close by my head—others have stoned my house and frequently insult me in the streets."[52]

Evangelists also encountered extensive criticism from the press. Charles Finney was the object of several scurrilous articles in Camden newspapers. Boston newspapers attacked the Baptist preachers, Swan and Knapp. Henry Ward Beecher was ridiculed by the

---

[49] G. W. Burrett to Finney, May 12, 1827 (Finney Papers).
[50] Quoted in Basil Miller, *Charles G. Finney, He Prayed Down Revivals*, p. 58.
[51] Mrs. Elizabeth White to Mrs. Finney, Nov. 6, 1830 (Finney Papers).
[52] Samuel Schaeffer to Finney, May 28, 1832 (Finney Papers).

press on several occasions. In 1840 Bennett's New York *Herald* devoted much space to a burlesque of Knapp's revivals in the Tabernacle Church.

One evangelist who suffered particularly at the hands of the press was John Newland Maffitt.[53] He was wildly praised by his admirers and brutally condemned by his opponents. He has been called a great evangelist by some, and by others a "theological tadpole" and a "clerical buffoon." He has been pictured as "a child of wayward genius, nurtured on novels, wrapped in gorgeous reveries, with thoughts dipped in diamond clouds."[54]

Maffitt was born in Dublin, Ireland, in 1794 of middle-class parentage and was trained to be a merchant-tailor, a profession of which he was ashamed. His conversion, it is claimed, bore a close resemblance to that of John Bunyan. At any rate, he had his full quota of strange visions and "hand to hand conflicts with Apollyon in the Valley of Humiliation."[55] In spite of the efforts of his mother and his beautiful wife, whom he married when he was twenty, he joined the Methodist Church of Ireland, a hopelessly small religious minority. Thereafter, Maffitt, a handsome man with a pleasant face, dark curly hair, large eyes, and a straight long nose, supplemented his mercantile trade by preaching on street corners hurling "unusual quantities of brimstone . . . at the heads of his Catholic neighbors."[56] Several times he was severely stoned for his efforts to convert the Irish nation. He must have found the stones thrown by his Catholic neighbors a bit more effective than Apollyon's fiery darts!

---

[53] Biographical material on Maffitt is slight. The most authoritative source is his own autobiography, *Tears of Contrition; or, Sketches of the Life of John N. Maffitt.* Although she deals primarily with Maffitt's seafaring son, Mrs. Emma M. Maffitt, *The Life and Services of John Newland Maffitt,* has valuable material in the early chapters. Elsemore, *An Impartial Account of the Life of Rev. John Newland Maffitt,* attempts to give an objective picture of his private life. See also Redford, *Western Cavaliers.*

[54] "Candour," *Theological Pretenders,* p. 8, 11; Elsemore, *An Impartial Account of the Life of Rev. John Newland Maffitt,* p. 28.

[55] Emma Maffit, *The Life and Services of John Newland Maffitt,* p. 20. Apollyon, it will be recalled, was the angel of the bottomless pit armed with fiery darts whom Christian overcame in *Pilgrim's Progress.*

[56] Elsemore, *An Impartial Account of the Life of Rev. John Newland Maffitt,* p. 4.

After two failures in business, Maffitt took his brother's advice and embarked for America in 1819. Finding his mercantile prospects in New York City as slim as they had been in Dublin, he turned to the ministry and in 1825 in New London, Connecticut, was admitted on trial as an itinerant minister in the New England Conference. During the rest of the 1820's he roamed through New England. In 1827 he preached in Boston and the following year Portsmouth felt his wrath. The 1830's took him southward and westward. One of his biographers has claimed, "There was not a single large town in the north which escaped the whirlwind everywhere raised by his eloquence." [57]

In 1833 Maffitt left New England to join the Tennessee Conference of the Methodist Church. In addition to his ministerial duties he was appointed an agent for La Grange College, a Methodist school in Georgia. The following year the college named him professor of belles lettres for a two-year term. In 1833 he also got out, with the assistance of Louis Garrett, the *Western Methodist*, a weekly religious journal.[58] In 1841 he was elected chaplain to the House of Representatives, receiving the votes of Southern and Western members in a sectional struggle for that office. Fortunately for Congress, he seems to have tempered his usual brilliant eloquence while in Washington. In the 1840's he moved on to New York City and stayed there until trouble within his church sent him across the river to Brooklyn. There, at about the same time Henry Ward Beecher was arriving at Plymouth Church, Maffitt was holding meetings that attracted over three thousand persons. There, too, he ran into personal difficulties that culminated in a tragic second marriage, the odium of scandal and persecution by a portion of the press.[59]

[57] *Ibid.*, p. 7.

[58] The paper has been known by a number of names, the most familiar of which was the *South Western Christian Advocate*, the chief organ of the Methodist Church South.

[59] The charges of personal misconduct against Maffitt were carried in the columns of the *Christian Advocate and Journal* and the *National Police Gazette*. His defense can be found in the *Sunday Morning News*.

Maffitt moved from New York to Arkansas and in 1850 conducted a tour of the Gulf cities, but Southern newspapers copied the sensational stories about his personal conduct and the death of his second wife. The accusations and insinuations were too much for him and he died of a heart attack that was directly traced to the charges laid against him.[60]

More important than the persecution of the press, however, was the opposition that arose against evangelists within the churches themselves. The spread of new measures caused considerable criticism. One of the first to complain against Finney's successful measures was William R. Weeks, Congregational minister in western New York, who helped form the Oneida Association which published pamphlets against Finney and which was instrumental in rousing Eastern antagonism against him.[61] Another minister who disapproved of Finney's methods was Asahel Nettleton, who in 1826 was the dean of all evangelists. He was so disturbed, in fact, that he journeyed to Albany from New York City to see Finney and ascertain for himself how serious a threat he was to the cause of religion. What he discovered after two conferences with the younger enthusiast appalled him. "I learned they had adopted and defended measures which I have ever regarded as exceedingly calamitous to the cause of revivals." [62]

Finney was not the only evangelist to whom there was objection. In Troy, Nathaniel S. S. Beman was having similar trouble. "A paper has been secretly circulating for some time . . . stating that on the ground of expediency Mr. B. had better leave, that a majority of the church and congregation are dissatisfied, and that there is no other way of restoring peace and harmony to a distracted and divided society." [63] One of Finney's disciples ran into

---

[60] Hibbard, *Startling Disclosures Concerning the Death of John N. Maffitt*, p. 22.

[61] Weeks later wrote a satire on revivals and new measures entitled *The Pilgrim's Progress in the Nineteenth Century*. For Finney's opinion of Weeks, see Finney, *Memoirs*, p. 144.

[62] Asahel Nettleton to S. C. Aikin, Jan. 13, 1827. Quoted in Lyman Beecher, *Letters of the Rev. Dr. Beecher and Rev. Mr. Nettleton on the New Measures in Conducting Revivals of Religion*, pp. 20-21.

[63] Julia F. Tracy to Mrs. Finney, Aug. 27, 1827 (Finney Papers).

difficulty in Trenton.   According to his report, "there is a secret, deep-rooted and inveterate opposition . . . of moral men, and of men of influence.   If this breaks forth as we expect it will, the whole city will be in an uproar." [64]

Opposition to new measures soon came to a head when in 1827 Eastern ministers under the leadership of Nettleton and Lyman Beecher met with Western evangelists to hammer out the question of their place in revivals.   This meeting was called "to see in what respect there is an agreement between brethren from different sections of the country, in regard to principles and measures in conducting and promoting revivals of religion." [65]   The person most instrumental in bringing about the conference was Lyman Beecher.   Hotly engaged in his struggle against the Unitarians in Boston, Beecher feared that the sudden wave of revivals spreading out from the West would threaten a new schism within the ranks of the embattled Calvinists themselves.

Much of the opposition to evangelists was based on personal grounds.   Strong-willed, individualistic revivalists made many personal enemies, and men such as Maffitt, Cartwright, Beecher, and Finney faced personal abuse throughout their careers.   Even after the New Lebanon Convention settled their differences, Lyman Beecher rebuked Finney for his "spirit of fanaticism, of spiritual pride, censoriousness, and insubordination to the order of the Gospel." [66]

The major figures in the field repudiated the perversions of revivalism which brought discredit to their profession.   Finney, for instance, wrote a friend, "I object as strongly as you can to that class of efforts to which you object.   We have had them in America, much to the disgrace of revivals. . . . But the frothy efforts I have always distinguished . . . from healthy efforts to

64 Herman Norton to Finney, Feb. 11, 1828 (Finney Papers).

65 Minutes of the New Lebanon Convention, New York *Observer*, Aug. 4, 1827. For a study of this conference and its results, see "The New Lebanon Convention" in *New York History*, XXI, No. 4 (1950), 385-397.

66 Lyman Beecher to N. S. S. Beman, Dec. 15, 1827, in Lyman Beecher, *Letters of the Rev. Dr. Beecher and Rev. Mr. Nettleton on the New Measures in Conducting Revivals of Religion*, p. 80.

promote the revival of true religion." [67]   The line between what was "frothy" and what was "healthy," however, was sometimes indistinguishable.

One form of criticism leveled against revivals was best developed by Horace Bushnell, who felt that there was a danger that new measures and extraordinary means would be overdone by churches.   To offset this overemphasis he underlined other means of salvation, pointing out other doors to a religious life.   It was not opposition so much as self-criticism.   He did not attack the techniques so much as the assumptions on which revivals rested. Bushnell's line of reasoning on this point was developed in *Views of Christian Nurture*, published in 1847, which was a collection of articles and sermons on the religious development of the individual.   In speaking of the nurture of the Christian, Bushnell asserted that if children were brought up in the faith there would be a far more rapid increase in church membership than there was under a system of periodic revivals.   He deplored those revivals which were "our scenes of conquest—valued of course according to the hopes rested in their power.   Let me not be understood as rejecting revivals of religion," he added, "though I heartily wish the name were yet to be invented; for it is a source of indefinite mischief." [68]

Gradually the opposition lost ground.   The success of the Finneys and Beechers, the changing theological conception, and a general acceptance of enthusiastic religion in the more sedate urban sectors served to diminish the hostility.   Finney thought public reaction to revivals improved after the New Lebanon convention. It was not until about 1831, however, that assurances were sent him that "Prejudices against Finneyism seem . . . to have almost wholly given way." [69]   This was corroborated from friends in Philadelphia.   "There is a vastly different feeling here now on the subject of revivals to what there was when you were here."   The

---

[67] Finney to Robinson, Feb. 5, 1859 (Finney Papers).   Adverse criticism by foreign visitors of the extremes in evangelism are found in Mackay, *The Western World*, pp. 268, 270; Marryat, *A Diary in America, 1837-1838*, III, 126-127.

[68] Bushnell, *Views of Christian Nurture*, p. 113.

[69] Rev. Ingersoll to Finney, Dec. 20, 1830 (Finney Papers).

opposition never completely died out and even as late as 1850 the
Puritan Recorder was taking pot shots at Finney, whom they considered "a terrible man." [70]

For the most part, these successive waves of religious excitement
attracted the attention of those already acquainted with the church
rather than those completely divorced from religious associations.
Although conversion meant a completely different life for a small
percentage of those affected, Gilbert H. Barnes is correct in pointing out that for the large majority conversion meant a change in
emphasis and attitude rather than a revolution in their way of
life.[71]   It is evident too that the majority of those converted in the
1830's were women.   Women made up a sizable percentage of
church membership, although Henry Ward Beecher's church at
Lawrenceburgh, Indiana, consisting of nine women and one man
was not quite the norm.   Maffitt's proselytes seem to have been for
the most part young women.   As one of his critics put it, "We
are informed that of the hundreds who have recently been 'hopefully converted,' there is but one male in the whole number.   Some
have even marvelled at this solitary instance." [72]   Davenport in
his study, *Primitive Traits in Religious Revivals,* asserted that those
who first fell under the evangelist's influence were "the relatively
impulsive, less rational, less responsible elements in the audience,"
and Mrs. Trollope's evidence on the great number of young,
fashionably dressed women occupying the anxious benches would
seem to bear him out.[73]

But giddy young girls were not the only converts.   Finney
boasted often of the many "lawyers, merchants and physicians
. . . brought in" in his Rome and Rochester revivals.   The same
was true of New York City where there were "many conversions
of intelligent men, physicians, lawyers, merchants and others." [74]

---

[70] Caspar Schaeffer to Finney, Feb. 20, 1831; John Campbell to Finney, Nov. 13,
1850 (Finney Papers).

[71] See Gilbert H. Barnes, *The Antislavery Impulse,* p. 25.

[72] "Candour," *Theological Pretenders,* p. 8.

[73] Davenport, *Primitive Traits in Religious Revivals,* p. 242; Trollope, *Domestic
Manners of the Americans,* I, 113.

[74] Lewis Tappan to Benjamin Tappan, June 1, 1831 (Benjamin Tappan Papers).

To Finney this was testimony that "the Lord was aiming at the conversion of the highest classes of society." It perhaps did not occur to him that the lower classes could not afford the luxury of pew rent nor the time it took to attend regularly one of his protracted meetings! [75]

Outside the church revivals sometimes had an immediate effect. For instance, Beardsley describes what happened during the Rochester revival in 1831:

Grog shops were closed. Crime decreased and for years afterwards the jail was nearly empty. The only theatre in the city was converted into a livery stable and the only circus into a soap and candle factory. A large number of men prominent in business and social life were brought into the churches.[76]

Similar results were observed after Daniel Baker's revival in Savannah at about the same time. Peter Cartwright, in describing the 1842-1843 revival in Naples, Illinois, boasted, "Deism gave way, Universalism caved in, skepticism, with its coat of many colors, stood aghast, hell trembled, devils fled, drunkards awoke to soberness, and, I may safely say, all ranks and grades of sinners were made to cry out." [77]

The evangelists themselves have made the most sweeping claims as to their own success. According to Lyman Beecher, "Whole towns, in some instances, were said to be converted." [78] Finney's account of the 1855 Rochester revival approaches exaggeration:

Merchants arranged to have their clerks attend, a part of them one day, and a part the next day. The work became so general throughout the city that in all places of public resort, in stores and public houses, in banks, in the street and in public conveyances, and everywhere, the work of salvation that was going on was the absorbing topic.[79]

There was, however, a certain impermanence to these revivals. Few expected the religious excitement to stay continuously at a

[75] Finney, *Memoirs*, pp. 166, 289, 306-307, 437.
[76] Beardsley, *A History of American Revivals*, p. 142.
[77] Cartwright, *Autobiography*, pp. 392-393.
[78] Lyman Beecher, *Autobiography*, II, 89.
[79] Finney, *Memoirs*, pp. 437-438. For a similar statement, see Colton, *History and Character of American Revivals of Religion*, pp. 26-27.

high pitch. But once converted, individuals were not supposed to revert to their old ways. There is abundant evidence to suggest that the closed taverns reopened, the jails refilled, and the merchants went back to making money almost on the heels of the departing itinerants. One of Finney's followers in Rome complained shortly after he had left them, "Christians appear to be sinking down in coldness and stupidity . . . what a contrast between the present state of feeling and that of last winter." [80] The same thing happened in Boston after one of his tours.[81]

Revivals in the 1830's, however, did produce a number of important results. Figures on membership increases already cited indicate the impact of this wave of revivals. The relative number of churches also increased. In 1800 there was one church organization for every 1,740 inhabitants, while in 1850 there was one for every 895 of the population.[82] Revivals also strengthened religious activity. They gave an impetus to organizations in the church. Sunday Schools and Infant Schools were aided; prayer meetings and maternal societies became popular. "Our Infant school is going on very well," one devout reported, "—'tis called the 'Finneyite' school." [83] Revivals also modified church services. They tended to popularize the use of hymns and other forms of audience participation.[84] The concept of the "activity church" engaging in all sorts of campaigns for improving morality or bettering social conditions came to the fore. Societies were formed to promote revivals, collect data, and disseminate information about them.[85] Revivals were also an impetus to religious literature.

[80] Fanny N. Dunton to Mrs. Finney, Oct. 6, 1826 (Finney Papers).

[81] See Mary S. Parker to Finney, Nov. 12, 1832; Lewis Tappan to Finney, Aug. 29, 1833 (Finney Papers).

[82] See Beardsley, A History of American Revivals, pp. 211-212.

[83] Nancy O'Brien to Finney, Nov. 1, 1829. Infant Schools were established by churches to give religious instruction to "little charity scholars." Mrs. Maria Cushman to Mrs. Finney, May 27, 1828 and Jan. 29, 1829; Mrs. Amelia Norton to Mrs. Finney, March 8, 1829 (Finney Papers).

[84] For a discussion of the connection between hymns and revivals, see Loud, Evangelized America, p. 110 ff.

[85] For a copy of the constitution of one of the more prominent groups, see Association for the Promotion of Revivals to Finney, May 27, 1830; Feb. 3, 1831 (Finney Papers).

The Revival Tract Society, whose leadership included evangelists Finney, Lansing, Joel Parker, Joshua Leavitt, and laymen such as Lewis Tappan, printed publications on the subject. The extension of missions, the antislavery drive, the temperance crusade, indeed the whole formation of national moralistic societies were connected with this phenomenon of the 1830's. To cite but one example, Jacob Knapp boasted that the Washingtonian temperance movement was an indirect result of his revival in Baltimore in 1839.[86]

But while there were obviously beneficial results in the quickened religious zeal and in the impetus to moral reform, there were a number of deleterious effects as well. Francis Lieber made a point when he remarked that camp meetings and revivals had a deplorable effect "on health, domestic happiness, industry and national wealth." [87] The engendering of excessive religious fervor infected people with an emotional dogmatism that, when carried to political or economic affairs, may well be disastrous. Davenport quite convincingly links the incidence of religious fanaticism and lynching. It was Logan County, Kentucky, that witnessed the 1800 revival, and it was Logan County with one eightieth of the population that perpetrated one eleventh of the lynchings in that state.[88]

Although it is difficult statistically to indicate such a correlation, a number of observers have alluded to the possibilities of increased immorality as one of the by-products of revivals. Francis Lieber thought it to be expected that licentiousness would increase during and immediately following camp meetings.[89] Davenport, while admitting there had been a certain amount of exaggeration, declared that "human love passion and the spiritual love passion appear . . . to be delicately interwoven . . . and the kind of spiritual excitement which a super-emotional revival generates is

[86] See Beardsley, *A History of American Revivals*, p. 167.

[87] Francis Lieber, *Letters to a Gentleman in Germany, Written after a Trip from Philadelphia to Niagara*, p. 321.

[88] See Davenport, *Primitive Traits in Religious Revivals*, p. 304.

[89] See Lieber, *Stranger in America*, II, 229-230.

likely to be more harmful than helpful to the self control." [90]   Mrs. Trollope, with a woman's love for gossip, lent evidence to this impression in her accounts of sexual irregularities during a revival season.   Speaking of an itinerant preacher's influence over a young girl, she remarked that her feelings for him "seem to have been a curious mixture of spiritual love and earthly affection." [91]

If we may read between the lines there is some evidence that revivals engendered a love of the earthly as well as a spiritual sort. But whether an intensified religious zeal and the close companionship of the sexes made possible by camp meetings and protracted services contributed to extracurricular sexual activity is after all unimportant.   What is interesting, however, is the fashion in which these nineteenth-century religious folk expressed their quasi-physical adoration of a spiritual figure.   One woman writing to the wife of an evangelist with whom she had worked put her feelings in these words:

I so often tell you I do not love you as well as I do your husband, yet I do love and highly esteem you for your own sake as well as his.   I do love him and I wish I could be more engaged if it were *only to please him*.[92]

There is another possible influence of revivals upon which we may speculate.   Frederick Davenport, in the work already cited, suggested that England escaped the excesses of a French Revolution partly because of the released volume of emotional energy in the Wesley revival.[93]   Perhaps there is an American parallel.   Although the American counterpart was more a middle-class phenomenon, and although the United States in the 1830's did not witness a volume of social unrest equal to that in England in the eighteenth century, nevertheless, the channeling of emotional energy into song, prayer, and conversion undoubtedly acted as a safety valve for the population as a whole.   The impetus to moral reform through the agency of religiously inspired societies diverted dissent and individual action into a respectable co-operative

90 Davenport, *Primitive Traits in Religious Revivals*, p. 81.
91 Trollope, *Domestic Manners of the Americans*, I, 96.   See also pp. 80-81.
92 Mrs. L. M. Gilbert to Mrs. Finney, Feb., 1828 (Finney Papers).
93 See Davenport, *Primitive Traits in Religious Revivals*, p. 177.

effort which at the start made for moderation, less sweeping change, and less violent methods. In a nation wasting enthusiasm and energy in periodic revivals, it was difficult to accumulate sufficient head of steam to try out Jefferson's dictum of a rebellion now and then.[94] And while the revolutions of 1830 and 1848 on the continent and the European flirtation with Marxian Socialism were improbable in this country, the successive waves of revivals rendered them impossible.

We must remember, however, that in speaking of the results of revivals, there is a tendency to overestimate their lasting effect on society. Their hold on individuals and on churches was for the most part temporary; their stamp on society tended to be, if not always evanescent, at least transitory. One might apply Professor Schneider's evaluation of the results of the Great Awakening to all revivals: "Desperate means seldom accomplish permanent results." [95]

[94] "I hold it, that a little rebellion, now and then, is a good thing, and as necessary in the political world as storms in the physical," Thomas Jefferson to James Madison, Jan. 30, 1787, in Padover, *The Complete Jefferson*, p. 270.

[95] Schneider, *The Puritan Mind*, pp. 125-126.

IV. SOCIAL AND MORAL REFORM

The Americans are Society mad . . . the zeal or fanaticism . . . with which many, if not all, of them are carried on, is too remarkable a feature in the American character to be passed over without comment.[1]

It cannot but be indifferent to me what dish of meat you select, but if I think you are losing your soul it is my duty to attempt to save you.[2]

EMERSON DAVIS, the nineteenth-century historian, in speaking of his times observed, "There has been . . . a more perfect development of the benevolent spirit of the gospel in the souls of men than has been known at any previous time since the age of the apostles."[3] Benevolence, the desire to do good, the urge to reform was indeed a trait of American society during these years. Historians have only recently begun to consider this phenomenon of social action in the light of the nation's cultural development and to give it the prominence it deserves.[4]

The drive against evils in the form of poverty, delinquency, licentiousness, the campaigns for temperance, women's rights, and antislavery reflected a new spirit in the minds of men and received their major impulse from those who conducted religious revivals and stirred up the thoughts and emotions of the nation's devout. Indeed, almost all these reform movements copied the arguments, ideals, and methods of the roving revivalists, their tenor and machinery were religious, and they partook of the emotional, extravagant atmosphere of revivals. Furthermore, many of the leading evangelists were actively engaged in the front ranks of the various reform drives.[5]

[1] Marryat, *Diary*, III, 172.
[2] Lewis Tappan to Benjamin Tappan, Aug. 21, 1830 (Benjamin Tappan Papers).
[3] Davis, *The Half Century*, p. 343.
[4] The classic work on this subject is Gilbert H. Barnes, *The Antislavery Impulse.* See also Tyler, *Freedom's Ferment.*
[5] See Addison, *The Clergy in American Life and Letters*, p. 23.

There were, of course, reform movements apart from those generated by the 1830 revivals. Radicalism of the nonreligious sort was deeply ingrained in the American tradition and we have only to think of Thomas Paine, Charles Brockden Brown, Robert Owen, and Frances Wright to recognize the existence of a reform element that was strongly anticlerical in its outlook. Nor must we overlook the influence of the Enlightenment, the ideas of English and French reformers, and the impact of the industrial revolution, all of which were important contributory factors in the rise of humanitarianism. But radicalism of this extreme never achieved substantial popularity with the American public. It remained for those standing on the rock of piety to bring changes in society. This second wave of reformers—such as Theodore Weld, the Tappans, and Gerrit Smith—stole the thunder, if not the blueprints, from the pioneering, antireligious radicals.

There always had been a reform society or two active in American religious circles. In 1710 Cotton Mather spoke of forming "Societies for the Reformation of Manners and for the Suppression of Vice." [6] Lyman Beecher, in one of his many essays on the subject, described a society to suppress vice founded in Maryland in 1760 "to aid the civil magistrate in the execution of the laws" and patterned after a similar organization in London that dated its existence from 1697.[7] One of the earliest such societies after the nation's independence was founded at Yale in 1797 by Timothy Dwight. A secret organization consisting at first of twenty-three members, it was known as the Society for the Prevention of Vice and the Promotion of Good Morals, or the Moral Society for short, and its aim was "to revive the older standards and to bring questionable conduct under surveillance and reproof." [8]

Dwight helped form a similar organization in Litchfield in 1812 and joined Beecher, Heman Humphrey, Tapping Reeve, Asahel Hooker, and others in forming a committee of inquiry and correspondence.[9] At about the same time the young Joshua Leavitt,

[6] Cotton Mather, *Essays to Do Good*, pp. 132-133.
[7] Lyman Beecher, *A Reformation of Morals Practicable and Indispensable*, pp. 11, 13.
[8] Rourke, *Trumpets of Jubilee*, p. 25.
[9] Lyman Beecher, *Autobiography*, I, 255.

then a student at Yale, was instrumental in setting up the Yale
College Benevolent Society "for the purpose of assisting indigent
young men of promising talents and good morals in acquiring a
college education."[10]   Justin Edwards, also engaged in organizing
such groups, was active in the Andover South Parish Society for
the Reformation of Morals, better known as the "Doing Good"
Society, which met quarterly with a membership of seventy men
and had as its object "to discountenance immorality, particularly
Sabbath-breaking, intemperance, and profanity; and to promote
industry, temperance, order, piety, and good morals."   The women
in the congregation, all 150 of them, were not to be outdone by
the men.   They soon formed the Andover South Parish Female
Charitable Society.   By 1825 there was even a Penitent Females'
Society active in Boston.[11]   One of the more energetic groups was
the New Jersey Society for the Suppression of Vice and Immorality, which in 1819 worked for reform in the conditions of the
state's traveling coaches and urged the publication of a catalogue
of crime and vices punished by the state.[12]

These were isolated examples, however, and do not reflect popular opinion toward such subjects before 1825.   Prior to that date,
in terms of theory and practice, religion and organized reform were
not to be mixed.   After 1825, the rationale for such an admixture
was not lacking and as revivals increased in intensity so too did the
idea of organized reform.

The subject of moral reform may be broken into three major
divisions, the idea behind it, its pattern, and its examples.   Considering first the idea behind the movement, the writings of evangelists and religious figures are full of justifications for such activity.   Calvin Colton set the keynote for this vast reforming drive
when he wrote, in describing the design of Christianity, "It is to
reduce the world . . . by a system of moral means and agencies.
This is a stupendous scheme, a sublime enterprise."[13]   Of course,

[10] Joshua Leavitt to his father, July 20, 1813 (Leavitt Papers).
[11] Hallock, *Light and Love, a Sketch of the Life and Labors of the Rev. Justin Edwards*, pp. 44-46, 193.
[12] *Christian Spectator*, I, No. 12 (1819), 663.
[13] Calvin Colton, *History and Character of American Revivals of Religion*, p. 28.

the tradition of what Perry calls "evangelical moralism" is deep-rooted. Cotton Mather's stern warning, "I will be very inquisitive and solicitous about the company chosen by my servants" was re-echoed time and again.[14] Justin Edwards sent many a letter of admonition to his college sons, directly pointing out the evils of wine, cards, profanity, and tobacco and warned, "Whoever nibbles [at these baits of the Devil] may expect to be caught. Avoid soda, mead, confectionary, and everything which tends to generate an artificial appetite of any sort." [15] Lyman Beecher had an equal concern for the salvation of his sons. "Is not the present your time?" he wrote Edward in 1820. "I cannot endure the thought that, amid such excitements to seriousness, you should continue unawakened and unconverted to God." A year later he wrote, "Oh, my dear son, agonize to enter in. You must go to heaven; you must not go to hell!" [16]

Ministers were not the only ones to express concern over the spiritual welfare of others. The conscientious Arthur Tappan mentioned his brother's soul in almost every letter he wrote to him. As he put it, "I consider the subject of importance beyond all comparison, and so dear is your soul to me that if all I am worth would buy its eternal happiness I would gladly give it and consent to be poor as regards this world." [17] Considering Arthur's wealth at that time he was offering a high price indeed. Nor did Lewis Tappan hesitate to look into the salvation of others. Lewis, who would rather have seen his brother "a Teacher in the Sabbath School" than United States Senator wrote Benjamin, "You ask why I cannot keep my religion to myself? I will tell you, my dear brother. Because I see you are in danger of eternal damnation." [18]

One of the earlier expressions of this urge to do good is found in the writings of Nathaniel Emmons, who possessed a stern pater-

---

[14] Quoted in Perry, *Puritanism and Democracy*, pp. 323-324.

[15] Justin Edwards to his sons in college (n.d.), in Hallock, *Light and Love, a Sketch of the Life and Labors of the Rev. Justin Edwards*, p. 427.

[16] Lyman Beecher to Edward Beecher, Aug. 25, 1820, and April 7, 1821 in Lyman Beecher, *Autobiography*, I, 431, 460.

[17] Arthur Tappan to Benjamin Tappan, Feb. 19, 1827 (Benjamin Tappan Papers).

[18] Lewis Tappan to Benjamin Tappan, Jan. 8, 1833 (Benjamin Tappan Papers).

nal concern for the welfare of his fellow men. He did not, however, share the enthusiasm for combined action which was so pronounced after his time. His interpretation of moral reform was
on an individual basis.

From the great influence of example, we learn how easy it is, to effect a
reformation of morals among any people. Example alone will do it. . . .
If men of influence among any people, would only set good examples
themselves, they would insensibly and gradually promote a reformation
of morals. There is a few in every town and parish, who carry the
power of reformation in their own conduct.[19]

Lyman Beecher's impression of a reformer was somewhat more
energetic than that of Emmons. As he put it, "when I saw a rattle-
snake in my path I would smite it. I talked to my deacons about
it, and with my people, and roused public feeling." Of all evangelists, Beecher was the most outspoken in enunciating the idea of
moral reform. He considered the regeneration of society possible
in several ways. First, public attention must be called to the subject. The second step was the improvement of what he called "the
better part of the community," the religious element in society.
The third was attention to "the religious education of the rising
generation." The youth must be trained in the precepts of his
church. The schooling must start early and continue unremit-
tingly until the new generation was as holy as Lyman Beecher.
More important than the training of the youth was "the indispensable necessity of executing promptly the laws against immorality." [20]

Beecher did not question the wisdom of such laws. Indeed, he
assumed the right of the civil authority to legislate morals. The
state was the handmaiden, if not of the entire church, at least of
Lyman Beecher. It was rather with the enforcing of these laws
that the Connecticut divine was concerned. The usual law en-
forcement powers were not enough, he believed. To make certain
that laws against immorality were enforced an influence was needed

[19] Nathaniel Emmons, *A Discourse, Delivered Sept. 3, 1792 to the Society for the
Reformation of Morals in Franklin*, pp. 21-22.
[20] Lyman Beecher, *A Reformation of Morals Practicable and Indispensable*, pp. 13,
14, 17.

"distinct from that of the government, independent of popular suffrage, superior in potency to individual efforts, and competent to enlist and preserve the public opinion on the side of law and order." The banding together of individuals could effect more change than the sum of all their separate efforts, he declared. What was needed were "local voluntary associations of the wise and the good" to aid the civil magistrate enforce laws. These groups could control public opinion "and by the sermons, the reports, and the conversations they occasion, diffuse much moral instruction." [21]

It was Beecher's opinion that these voluntary associations should not limit their activities to preaching and persuasion. There were other means of improving men's morals and of checking vice. There was even a hint of force in his suggestion:

If beside these local associations, a more extended concert could be formed of wise and good men, to devise ways and means of suppressing vice and guarding the public morals; to collect facts and extend information, and in a thousand nameless ways to exert a salutary, general influence; it would seem to complete a system of exertion, which we might hope, would retrieve what we have lost, and perpetuate forever our civil and religious institutions. [22]

Beecher's stern, Matherlike insistence on running the affairs of his neighbors was not the only justification advanced for forwarding the cause of moral reform. There was a reason inherent in the modifications of theology which Finney and others defended. To the New School evangelist the piety of a Christian should be exercised in doing good to others. The reformation of society, therefore, followed from the inward consecration of the individual. [23]

Others joined in preaching moral reform. Horace Bushnell saw "a fixed relation between the temporal and the eternal, such that we shall best realize the eternal by rightly rising the temporal." New times demanded new approaches to morality, he believed, adding that nineteenth-century material and intellectual improvements made "old practices more destructive, old vices more in-

---

21 *Ibid.*, p. 18.

22 *Ibid.*, p. 19.

23 For Finney's theological rationale of reform, see Oberlin Maternal Association, MS Minutes, Oct. 22, 1844 (Finney Papers), and *The Oberlin Evangelist*, VII, No. 20 (1845), 155.

curable." [24]   Edward Beecher in his *The Conflict of Ages* justified
working for "the moral renovation of man." [25]   Evangelists were
not the only ones to defend the idea of organized action against
evil. "I have great faith in the influence of the Literary and
Philanthropic Associations of our day," wrote Angela Grimké.
"All nature reads us an instructive lesson on the power of combi-
nation.   In every object we behold we see the beauty and utility
of this all pervading principle." [26]

This impetus to moral reform followed a pattern.   After revivals had kindled religious zeal and the religious community had
strengthened its own ranks through conversions, the first wave of
activity was in the form of missionary enterprises.   Missionary
societies were organized on a local and national basis; support was
solicited and workers were sent out to spread the gospel, first at
home and then abroad.   The second wave took the form of Bible
and tract societies, designed to facilitate the distribution of the
Scriptures and to serve as a propaganda mill for other phases of the
combined effort to remake society.   The third stage was reached
with the establishment of Sunday Schools and education societies to
train the youth and work at reform through the younger generation.   The habit of joining societies now well established, the
fourth step included the various attempts at moral reform, at
eliminating vice, licentiousness, juvenile delinquency, and the like.
Finally, the last stage was the development on the national scale of
the great humanitarian crusades such as temperance, peace and
antislavery.   So powerful did these various societies become that

[24] Bushnell, *Sermons on Living Subjects*, p. 270; *A Discourse on the Moral Tendencies
and Results of Human History*, p. 16.
[25] Edward Beecher, *The Conflict of Ages*, p. 2. Lyman Beecher's second oldest son,
Edward (1803-1895), was licensed to preach in 1826, was pastor of the Park Street
Church in Boston until 1830, became the first president of Illinois College, went back
to Boston in 1844 until 1855, when he took up ministerial duties in Galesburg, Illinois.
Edward was the first Beecher to espouse antislavery and his *Narrative of the Riots at
Alton* provided his generation with the most complete account of Lovejoy's martyrdom.
An ardent anti-Catholic, he was editor of the *Congregationalist* for six years after its
founding in 1849.
[26] Angela Grimké to D. L. Dodge, July 14, 1836 (Weld Papers).

by 1834 the total annual receipts of the benevolent societies equaled some nine million dollars.[27]

Many of these societies overlapped in membership and objectives. They held their annual meetings at the same time and place. The close affiliation of the various groups is revealed in one of Justin Edwards's letters. "In the morning," he writes, "we found ourselves at New York. I attended the meetings of the American Home Missionary Society, the American Tract Society, the Bible Society, and the Education Society." [28] Travelers noted with interest the continued popularity of these anniversary meetings, which by 1839 numbered sixteen. In that year Combe wrote:

The annual meetings of the great benevolent and religious societies of the Union are now taking place in New York, and they present striking evidence that, however active the acquisitive and ambitious propensities of this people may be, their benevolent and religious sentiments are far from being dormant. The crowds of persons in attendance, and the large sums of money contributed, bespeak a vigorous and general activity of the moral faculties.[29]

Edwards, indeed, strongly favored tightening the lines among the many groups. "Our benevolent operations," he wrote, "should combine and consolidate as much as possible." [30]

This interconnection cannot be overemphasized. As Gilbert H. Barnes has pointed out, there was a "benevolent empire" of leading laymen, most of whom were wealthy merchants, who together with the major evangelists led in the concerted efforts to remold society. Men like the Tappan brothers, Gerrit Smith, William Jay, Anson Phelps, and others controlled through a series of "interlocking directorates" the policies and activities of the major societies for the promotion of moral reform, and as Barnes has indicated, this movement was dominated by New School Presbyterians, leaders in the 1830 revivals.[31] This group, who listened to Finney,

[27] Marryat, A Diary in America, 1837-1838, III, 171-172.
[28] Justin Edwards to Mrs. Edwards, May 15, 1826, in Hallock, Light and Love, a Sketch of the Life and Labors of the Rev. Justin Edwards, pp. 213-214.
[29] Combe, Notes on the United States of America, II, 39.
[30] Justin Edwards to the Rev. William A. Hallock, Aug. 28, 1823, in Hallock, Light and Love, a Sketch of the Life and Labors of the Rev. Justin Edwards, p. 189.
[31] Gilbert H. Barnes, The Antislavery Impulse, p. 18.

followed his preaching and supported the vast network of local groups and national societies influenced immeasurably the course of moral reform in the ante-bellum era.

One of the first things this group of wealthy businessmen did in the cause of reform was to help establish in New York a weekly paper of their own. A crusade needs a sounding board to publish its views. Finney and Finney's followers had found the columns of the orthodox religious journals closed to them. To defend new measures, disseminate news about revivals, and seek support for the rising reform societies, there was founded the New York *Evangelist*, which later under Joshua Leavitt's editorship had such a stormy career.

Turning to the various examples of reform, an early indication of the way in which the crusading evangelists were to go about removing the evil in society is seen in the religious attack on dueling, a quaint custom which was, for practical reasons, disappearing in the nineteenth century. The fight against dueling had its philippic in the form of Lyman Beecher's curious work, *The Remedy for Duelling*, first delivered as a sermon in 1806 and published in 1809. It had its society, the Anti-duelling Association, which was established in New York in 1809, and it had its repercussions in the lingering apathy many moralists felt against duelers, strong enough in 1844 to lose Clay a number of votes.

Beecher's *Remedy for Duelling* singled out for criticism the elevation of the duelist to power. He opposed the election to public office of anyone who had ever engaged in a duel, believing them unfit for office. "The duellist is a murderer," he maintained, and to vote for him was a blow against civil society, against the sanctity of government, and against the word of God.[32] Support for such a man encouraged the crime, and the sober evangelist considered those who voted for him just as guilty as the dueler himself.

Lyman's argument is illustrative of the overwhelming self-assurance of the reformer. It is indicative of the fanatic's sweeping statements, of the gross lack of perspective which characterized the pious enthusiast intent on moral reform. In his conclusion he declared,

32 Lyman Beecher, *The Remedy for Duelling*, p. 5.

But why so inveterate against duelling in particular? Because at present it is a great and alarming national sin. Because no other crime, with such shameless effrontery, bids defiance to the laws of God and man. Because no other crime is so palliated, justified, and with such impunity sanctioned by the example of the great; and of course no other crime has so alarming an aspect upon the principles of our young men, and the moral sensibilities of our country.[33]

That a man of Beecher's intelligence could write in such sweeping terms at a time when the United States was in the midst of a commercial war, when Jefferson's embargo was still in most men's minds and when the nation was on the brink of a conflict with England was indicative of the evangelist's peculiar lack of perspective.

One of the more curious of the agitations designed to effect a change in society was the Sabbatarian movement, the drive to make Sunday a more holy day.[34] As part of the Puritan heritage the observance of the Sabbath was maintained by the pious with great strictness. As the nation developed, however, and as people became less religious, the colonial observance of the Sabbath began to disappear. Nineteenth-century ministers endeavored to repair the damage of time and restore Sunday's sanctity with all its restrictions and regulations. Justin Edwards, one of the leaders in the Sabbatarian movement, attempted to justify the return to the ways of the past on constitutional as well as religious grounds. His *Sabbath Manual*, used by his followers as their Bible, sounds strangely like a declaration of independence:

All have a right to rest one day in seven, because God has given that. . . . This right does not come from men. It comes from God. Like the right to live, to see the sun, and breath the air, it vests in humanity, and is inalienable. No human government gave it, and no human government, without deep injustice, can take it away. There is not a laborer on the canal or railroad, in the manufactory or workshop, or in any department of worldly business, who has not [this] right.[35]

[33] *Ibid.*, p. 34.
[34] The most complete study of this nineteenth-century phenomenon is found in Bronner, "The Observance of the Sabbath in the United States," *Harvard Summaries of Ph.D. Theses 1937.* This movement had its political side which will be considered in Chap. V.
[35] Edwards, *The Sabbath Manual*, pp. 26-27.

Later in the century Francis Wayland in writing on the observance of this day asserted that the law of the Sabbath forbade "all
labor of body or mind, of which the immediate object is not the
worship of God, or our own religious improvement." This ex-
cluded "the pursuit of pleasure, or of any animal, or merely intellectual, gratification" as well as any activity of an economic
nature.[36]

It was this latter that was particularly distressing to the pious
evangelist. Economic activity on Sunday was increasing in the
nineteenth century. One especially obnoxious enterprise in the
minds of the devout was the transportation of mail on the holy
day, and it was this practice that became the rallying cry for the
entire Sabbatarian movement. Much of the reason behind the
attack on Sunday mails hinged on the political views of orthodoxy.
The Protestant sects were rapidly losing their favored position of
influence over the affairs of state, and the Sabbatarian movement
was, in a sense, the last counteroffensive of a theocracy routed
generations before.

Early protests against the transportation of mail on Sunday came
from Philadelphia churches prior to 1811. The following year the
Presbyterian Synod at Pittsburg opposed the practice, while in
1813 other portions of the country were heard from. In 1814
some seventy-three petitions were sent to the House of Representatives on the matter. Presbyterianism in central New York took
an especially outspoken stand. In 1812 and 1814 the General
Assembly instructed the several presbyteries to call on their
churches to send petitions to Congress. The Oneida Presbytery,
later to be Finney's famous stamping ground, "responded at
once." [37] Meanwhile in Connecticut Lyman Beecher was active in
the cause, although he hardly deserves all the credit he claims in
his *Autobiography* for originating the movement:

We really broke up riding and working on the Sabbath, and got the victory. The thing was done, and had it not been for the political revolu-

---

36 Wayland, *Elements of Moral Science*, pp. 195-196.

37 Fowler, *Historical Sketch of Presbyterianism within the Bounds of the Synod of
Central New York*, p. 142. For details on the petitions to Congress, see McMaster,
A History of the People of the United States, VI, 95-96.

tion that followed, it would have stood to this day. We took hold of it in the Association at Fairfield, June, 1814, and I brought in a report, which was adopted, recommending, among other things, a petition to Congress. That was the origin of the famous petitions against Sunday mails.[38]

All this at a time when the nation was at war.

What was called the Christian party in politics kept up the fight. Devout individuals signed petitions and refused to post letters on Sunday. Josiah Bissell of Rochester helped establish a "Pioneer Line" of stages which did not run on the Sabbath. Opposition to Sunday activities extended to "abolition agitation and funerals on Sunday." [39] There was even hostility against Sunday cheesemaking!

The flames of controversy were fanned in 1825 when a law was passed requiring all post offices where mail was delivered on Sunday to stay open the entire day. By 1828 the stage was set for a nationwide organization. In May of that year, conveniently scheduled to attract attendance from the anniversary meetings of the religious groups, a convention of ministers and laymen organized the General Union for Promoting the Observance of the Christian Sabbath. The convention was generously sprinkled with affluent businessmen and the Connecticut orthodoxy was well represented. None other than Arthur Tappan was named treasurer. For the next two years the tempo of agitation was stepped up. Lewis Tappan was kept busy atending meetings the object of which was "memorializing Congress to stop the transportation of mails on the Sabbath." [40] By 1829 petitions had been presented to Congress from all parts of the Union. The answer of the lawmakers came in March, 1830, with the famous report by Richard M. Johnson, a classic, though little read, statement on the freedom of conscience.[41]

[38] Lyman Beecher, *Autobiography*, I, 268-269.

[39] Fowler, *Historical Sketch of Presbyterianism within the Bounds of the Synod of Central New York*, p. 143.

[40] Lewis Tappan Diary, Nov. 28, 29, Dec. 27, 1828, pp. 57, 61 (Lewis Tappan Papers).

[41] See Richard M. Johnson, "Report of the Committee of Post Offices and Post Roads of the United States House of Representatives," *Reports of the 21st Congress, First*

Thereafter the attack was more sporadic. The Sabbath Union declined in numbers and influence but the petitioning continued. Herman Norton did what he could to get Reading interested in the question. "A meeting . . . has been called to take into consideration the propriety or impropriety of stopping the Sunday mail. . . . If our Lawyers will not go and stand up for the Sabbath of the Lord, I think I shall feel a duty to go myself," he wrote to his close friend, Charles Finney.[42] Finney himself was strongly in favor of the movement although his participation on its behalf was limited to sermonizing. It was his opinion "that unless something is done, and done speedily . . . to promote the sanctification of the Sabbath by the church, the Sabbath will go by the board." He feared that not only would the mails be running and the post offices open but also in time the courts of justice and the halls of legislation would be opened wide. "And what can the church do, what will this nation do, WITHOUT ANY SABBATH?"[43]

The movement still had sufficient impetus to rally the faithful to form the American and Foreign Sabbath Union in April of 1843. Chief Justice Williams of Connecticut was named president and Justin Edwards secretary. During the ensuing year Edwards visited ten states on behalf of the cause, wrote numerous articles for the press, and issued his *Sabbath Manual,* in which he asserted that the transportation of mails had been discontinued on a number of routes and predicted eventual victory. He also claimed that the number of those going to the post office, working, traveling, or engaging in amusements on Sundays had decreased. His work was applauded by the National Sabbath Convention, a group of 1,700 delegates from eleven states presided over by the aging John Quincy Adams, when it met in Baltimore in November, 1844.[44] Be that as it may, the Sabbatarian movement failed to accomplish

---

Session, No. 271. For a short critique of the Johnson Report, see Blau, *Cornerstones of Religious Freedom in America,* pp. 106-109.

[42] Herman Norton to Finney, Jan. 18, 1830 (Finney Papers).

[43] Finney, *Lectures on Revivals of Religion,* p. 280.

[44] Hallock, *Light and Love, a sketch of the Life and Labors of the Rev. Justin Edwards,* p. 465.

its objectives and remains a curious example of misdirected religious zeal.

Of equal importance in the eyes of many zealots was the tract society, established to print and distribute pamphlets and sermons among the population. The tract, a short, usually dogmatic, persuasively written leaflet was as much a part of nineteenth-century society as direct mail advertising is today. Religious groups used the tract as an inexpensive sounding board, and soon after the start of the century groups were organized to facilitate in the dissemination of these tracts. Costs of printing were met by donation and the sale of the pamphlets. Agents were sent out and were paid commissions for selling the publications. It was a convenient scheme for extending religious education and persuading the pious by the printed word.

One of the earliest such societies was the New England Tract Society, founded in Boston in 1814 on a subscription of $3,800. One of the founders, Noah Porter, had the idea of printing wholesome literature for the community at prices lower than the commercial booksellers. The society's management gradually fell into the hands of Justin Edwards, who became its corresponding secretary in 1821, several years before he turned to the temperance crusade. In 1825 the various local organizations united to form the American Tract Society, and the following year this group joined the growing list of those holding May anniversaries in New York and was well on its way to national prominence.

At first the American Tract Society confined its attention to purely religious books. Gradually, however, it joined forces with other reform organizations publicizing them and propagandizing for them. Missionary groups, temperance drives, and later antislavery agitation received the Tract Society's aid. The organization reached its peak in the 1830's, aided by the waves of revivals which increased its potential audience.[45] Auxiliary societies were

---

[45] In 1833 the Society devoted its time and money to the following uses: Five hundred dollars was appropriated to be paid to authors of the best ten approved tracts received by the society. Fourteen agents were planted throughout the country. Fifteen hundred dollars was donated for the use of "American Baptist Missionaries in Burmah." An equal amount went to missionaries in China, while a thousand was sent to those in Bombay, Ceylon, the Sandwich Islands, and the Mediterranean. European missionaries

formed, and these often fulfilled social and religious functions as well as the literary one. Allied women's groups, if they could not print, write, or distribute tracts, were at least able to meet and discuss them. Typical of the many invitations evangelists received from tract societies was this one addressed to Finney: "I am requested to ask the favor of your attendance and services at the annual meeting of the Union Ladies Tract Society, which will be held at the lecture room of Essex Street Church tomorrow p. m. at one-fourth past four o'clock." [46]

In the 1840's, as the time and energies of its followers were turned elsewhere, the American Tract Society declined in importance. Justin Edwards tried to rally it but with little success. Working with Edward N. Kirk and others, he endeavored to get the Society to publish the Bible with brief explanatory notes. He even worked on the notes himself, devoting the bulk of his time from 1849 until 1853 on this task. Some indication of the extent of the Society's growth can be seen in the reports it published in 1850. By that year some 700,000 copies of the Society's *Sabbath Manual,* printed in English, German, French, and Spanish, had been circulated. But the organization that at its height had been able to donate twelve thousand dollars a year to worthy causes could grant in 1850 a bare $2,421.77 "for the supply of emigrants . . . for missionaries, clergymen and others." [47]

But for many, writing and distributing pamphlets was not enough. There were other, more active "sublime enterprises" which attracted the religious reformers. If they were to remake the world in the image of their own church, the living conditions and standards of a large portion of the population had to be changed. If middle-class morals were to prevail, those of the masses must be remade. Consequently, a variety of groups as-

---

in Greece received five hundred dollars from the group, as did the Lower Saxony Tract Society in Hamburg. The Paris Religious Tract Society was the recipient of fifteen hundred dollars, while "William Ropes, Esq., St. Petersburg, Russia" was sent five hundred more. See "Objects Now Before the American Tract Society," *American Tract Society, Annual Report,* No. 8 (1833).

[46] Elizabeth Cadman to Finney, April 10 (1830?) (Finney Papers).

[47] Hallock, *Light and Love, a Sketch of the Life and Labors of the Rev. Justin Edwards,* p. 496.

signed to themselves the task of elevating the poor, cleansing the criminal, purifying the prostitute. Not concerned with the reasons for the existence of poverty, crime, and immorality, the nineteenth-century religious reformers set about to force all men—and women—to live as they.

Typical of this endeavor was the work done to elevate the morals of the poor. As early as 1816 there was organized a Society for the Prevention of Pauperism that addressed itself to the problem of juvenile delinquency. In 1825 the House of Refuge was built to hold between two and three hundred youths who had been saved from a life of crime. A similar structure was built in Boston the following year, and in 1828 one was organized in Philadelphia. Religious instruction was given them; orphanages were founded and financial aid was rendered. In 1837 New York City was spending almost $280,000 a year to aid its poor.[48]

The care of the poor was a perfect field for humanitarian endeavor, although the Puritan tradition put upon idleness a certain sinful connotation. The efforts of reformers were directed to preaching and praying rather than eradicating the roots of poverty. Salvation was more important than economic security. Indeed, salvation was the only security. One of Finney's correspondents indicated this state of mind in describing a plan to aid the poor in Salem, Massachusetts:

The object is to raise up Local missionaries to visit and read the Scriptures, and preach to the *poor* in our own neighborhood. Brethren and Sisters are to join—each to visit etc. to a certain number of Families once in two weeks and meet for prayer, searching the Scriptures and make reports to a Superintendent weekly. Every member *must work or quit*. No honorary members.[49]

Many were the groups formed to improve mankind. The prison-reform movement was aimed at elevating the morals of the nation's neglected, and the Boston Prison Discipline Society of 1825 and the New York Prison Association of 1845 were highly moralistic in

[48] Tyler, *Freedom's Ferment*, p. 257; Davis, *The Half Century*, p. 176; Billington, *The Protestant Crusade*, p. 35; For a description of the New York House of Refuge, see Hall, *The Religious Background of American Culture*, I, 24 ff.

[49] John Brooks to Finney, Nov. 9, 1830 (Finney Papers).

character. In 1847 in New York City a society was organized
with Finney's blessing to erect a "Home for the friendless" in
order to prevent crime. Its object was to provide facilities "for
benefiting the bodies and saving the souls of the needy."[50] Various programs were advanced to care for underprivileged children.
William C. Chapin, wealthy merchant and Rhode Island politician,
advanced one such plan for "the education of idiotic and feeble
minded children." [51]

Other underprivileged segments of society were not overlooked.
The sailors received their full share of attention. As a result of
the increase in revivals, Bethel meetings were held to save sailors'
souls. In his diary for October 18, 1829, Lewis Tappan recorded
one of his less successful endeavors in this direction:

Went to the Tow Boat where Mr. Leavitt and myself have had Bethel
meetings, but the season is too far advanced to have them on deck, and
no convenient place is yet found in which to hold them. We conversed
at length upon exerting outselves systematically for the good of the poor
and ignorant in the city.[52]

In 1846 the American Bethel Society was organized to give religious instruction to canal workers. Another group active in the
field was the Western Seamen's Friend Society.

Preaching to the poor and praying to sailors were thankless
tasks, and, despite the extravagant claims and rows of statistics
given out by the reform societies, little in the shape of a millennium was to be observed from all the effort in this direction. But
if proletarian purification proved fruitless, there was one field in
which the forces of morality could defeat the adversary. To the
nineteenth-century evangelist the theater was Satan's stronghold.

If the number of theaters in the 1830's was any indication of
Satan's power, however, it was languishing. In 1839 New York
City had three theaters and an Italian opera house. Earlier in
the decade the Chatham Theater was open but it was, as Mrs.
Trollope discovered, "so utterly condemned by bonton, that it

---

[50] Mrs. S. R. Ingraham to Finney, Jan. 16, 1847 (Finney Papers).
[51] William C. Chapin to Finney, Feb. 6, 1851 (Finney Papers).
[52] Lewis Tappan Diary, Oct. 18, 1829 (Lewis Tappan Papers).

requires some courage to decide upon going there." [53]   It was no
wonder the Finneyite forces were able to buy it out and open a
church in its place. Philadelphia also boasted three theaters, while
Boston had two. Baltimore, Washington, and Cincinnati each had
one, and New Orleans contained one English-speaking house, "a
very good French Vaudeville and Opera Comique."[54]   This for a
nation of fifteen million was rather meager.

Since the theaters were a rival institution competing for the attention of the populace, it was understandable that ministers would
oppose the establishment of them.   Opposition to them, however,
was also based on religious principles.   The chief object of theaters
was amusement, not the spiritual elevation of man; their actors
were individuals of questionable reputation; their habitués were
men of shady morality.   As one cleric put it, "licentiousness en-
courages the establishment of theatres and opera houses.   Such
buildings are consecrated to the dissemination of loose principles
in morals, and the promotion of every infamous vice." [55]   Henry
Ward Beecher, who considered such a place "the gate of debauch-
ery, the porch of pollution," once remarked, "It is notorious that
the theatre is the door to all the sinks of iniquity." [56]

The various evangelists may have differed on points of theology
or ways to win souls, but on this question there was unanimity.   It
is interesting to compare the pronouncements of the Beechers,
father and son, on this subject.   Lyman in 1827, speaking about
"crime in its varied forms," had this to say about the theater:

Theatres, those "schools of morality", falsely so called, shall cease to be-
guile unstable souls, whose feet go down to death, whose steps take hold
on hell.   Christianity, as she prevails, will form a public sentiment that
will make virtue blush at the thought of meeting within the same walls,
and breathing the same polluted air, and applauding the same exhibitions,
with the most debased and wretched portion of the community.[57]

---

[53] Trollope, *Domestic Manners of the Americans*, I, 193-194.
[54] Grund, *The Americans*, p. 76.
[55] *McDowall's Journal*, I, No. 5 (1833), 37.
[56] Henry Ward Beecher, *Lectures to Young Men*, p. 235.
[57] Lyman Beecher, *Resources of the Adversary*, p. 9.

Many years later, Henry Ward, having revolted from his father's
generation in terms of theology, still stuck to the same theme.

> If you would pervert the taste—go to the Theatre. If you would
> imbibe false views—go to the Theatre. If you would efface as speedily
> as possible all qualms of conscience—go to the Theatre. . . . If you would
> be infected with each particular vice in the catalogue of Depravity—go
> to the Theatre. . . . We pay moral assassins to stab the purity of our
> children.[58]

The plays enacted on its stage were also condemned. Representative of evangelistic scorn were the words of John Newland
Maffitt who, in his autobiography, confessed to having visited
"that nest of malignant blandishment" as a youth:

> Here allow me to warn the youth of both sexes, and point out the awful
> consequences that accrue to those who make it their study to visit such
> places, and, putting the curtain aside, detect the cursed evil that lurks
> unseen in the representation of all pieces within the range of drama.[59]

Albert Barnes was another who in his lighter moments turned
critic. "When has the drama contributed to public virtue?" he
asked in one address. "In what place has it existed where it has
not been patronized by the effeminate, the unprincipled, the licen-
tious? Where has it left men better than it found them?" His
conclusion was that youth did not need what the theater had to
offer them. Theirs was a better task standing as they did on the
threshold of Barnes's millennium. "Talent is demanded here for
useful purposes; and our country demands the aid of her sons to
carry out her great and noble plans of liberty and virtue." [60]

Evangelists not only preached and wrote against the theater;
they also prayed for its destruction and worked to turn theaters
into houses of worship. During the Rochester revival of 1830
Finney claimed that he transformed the only theater in town into
a livery stable. Shortly after the Tremont Theater was opened in
Boston Justin Edwards campaigned against it on this theme:

> It was suggested to my mind in passing the new theatre . . . whether it is
> not the will of God that his people should agree together to pray that the

---

[58] Henry Ward Beecher, *Lectures to Young Men*, pp. 237, 246.
[59] Maffitt, *Tears of Contrition*, p. 22.
[60] Albert Barnes, *Literature and Science in America*, pp. 16-17.

building may be . . . consecrated as a temple for the worship of the living God; and that instead of its being . . . a place in which multitudes . . . will be ripened for perdition, it may be a place in which multitudes . . . shall be prepared for glory.[61]

Fifteen years later Edwards got his wish. The Tremont Theater was bought and turned into a free Baptist evangelical church. The "friends of morality and religion" rejoiced at the news, especially when they learned that the enterprise had lost ten thousand dollars the last three months it was open.[62]

The theater was only one form of amusement which suffered at the hands of the evangelists. Indeed, all semblance of levity and frivolity was suspect. Peter Cartwright opposed in the strongest words what he called frivolousness in dress. Finney was known to bawl out from his pulpit the ladies in the congregation whose finery in fashion displeased him. "There is no way in which you can bear a proper testimony by your lives against the fashions of the world but by dressing plain," he told them.[63] Card playing was, of course, taboo. "I should rejoice," wrote Justin Edwards to his daughter, "should each one of my children be able to say, at the close of life, that they never knew how to play cards." [64] And dancing was the instrument of the devil! The dance floor was Cartwright's favorite place for impromptu revival meetings, and many a convert, if Finney, Cartwright, Finley, and others are to be believed, was saved from perdition by an evangelist's awesome presence at a dance.[65] Perhaps the most vocal opponent of dancing was Albert Barnes. In a short piece entitled *On Dancing* he detailed all the evils connected with this form of amusement. His peroration sounded a despairing note:

---

[61] Justin Edwards to Secretary of the Tract Society, May, 1827, quoted in Hallock, *Light and Love, a Sketch of the Life and Labors of the Rev. Justin Edwards*, p. 229.

[62] Knapp, *Autobiography*, p. 135.

[63] Finney, *Lectures to Professing Christians*, p. 107.

[64] Justin Edwards to Elizabeth Edwards (n.d.), quoted in Hallock, *Light and Love, A Sketch of the Life and Labors of the Rev. Justin Edwards*, p. 478.

[65] Maffitt related with pride his experience in interrupting a party to preach. To him, "the practice of dancing is so subversive to the cause of Christianity—so opposite to the language of the holy writ—and so entirely subservient to the ends of the prince of darkness." Maffitt, *op. cit.*, p. 109. See also Finney, "Innocent Amusements" (MS article, Finney Papers).

Dear Youth! Candidate for heaven! The ball-room is not far from the grave; and from the scenes of hilarity in the one you will soon go to the gloom of the other. . . . Will you still rejoice at the sound of the lute, and regard life as designed only for gaiety and vanity? [66]

Profanity was another of the vices to be fought. Societies were formed to remove this blemish on society. Even the young were enlisted in the campaign, as George Combe discovered while visiting a school in South Boston:

The children have been formed in "An Association for the Suppression of Profanity" which the teacher said had been eminently successful in banishing not only oaths, but rude language and violence from the school. The organization is very similar to that of a temperance society.[67]

No survey of evangelistic reform would be complete without mention of the temperance crusade. Here again the evangelists played a leading part, and the drive against intemperance was an integral part of the expanded revivalism of the 1830's. Daniel Dorchester, whose monumental though unsatisfactory tome was one of the first studies of American church history, gave heavy credit to the religious roots of the drive, declaring that it developed out of the religious life of the churches.[68] The temperance movement spread with revivals. Temperance societies gained their staunchest supporters from among church members. Their methods were often those of revivals; their agents and lecturers were associated with the other religious reforms of the day. Some churches were so identified with the movement that an abstinence pledge was a prerequisite for membership.

There is some evidence that a temperance crusade was needed in the United States. Critical travelers, moralistic though some of them were, pointed out the extensive popularity of what the nineteenth century so picturesquely called "ardent spirits." The English aristocrat, Basil Hall, believed that "a deeper curse never afflicted any nation. The evil is manifested in almost every walk

[66] Albert Barnes, "On Dancing," *The American National Preacher*, XVIII, No. 1 (1844), 22, 24.

[67] Combe, *Notes on the United States of North America*, I, 109.

[68] Dorchester, *Christianity in the United States*, p. 441. Similar views are held by Tyler, *Freedom's Ferment*, pp. 316, 318, and Ludlum, *Social Ferment in Vermont*, pp. 69, 70. See also Grund, *The Americans*, pp. 180-194.

of life, contaminates all it touches." Hall was especially critical of the "bars" which he found on steamboats, in theaters and hotels, near museums, and at almost every turn. The Dutch visitor, De Roos echoed Hall's comments, while Francis Wyse declared that Americans consumed more "spirits of all kinds" proportionately than any other people.[69]

If we can believe Albert Barnes, there were a number of reasons why intemperance existed in nineteenth-century America. According to the Philadelphia clergyman, intemperance was caused by the nation's abundant land, which made the people wasteful. It was the result of American views of liberty. National habits, the respectability of those dealing in liquor, and the protection of the laws all had their part.[70] Be that as it may, as religious reformers attacked social and moral evils they began to realize more and more that intemperance was closely connected with pauperism, delinquency, crime, and vice. As Barnes put it, "It stands in the way of revivals. . . . Every drunkard opposes the millennium; every dram-drinker stands in the way of it, every dram-seller stands in the way of it . . . there is no hope of the conversion of a man who habitually uses ardent spirits." And Finney quickly added, "Resistance to the temperance reformation will put a stop to revivals in the church. . . . The man's hands are RED WITH BLOOD who stands aloof from the temperance cause." [71]

None of the men of God were more enthusiastic in their temperance fervor than Lyman Beecher. Heavily indebted to Benjamin Rush and to the English example of temperance crusading, Beecher's biggest attack on drunkenness came in six sermons on *The Nature, Occasions, Signs, Evils and Remedy of Intemperance,* delivered in 1825 and published in 1827. Earlier in his career he had revolted against excessive drinking at ministerial meetings, and in 1812, in the Congregational General Association of Con-

---

[69] Hall, *Travels in North America in the Years, 1827 and 1828,* II, 84, I, 125-126; De Roos, *Personal Narrative of Travels in the United States and Canada in 1826,* p. 6; Wyse, *America, Its Realities and Resources,* I, 309.

[70] Albert Barnes, *The Causes of Intemperance in Cities and Large Towns; The Immorality of the Traffic in Ardent Spirits,* pp. 27-30.

[71] *Ibid.,* p. 44; Finney, *Lectures on Revivals,* p. 265.

necticut, he was named to a committee that recommended among other things that drinking at ecclesiastical meetings be stopped, that church members cease to sell, buy, or use "ardent spirits," and that voluntary associations be formed to preach temperance. Lyman gave the cause his constant support, preaching sermons on its behalf, urging membership in its societies, and even writing pledges for followers to sign.[72]

Beecher took the position that the daily use of any strong drink was intemperance. With medical completeness and sardonic enthusiasm he described what happened to the human body when alcohol affected it. The moral agonies of the soul lost to drink, however, were far worse than the physical infirmities, he maintained. "Intemperance is the sin of our land," he asserted, "and if anything shall defeat the hopes of the world, which hang upon our experiment of civil liberty, it is that river of fire, which is rolling through the land, destroying the vital air, and extending around an atmosphere of death." [73]

In considering the remedy for intemperance, Lyman demanded that the liquor traffic be made unlawful. He also recommended that statistics on its extent should be gathered and published widely, thus anticipating the fact-finding approach popular with reformers. But more important, "Let the temperate part of the nation awake, and reform, and concentrate their influence in a course of systematic action." By this Beecher meant a society founded for the special purpose of superintending the project "whose untiring energies shall be exerted in sending out agents to pass through the land and collect information, to confer with influential individuals and bodies of men, to deliver addresses at popular meetings, and form societies auxiliary to the parent institution." [74]

Noteworthy in Beecher's work is the connection he made between the evils of intemperance and slavery. The sale of ardent spirits, he believed, was just as vicious as the slave trade and the

---

[72] See Lyman Beecher, *Autobiography*, I, 245-251, II, 220-221.
[73] Lyman Beecher, *The Nature, Occasions, Signs, Evils and Remedy of Intemperance*, p. 3.
[74] *Ibid.*, pp. 25, 26.

fight for the abolition of the enslavement to drink just as noble as the plea for the cause of the Negro. Both were enormities that had to be eradicated. The horrors of the middle passage are outdone, he maintained, by the middle passage "from time to eternity" that carries the intemperate to "darkness, and chains, and disease, and death." [75]

This work earned Beecher a reputation throughout New England and put him in the forefront of the temperance cause. Nevertheless, it has been highly overrated. Leonard Bacon certainly exaggerated when he said of the sermons, "They had a circulation and effect, and obtained a celebrity, far beyond the aspirations of ordinary authorship. They have been carried to barbarous races. They have been read with tears of thoughtfulness by Hottentots in Southern Africa." Anson Phelps Stokes is more temperate in his evaluation of Beecher's role in the crusade but nonetheless asserts that he probably did more for the cause than anyone else during the years from 1825 to 1850. [76]

One of the earliest and most constant supporters of the drive was Justin Edwards, who started preaching against intemperance in 1814. In 1816 he enunciated what a decade later became the chief principles of the American Temperance Society. In 1822 he launched a series of sermons to persuade the moderate consumers of alcohol to give up drinking. In 1829 he devoted most of his energies to the crusade, preaching complete abstinence from all intoxicating beverages. As general agent and secretary of the American Temperance Society he was instrumental in shaping the course of the movement in its early years. [77]

While there were many protests against the evil, and feeble efforts to organize before 1825, association on a national scale did not get under way until 1826. In January and February of that

[75] *Ibid.*, pp. 19, 21. For corroboration on this association between temperance and antislavery, see Lyman Beecher, *Autobiography*, II, 35, and Humphrey, *A Parallel between Intemperance and the Slave Trade.*

[76] Bacon, *Sermon at the Funeral of Rev. Lyman Beecher*, p. 20; Stokes, *Church and State in the United States*, II, 40.

[77] See Hallock, *Light and Love, a Sketch of the Life and Labors of the Rev. Justin Edwards*, pp. 62, 106, 312 ff.

year, a group of prominent ministers and laymen already active in support of missions and the American Tract Society, responded to Justin Edwards's invitation to form a new group to be named the American Society for the Promotion of Temperance. The organization's constitution was patterned after that of the American Board of Commissioners for Foreign Missions. That seven of the original sixteen members were ministers illustrates the close connection between the drive and the unfolding moral reform movement. Before breaking up, the members of the new body took a pledge to abstain personally from the use of all distilled liquors. The issue of abstinence, therefore, was raised early in the temperance campaign. Edwards greeted the founding of the society with high hopes. Victory, he was sure, was inevitable and with the removal of drunkenness came most certainly the renovation of the world!

> We are at present fast hold of a project for making all people in this country, and in all countries, temperate; or rather, a plan to induce those that are now temperate to continue so. Then, as all who are intemperate will soon be dead, the earth will be eased of an amazing evil.[78]

With the spread of revivals and under the constant prodding of the national organization, temperance societies mushroomed throughout the country. By 1829 a thousand, comprising a membership of 100,000, had been formed. Two years later there were 2,200 societies. Temperance lecturers, such as Theodore Weld, toured the country making long addresses on the "sin of drunkenness." In 1833 there were 4,000 temperance groups with a half million membership. The following year found 5,000 societies with a million members. Some local groups included in their membership almost the entire population of the town. Sometimes Weld would garner a hundred pledges at one meeting.[79]

These temperance societies also fulfilled religious and recreational functions. Associated as many of them were with the churches, they became another group to which the pious person in search of

---

[78] Justin Edwards to William A. Hallock, Feb. 10, 1826, in *ibid.*, p. 195.

[79] Sarah M. Beebe to Mrs. Finney, Feb. 24, 1830 (Finney Papers). For a description of Weld's work on behalf of temperance, see Milton Brayton to Finney, Nov. 18, 1829; Sylvester Eaton to Finney, Jan. 21, 1831 (Finney Papers).

religious satisfaction and mid-week attraction could go. "We meet to pray," wrote one enthusiast, "we go occasionally with tracts and converse with our fellow sinners." [80] Propagandizing neighbors was also an important function. Tracts supplied by the national body provided the devout with ammunition.

In the 1830's the national organization became more radical, especially after such men as Beecher and Edwards obtained acceptance of their program. Typical of Edwards's ultraism was his assertion that laws authorizing the liquor traffic were morally wrong and politically inexpedient. Typical also was his list of "hints" for temperance workers, which included the advice to abstain not only from liquor but also from tobacco, snuff, "and all needless things" and to be "temperate in the use of tea, coffee, and every kind of food and of drink." [81] As the crusade grew in strength it began more and more to stress total abstinence and to demand the immediate end of all liquor production. This eventually led to a decline in its influence. The fact that its leaders were associated with abolitionism did the cause little good. The revivalistic phase of temperance ended in 1840 and with the founding of the Washington Temperance Society in Baltimore that year, the leadership of the drive passed into the hands of laymen. It is noteworthy, however, that a revivalist took credit for initiating the Washingtonian reform. [82]

No evangelist agitated more on this subject than Albert Barnes, who looked on intemperance "as the source of most of the evils in this land, including those of pauperism, and theft, and assaults, and murders, and suicides, and irreligion." It was his opinion that America was "fast becoming a nation of drunkards," three hundred thousand of which, Barnes asserted, peopled the country. [83] The Philadelphia minister linked temperance with the nation's freedom,

---

[80] Mrs. Amelia Norton to Mrs. Finney, July 4, 1829 (Finney Papers).

[81] Quoted in Hallock, *Light and Love, a Sketch of the Life and Labors of the Rev. Justin Edwards*, pp. 322-323.

[82] See Knapp, *Autobiography*, p. 136.

[83] Albert Barnes, *The Immorality of the Traffic in Ardent Spirits*, p. 3; "Revivals of Religion in Cities and Large Towns," *The American National Preacher*, XV, No. 1 (1841), 23.

with the future of the Constitution, with the hope of American civilization. Republican freedom, which the founding fathers fought so hard to obtain, was only possible, he was sure, in a society purged of drunkenness. That so many of the founding fathers imbibed heavily Barnes seems to have overlooked! According to the evangelist, temperance enhanced the diffusion of intelligence. It encouraged public education, led to respect for the laws, aided in the inculcation of patriotic sentiments. And it also enhanced the true worship of God.[84]

Barnes based his temperance argument on grounds of an economic philosophy. He believed that every man was bound to pursue such a business or profession as to give back to society something in value equal to what he received from others. The merchant, the manufacturer, the physician, the farmer produced goods or services which had an absolute beneficial value and which could be measured against what the individual in question consumed.

But it is not so with the dealer in ardent spirits. He obtains the property of his fellow men, and what does he return? That which will tend to promote his real welfare? That which will make him a happier man? That which will benefit his family? . . . None of these things. He gives them that which will produce poverty and want, and cursing, and tears, and death.[85]

Perhaps the most curious arguments in favor of temperance were those advanced by N. S. S. Beman, staunch Finneyite and Presbyterian revivalist from Troy. Beman, whose stormy career included a number of tours on behalf of temperance, was struck by what he considered was a close connection between drunkenness and the cholera which gripped the East in 1832. In a work filled with statistics and dire descriptions of the disease, Beman pleaded for the suppression of what he called "nocturnal dissipations" and called for regulations curbing the retailing of ardent spirits. It was his firm conviction, shared by many pious souls, that "persons who hurry into excess and dissipation become the first victims of the cholera," and he concluded that "from five-

---

[84] Albert Barnes, *The Connection of Temperance with Republican Freedom*, pp. 11-17.
[85] Albert Barnes, *The Immorality of the Traffic in Ardent Spirits*, p. 12.

sixths to nine-tenths of the destructive power of the cholera, is generated by ardent spirits." [86] How shocked he must have been when his idol, Finney, was stricken with the cholera that year.

Finney's attitude toward the subject was just as outspoken as that of Edwards and Beecher. Contrary to his usual subordination of moral reform to revivals, Finney singled out intemperance as an object of particular concern. "It is not needful that a person should rail at the cold-water society, in order to be on the best terms with drunkards and moderate drinkers," declared Finney. "Only let him plead for the moderate use of wine . . . and all the drunkards account him on their side." If the man refuses to support the temperance cause, he is helping the opposition. What ministers and churches must do with such men is clear. "They must cast out from their communion such members as, in contempt of the light that is shed upon them, continue to drink or traffic in ardent spirits." [87] The churches had it in their power, he believed, to do away with the "death-dealing abomination." If they would close their doors against anyone having anything to do with the evil, if they would speak out against it, the temperance cause would be triumphant.

Finney demanded the right to intrude into the affairs of liquor dealers and distillers. When a man merchandised poison, it was Finney's business and, he added, "it is everybody's concern, and every man is bound to rebuke his crime till he gives it up, and ceases to destroy the lives and souls of his neighbors." [88] His solution was not moderation but total abstinence. His formula for

---

[86] Beman, *The Influence of Ardent Spirits in the Production of the Cholera*, pp. 2, 5. Beman appended this note to the second edition: "It is no part of the author's object to prove that all who die of the cholera are intemperate; but that a large proportion are of this description. . . . As far as my enquiries have extended, I have not been able to find one instance where the cholera commenced, in any place, among the temperate!" p. 5 n. Similar views were expressed by other pious Protestants. See Silas Mathews to Finney, Aug. 11, 1832 (Finney Papers). For Beman's temperance activities, see N. S. S. Beman to Finney, Nov. 16, 1829 (Finney Papers).

[87] Finney, *Lectures on Revivals*, p. 281.

[88] Finney, *Lectures to Professing Christians*, p. 55. Henry Ward Beecher favored similar treatment for liquor dealers but changed the epithets from "poisoners" and "death-dealers" to "counterfeiters" and "those suspected of treason." See Henry Ward Beecher, "The Search and Seizure Clauses," *The Independent*, VII, No. 330 (1855), 1.

defining a drunkard was simple. "He is drunk, if you can smell his breath." [89]

Heated opposition to their cause was generated by the temperance zealots. Those outside religious circles, the press and other secular leaders, were most vociferous in objecting to the self-appointed guardians of morality. Many were inclined to agree with William L. Stone when he remarked after one of Gerrit Smith's typical exploits, "A fool's tongue is long enough to cut his own throat. The teetotalers in Temperance, anti-slavery and religion are rapidly exemplifying this proverb." [90] Among ministers the mildest sort of reproach came from a group of whom Francis Wayland was representative. Wayland, who on occasion made addresses condemning drunkenness, believed the temperance advocates were misguided in their efforts at association and in their emphasis on the temperance pledge. He questioned the usefulness of the pledge and considered temperance agents and lecturers intolerant and overbearing.[91]

More forceful in his animadversions on the temperance crusade was Calvin Colton who in his *Protestant Jesuitism* poured all his eloquence and biting satire on the heads of the temperance reformers. Fully one third of what one cleric called "this obnoxious treatise" on organized reform dealt with the temperance movement. It was Colton's opinion that the drive was a failure, that it reflected the worst aspects of Protestantism, that it was merely a device of those in ecclesiastical power to maintain their hold over the moral and economic aspects of society. He asserted that scores of respectable citizens left the movement because of its excesses and that many others were repelled from it by its very fanaticism. He was convinced that the crusade did more harm than good, that "the whole system of the Temperance reformation, as now managed, is upon a false basis." [92]

89 Finney, *Lectures on Revivals*, p. 145.

90 W. L. Stone to Gerrit Smith, Feb. 16, 1836, quoted in Harlow, *Gerrit Smith, Philanthropist and Reformer*, p. 77.

91 Wayland, *Limitations of Human Responsibility*, pp. 112-114. For a characteristic exposition of his views, see "Address on Temperance" in *Occasional Discourses*, pp. 343-368.

92 Calvin Colton, *Protestant Jesuitism*, p. 68. For caustic comments on this work, See Waylen, *Ecclesiastical Reminiscences of the United States*, p. 186.

Colton's argument was based on an appeal to reason and common sense. Drunkenness was an evil, but each man should come to that conclusion himself and not be forced to it. Temperance was a virtue but the fanatical actions of temperance reformers were not conducive to virtue. "Give us light," he pleaded, permit our consciences to have full sway, eradicate the "extravagance and mischief of the Temperance quackery," and let men be free.[93]

It was not the moralist's intention for man to be free, however, for he had to be pious, protestant, and pure. The evangelists regulated the religious life of their followers; they told them what not to eat and what not to drink. They also tried to control their sex life. Perhaps the most curious of these religiously inspired campaigns associated with the 1830's was that which went by the polite title of moral reform but which aimed at the eradication of the world's oldest profession. Moral reform, in its limited sense, was used by the nineteenth century to describe the reformation of those who violated the seventh commandment and the steps taken to prevent its violation.

The leading light behind this movement was John R. McDowall, young Presbyterian minister, who in the fall of 1830 left Princeton Theological Seminary and journeyed to New York to help organize a society "for the moral and religious improvement of the Five Points." [94] Upon his arrival, the friend to reformers, Arthur Tappan, paid his board and McDowall seems to have devoted all his time to plans for the establishment of a Magdalen Asylum that was to be a place of refuge for wayward girls who wanted to return to a virtuous life.[95] He found no lack of support for his schemes. The habit of benevolence had taken hold. One of Finney's friends described the society's plans:

A number of individuals have formed themselves into a society here called the "Christian benevolent society". The object of which is to en-

---

[93] Calvin Colton, *Protestant Jesuitism*, pp. 91, 295.

[94] McDowall, *Memoirs*, p. 101. This work contains the essential details of his short career. Some autobiographical material is also found in *McDowall's Journal* and the *Advocate of Moral Reform*.

[95] The full title of this place was the "Asylum for Females Who Have Deviated from the Paths of Virtue."

deavor to reform depraved and abandoned females, and the profligacy in the vicinity of noted places of vice. The scene of our operations was commenced at the noted "five points". Two Sabbath schools have been in operation there for two months, one for white and one for colored persons of all ages. . . . A Magdalen asylum is provided for the accommodation of those depraved women who are willing to give up their profligate mode of life.[96]

In 1832 McDowall was licensed to preach and during the same year brought out his famous *Magdalen Report*. His continued activities on behalf of virtue stirred up considerable opposition, but he carried his crusade as far as the General Assembly of the Presbyterian Church, speaking before that august group in 1833. Three years later he was called before the Third Presbytery in New York to answer charges of impropriety brought against him, was unsuccessful in his appeal, and was suspended from the ministry. He died the same year.

McDowall's major effort was a lurid account of prostitution in New York City that was published under the title of *Magdalen Report*. Its sensational style rivaled modern tabloids. It was brash, clinically detailed, and overly pious. Its circulation dismayed the more conservative reformers who felt that McDowall had overdone it. Its statements were questioned, its conclusions debated. In spite of the storm of criticism provoked by the *Magdalen Report*, McDowall and his followers remained convinced of its accuracy. As Lewis Tappan wrote his brother, Benjamin,

Arthur was not imposed upon in the matter of the Magdalen Report. It was too true. The clamor was made by Infidels at first, and the timid christians joined in the cry. Intelligent men in European cities and in Philadelphia and Boston, corrobate the statements. But it must be observed that *not half of the* prostitutes are ever included in the census.[97]

In 1833 McDowall began his battle against licentiousness, in a jeremiadlike periodical titled *McDowall's Journal*, that lasted two years and that brought its editor more than he bargained for. Its main design was "to expose public immorality, to elicit public sentiments, and to devise and carry into effect the means of pre-

---

[96] Dr. L. Brown to Finney, Jan. 6, 1830 (Finney Papers).
[97] Lewis Tappan to Benjamin Tappan (n.d.) (Benjamin Tappan Papers).

venting licentiousness and vice." [98]   In one of the first numbers he reprinted his *Magdalen Report*, gave news of the society's meetings, and offered to turn his own house into a shelter for "helpless females, degraded by sin, and to establish among them a school of industry, cleanliness, chastity and religion." [99]   Most of the magazine was filled with long accounts of houses of prostitution and detailed descriptions of the city's vice.   The *Journal* was finally declared a nuisance by the New York Grand Jury.

Other organizations soon followed in the footsteps of the New York Magdalen Society.   In 1833 *McDowall's Journal* recorded the constitution of the American Society for the Prevention of Licentiousness and Vice and the Promotion of Morality, which, incidentally, was patterned after that of the American Temperance Society.   In January, 1834, a number of evangelists combined with the leading New York merchants to form the American Society for promoting the observance of the Seventh Commandment. This Seventh Commandment Society had its policies shaped by Lewis Tappan, William Goodell, William Green, and the evangelists Leavitt and Lansing.   Beriah Green, head of the Oneida Institute, was named president of the society and Theodore Weld was one of its many vice presidents.   Other evangelists lent their support to the crusade.   N. S. S. Beman in Troy sent McDowall $27, "as a donation from a few females," early in 1833; the Albany revivalist Edward Kirk sent encouragements; and Finney sent a mattress!   Even the conservative Timothy Dwight preached a sermon for the group.[100]

The most successful organization in this field, however, was the American Female Moral Reform Society, which was set up in May, 1834.   This group immediately started publication of the *Advocate of Moral Reform*.   At this point McDowall stopped his moribund *Journal* and threw his support behind the younger society.

In its first issue the *Advocate of Moral Reform* explained its purposes.   Other papers would not expose the vice, the *Advocate's*

[98] *McDowall's Journal*, I, No. 1 (1833), 1.
[99] *Ibid.*, I, No. 4 (1833), 32.
[100] *Ibid.*, II, No. 1 (1834), 6; I, No. 2 (1833), 14; I, No. 5 (1833), 34; II, No. 4 (1834), 29.   Marryat, *A Diary in America, 1837-1838*, III, 176.

editors declared, and it was their duty to "raise their voice in solemn warning." They intended to "publish names and places" and to draw public attention to the extent of licentiousness. When asked why such a task should be undertaken by women, the paper's reply was because "the men will not do it." "We shall therefore take peculiar pains to collect and publish facts in relation to the state of public morals . . . and thus endeavor to alarm the public mind, and turn public attention to this wide-spread and fast growing evil." [101] In order not to encounter the same odium associated with McDowall's efforts, the *Advocate* hastened to indicate that the Female Moral Reform Society would have nothing to do with the effort to create asylums. The group's work would be confined generally to meetings on Wednesday afternoons.

By 1835 the campaign had taken on sizable proportions. Donations poured into the Female Moral Reform Society. Mrs. Finney was a frequent contributor, and the *Advocate of Moral Reform* recorded receipt of a "cot and mattrass from Mr. C. G. Finney." Theodore Parker came to New York to see Charles Loring Brace and study the methods for fighting prostitution. Returning to Boston he joined Phillips, Edward Beecher, and others in forming a society "to rescue delinquent girls, instruct them in housework and place them in homes throughout the state." Others enlisted in the cause. Indeed, as early as 1833, if McDowall is to be believed, there was in operation the Boston Penitent Females' Refuge, while a Magdalen Asylum was going strong in Philadelphia.[102]

New York led the way in the formation of societies, however. A Mutual Praying Society attempted to attack the problem on a different front. Women's groups formed auxiliaries to the Seventh Commandment Society, and under the leadership of Finney's wife there was set up in the city the New York Female Moral Reform Society. Since the membership in these various groups overlapped to a great extent, it is difficult to gauge their strength. Some indication of the nature of the movement's support can be seen in

---

[101] *Advocate of Moral Reform*, I, No. 1 (1834), 1, 3.
[102] *Ibid.*, I, No. 1 (1834), 8; Commager, *Theodore Parker*, p. 177; *McDowall's Journal*, I, No. 5 (1833), 40.

the fact that there was regularly included in *McDowall's Journal* a column devoted to listings of "Prices Current," suggesting an interest on the part of its readers in mercantile trade. And in the minds of the general public, this movement must have been considered as much of a nuisance as the antislavery campaign because, although it is generally overlooked, McDowall's office received the same distinctive treatment in the July, 1834, riots as was accorded the home of the abolitionist Lewis Tappan.[103]

Not to be outdone by the fairer sex, the men produced more societies. In June, 1834, the Young Men's Moral Reform Society of New York was established. A year later Oberlin set up a similar organization. By 1836 the *Advocate of Moral Reform* had some ten thousand subscribers and towns the size of Rochester were boasting Moral Reform Societies of sixty odd members. In 1838 the American Female Moral Reform Society had some 20,000 members, with 361 auxiliaries and a subscription list to their paper of over 16,000.[104]

After that, however, the movement declined. The economic panic of 1837 took away much of its financial support; the Presbyterian schism left its mark, and the crusade encountered an experience common to other reforming activities in that it found itself swallowed up by the expanding antislavery movement. Finally, the public must have tired of hearing so much about licentiousness and prostitution, and the misguided souls who had striven to remove vice and salvage wayward girls probably discovered the futility of their endeavors.

There were other reasons for the movement's failure. Those who engaged in it incurred the unpopularity that comes to the reformer. "Brother Ingersoll is a good man," wrote one friend to Finney, "but he is unpopular in our church . . . his sermons upon Anti-Slavery and moral reform, more especially the latter, created

---

[103] *McDowall's Journal*, Extra, II, No. 2 (1834); II, No. 6 (1834), 42; McDowall, *Memoirs*, p. 232.

[104] *McDowall's Journal*, II, No. 6 (1834), 45; *Advocate of Moral Reform*, I, No. 8 (1835), 57; Mrs. H. C. Green to Finney, Aug. 1, 1836 (Finney Papers); Marryat, *A Diary in America, 1837-1838*, III, 174-175.

a dislike in the bosoms of some of the church." [105] Then too, the reformers were not all united on the means to be used in removing the evil. Those like McDowall and the New York Female Benevolent Society concerned themselves with rescuing reformed prostitutes. The leaders of the other faction, represented by the American Female Reform Society, refused to support asylums to reform wayward women. According to this latter group, "there is not enough hope of reforming this class of females to warrant the expense." [106]

In the last analysis, it was the shortsightedness of the reformers themselves that led to their failure. Endowed with religious zeal and high ideals, they attempted to erase an evil without regard to the conditions that produced it. Had the Don Quixotes of the Five Points devoted as much attention to the poverty and social dislocations of their city as they did to rescuing "abandoned females," they might have met with greater success.

In perspective, this rash of reform appears as the natural, though peculiar, result of the invigorated religious zeal of the 1830's. The plethora of societies serves only to underline the close alliance between the planners of a new social and moral order and the more advanced followers of evangelical religion. Moral reform of the middle period is more understandable when we reflect that it rested on four assumptions: first, that man was a base creature with a constant inclination to evil; second, that the elect had a responsibility to do something about this evil in man and society; third, that progress was considered inevitable and optimism was a matter of course; and finally, that the words of a man of God were not to be taken lightly. Characteristic of all these moral reformers was a strongly arrogant sureness of one's point of view. As Lewis Tappan wrote in keynoting the spirit of the times, "if I think you are losing your soul it is my duty to attempt to save you." [107]

---

[105] T. Brown to Finney, Oct. 7, 1834 (Finney Papers).
[106] *Advocate of Moral Reform*, I, No. 8 (1835), 64.
[107] Lewis Tappan to Benjamin Tappan, Aug. 21, 1830 (Benjamin Tappan Papers).

William Leete Stone, that grand critic of his age, in evaluating this religious zeal toward others that permeated so many of his generation, concluded:

In the solemn affairs of religion, moreover, instead of looking into our own hearts, and repenting of our own sins, we are striving to look into the hearts of others, and take care of them, in our own way, and to the danger, we fear, of our own souls . . . we are striving to raise hurricanes ourselves.[108]

Without condemning the social architects and religious reformers of the age, we can only wish more of them had listened to Francis Wayland when he pointed out, "moral questions cannot be decided by majorities, nor can the law of God be ascertained by the votes of conventions." [109]

[108] Stone, *Matthias and His Impostures*, pp. 322-323.
[109] Wayland, *Limitations of Human Responsibility*, p. 188. The subject of benevolence received ample treatment in his *Elements of Moral Science*, and *Occasional Discourses*.

V. POLITICS AND POLITICAL IDEAS

I therefore, as a Christian citizen, look upon the civil government and the civil magistracy with as unblenching an eye as I look upon anything else. . . . I may pronounce my opinion upon its enactments and measures just as I would express my opinions in any other case.[1]

It is the duty of the minister of the Gospel to preach on every side of political life. I do not say that he may; I say that he must.[2]

THOMAS NICHOLS, shrewd observer of the American scene, once stated that "A great number of American preachers . . . have no hesitation in introducing political or social topics into the pulpit. They are often candidates for office, and not infrequently take the stump in presidential electioneering campaigns." Addison, in his study of the American clergy, echoed this observation and held that it was expected that ministers would become deeply interested in public issues of the day, "entering boldly the arena of political life."[3]

Applying the word of the Gospel to contemporary political problems has always been characteristic of the American divine. It must be expected that a land whose tradition included a theocracy, whose clergy influenced the magistrates, should have its portion of political-minded ministers. The seventeenth-century election sermons that were part and parcel of Massachusetts political life set the stamp for later generations to follow. In colonial times the minister exerted great influence in the shaping of political forces and the tradition, if not the practice, was carried over into the young nation. A group whose members were certain of their God-given opinions and who felt it their duty to speak out on all issues did not hesitate to engage in the Federalist-Republican

[1] Wayland, *The Duty of Obedience to the Civil Magistrate*, p. 16.
[2] Henry Ward Beecher, *Freedom and War*, p. 295.
[3] Thomas L. Nichols, *Forty Years of American Life, 1821-1861*, p. 232; Addison, *The Clergy in American Life and Letters*, p. 10.

struggles, to use their pulpits as sounding boards during the War of 1812, and to pontificate on all political issues from the Missouri Compromise to the Civil War. To the American evangelist, the fate of his particular political party and the workings of divine Providence were often interconnected, and it was not considered unusual for a minister to make assertions in the manner of the Rev. Edward P. Humphrey who, preaching on the occasion of Zachary Taylor's burial, declared, "the death of the President was the act of God." [4]

The evangelists themselves were quick to justify this attention to political affairs and public issues. To Finney, politics was "an indispensable part of religion. No man can possibly be benevolent or religious without concerning himself to a greater or less extent with the affairs of human government." [5] Albert Barnes also defended probing into any matter that was touched with the public interest. "I have not a right to go into my neighbor's dwelling, and discuss and examine the private matters of his intercourse with his wife, and children; but everything in which he and I have a common interest may be the subject of the most free and full investigation." [6] Wayland took a similar stand. "I seem to myself," he wrote, "to be discharging a duty not improperly devolving upon a profession which is expected to watch with sedulous anxiety, every change that can have a bearing upon the moral or religious interests of a community." [7]

The rationale for political action by clerics was advanced particularly at Oberlin. "We are christian citizens," the Oberlin faculty declared; "[we] have christian duties towards our government; we feel bound to use our best endeavors to promote the election of good rulers. . . . We aim and endeavor to throw the power of our elevated and earnest christianity into the domain of politics." [8] It remained, however, for Henry Ward Beecher to give

---

[4] Humphrey, *A Discourse on the Death of General Taylor*, p. 8.
[5] Finney, *Lectures on Systematic Theology*, p. 431.
[6] Albert Barnes, *The Literature and Science of America*, p. 22.
[7] Wayland, *The Duties of an American Citizen*, p. 4.
[8] Faculty and Trustees of Oberlin to Finney, July 26, 1860 (Finney Papers).

the most eloquent justification for the preacher's political action. "When ministers meddle with practical life, with ethical questions and relations," he wrote, "they are meddling with just what they do understand. . . . The moment a man so conducts his profession that it touches the question of right and wrong, he comes into my sphere." [9]

Early in their careers the evangelists turned their attention to political matters. When he was working for the *Journal of Commerce* in New York, Bushnell had ample opportunity to gauge the true worth of politics and politicians. Commenting on a presidential election, he wrote, "I think there is quite too much iniquity in these political scuffles. . . . Real merit has very little to do with political elevation." [10] Finney had a similar distrust of politics. "I looked forward to the election day with considerable solicitude," he recalled, "fearing that the excitement that day would greatly retard the work." [11] It was ever his concern lest the suspense of balloting would disrupt his revivals, and he made a point of preaching election evenings. Even Joshua Leavitt, who filled many pages of letters from Yale with political observations and who was not averse to engaging in politics, condemned political action and scorned the politician. Washington, he believed, was a "hotbed of politics and sin." [12] One who did not share such a sentiment, however, was the incomparable Lyman Beecher, for whom elections had a special attraction. Beecher was interested enough in politics to travel six miles to vote the day before he set out to defend himself against charges of heresy.[13]

The political activities of the Northern evangelists went through a number of phases. At first there was the meddling in political fields for religious purposes. Political figures were in special need of ministerial attention, and the evangelists were not loathe to at-

---

[9] Henry Ward Beecher, "The Sphere of the Christian Minister," *Patriotic Addresses*, pp. 79-80.

[10] Bushnell to Cortlandt Van Rensaelaer, Dec. 23, 1827, in Cheney, *Life and Letters of Horace Bushnell*, p. 49.

[11] Finney, *Memoirs*, p. 230.

[12] Joshua Leavitt to Hooker Leavitt, Dec. 10, 1841 (Leavitt Papers).

[13] Lyman Beecher, *Autobiography*, II, 354.

tempt to convert them. Edward N. Kirk's interest in the New
York state legislature was typical of this concern. "The Legislature now attend my church in numbers," he wrote to Finney,
who was operating nearby. "If you come, I have no doubt they
will all attend, and you may strike blows which will be felt
throughout the State." Later Kirk's appeal became more urgent.
"I am exceedingly anxious to have you here while the Legislature
is in session." [14] Other ministers in Albany shared Kirk's views.
"Can't you come while the legislature is here?" one pleaded. "The
Speaker you know is a convert from Troy." [15] Other political
bodies were considered fair game for Finney. He was urged to
strike in New Hampshire through its office holders, while ministers
in Connecticut, referring to their legislature, affirmed, "By preaching to them you preach in the most direct manner to the whole
state." [16]

The second phase of political action occurred when the evangelists attempted to influence politics for other than religious purposes. The minister was never reluctant to enlist the support of
legislative bodies for his pet projects. Daniel Baker camped on
the steps of the Texas legislature session after session armed with
memorials in an effort to secure aid for his college. So persistent
was he that he was finally invited to the floor of the Senate to
express his views.[17] One of the chief features of the Sabbatarian
movement was the petitioning of Congress. The temperance
crusade did not overlook the political arena. Even before the
movement turned to lobbying for laws in its behalf, temperance
leaders put pressure on legislators. In 1830 Justin Edwards, who
was crusading through the Middle Atlantic states, devoted the
bulk of his time to Washington "with a special view to organize
a Congressional Temperance Society." [18] The place of the petition

[14] Kirk to Finney, Feb. 28, 1831, March 21, 1831 (Finney Papers).

[15] B. P. Johnson to Finney, Feb. 24, 1831 (Finney Papers).

[16] John Lawton to Finney, May 2, 1827; Rev. J. Hopkins to Finney, May 5, 1831
(Finney Papers).

[17] Baker, *The Life and Labors of the Rev. Daniel Baker*, p. 308.

[18] Hallock, *Light and Love, a Sketch of the Life and Labors of the Rev. Justin
Edwards*, p. 371.

in the antislavery campaign is well known, and it was on behalf of abolition that Joshua Leavitt labored so long among Washington lawmakers.

Leavitt also engaged in lobbying on issues not connected with moral reform. "I have not time to write much," he confided to his brother, "as I am hurrying to get ready to go to Albany to-night, in hopes of doing something to bring through the Bills now before the legislature." In the 1840's he interested himself in problems connected with railroad charters and indicated to his brother that with his lobbying experience, "I shall be happy to do any thing in my power to help your R.R." He also entered Massachusetts politics and in 1852 predicted victory for what was to become the Republican party in eight years, "if not in four." [19] His enthusiasm for Lincoln knew no bounds:

Mar. 2, 1861
12½ o'clock P.M.

Only 47½ hours—and then!
Hurrah for President Lincoln!

Dear Brother:

The above slipped from my pen spontaneously. I hope it won't hurt your feelings.[20]

The national and state arenas were not the only areas for the political endeavors of the evangelists. They engaged in local politics as well. Lyman Beecher helped organize the Hanover Association of Young Men in Boston in 1827 ostensibly to remove the influence of Unitarians in the operation of political patronage. The group "had committees on various important matters relating to state of city and things needing to be done." [21] They petitioned against the sale of liquor on the Common on public days, checked violations of the Sabbath, and had committees on Negroes, Irish, sailors, and other minority groups.

Western evangelists at times carried their political action even further than their Eastern colleagues. As William Warren Sweet

[19] Joshua Leavitt to Hooker Leavitt, May 17, 1841, Dec. 7, 1847, Nov. 12, 1852 (Leavitt Papers).

[20] *Ibid.*, March 2, 1861.

[21] Lyman Beecher, *Autobiography*, II, 145.

points out, it was normal to find itinerant preachers delving into politics and the ministerial profession contributed early governors to both Ohio and Kentucky.[22] The colorful Cartwright, who was "a simon pure Andrew Jackson Democrat," was a member of the Illinois legislature for two years and ran for Congress against Abraham Lincoln.[23] Some indication of the popularity of politics among Western preachers is seen in Duffield's notation in his diary concerning a meeting of his synod: "I endeavored to lead them to consider the impropriety of mixing themselves up with party politics but stood alone." [24]

Although he never ran for office, Henry Ward Beecher took to the hustings with as much enthusiasm as Peter Cartwright. In 1856 he took a leave of absence from Plymouth Church to fight for Fremont, speaking two and three times a week during the campaign. He did not exert himself on Lincoln's behalf, however, and, like Finney, he favored the selection of Benjamin F. Butler in 1864 and was an enthusiastic supporter of Grant, not only for one term but for two and three.

The political ideas of the evangelists, however, were more important than their activities in that field. Characteristically, one of the earliest to speak out on the subject in the nineteenth century was Lyman Beecher. As a resident of Connecticut and as a minister of the Gospel, Beecher enjoyed a certain amount of control in the political affairs of the state prior to the War of 1812. As Lyman put it,

[22] See Sweet, *The American Churches*, p. 50.

[23] Ross, *Lincoln's First Years in Illinois*, p. 26.

[24] Duffield's Diary, June 1856 in Lewis G. Vander Velde, ed., "Notes on the Diary of George Duffield," *The Mississippi Valley Historical Review*, XXIV, No. 1 (1937), 63. George Duffield (1794-1868), New School Presbyterian, graduated from the University of Pennsylvania in 1811 and was licensed by the Presbytery of Philadelphia in 1815. His first charge was in Carlisle, Pennsylvania where he stayed for nineteen years. In 1834 he was invited to the Fifth Presbyterian Church in Philadelphia and two years later was at the Broadway Tabernacle in New York. While in New York he was Finney's assistant but later became one of his severest critics. The last thirty years of his career were spent in Detroit. In addition to temperance work, he concerned himself with improving conditions in insane asylums and fostered railroad construction and the advancement of science. He was an authority on chemistry, geology, mechanics, and navigation, dabbled in agriculture, and in 1839 was appointed a regent of the University of Michigan.

The ministers had always managed things themselves, for in those days the ministers were all politicians. . . . On election day they had a festival. All the clergy used to go, walk in procession, smoke pipes and drink. And, fact is, when they got together they would talk over who should be governor, and who lieutenant-governor, and who in the Upper House, and their councils would prevail.[25]

By 1811, however, this hold over politics was slipping. That year the splitting of a coalition between ministers and lawyers brought about a Federalist defeat in Connecticut. Decisive in the campaign was the support given the anti-Federalists by the Episcopalians, who were piqued at the way the Federalists had distributed funds between their Bishops' Fund and Yale College.[26] Beecher was in the thick of the battle. "It was a time of great depression and suffering," he recalled. "It was as hard a day as ever I saw." [27]

Having been defeated at the polls, Beecher, Dwight, and others continued their fight on other fronts. One weapon they used was their organization in July, 1812, of the Society for the Suppression of Vice and the Promotion of Good Morals. Although ostensibly a moral reform society, the group discussed the political situation and measures they might take in a counterattack.[28] Beecher took to writing his friends on the matter. "I am persuaded," he wrote, "that the time has come when it becomes every friend of the State to wake up and exert his whole influence to save it from innovation and democracy. . . . My request is that you will . . . touch every spring, lay or clerical, which you can touch prudently." [29] The stand of the clergy and Federalists during the War of 1812 further discredited them, and by 1817 the dissenting sects, having joined anti-Federalists in forming the Toleration party, helped win the state; and the following year a new constitution overthrowing the

[25] Lyman Beecher, *Autobiography*, I, 259.   For a typical defense of the standing order, see Beecher's sermon "Building of Waste Places."

[26] See Lauer, "Church and State in New England" (Johns Hopkins University Studies in Historical and Political Science, 10th series), p. 100.

[27] Lyman Beecher, *Autobiography*, I, 344.

[28] See Greene, *The Development of Religious Liberty in Connecticut*, pp. 437-438.

[29] Lyman Beecher to Asahel Hooker, Nov. 24, 1812, in Lyman Beecher, *Autobiography*, I, 257.

standing order was adopted. This "revolution" was, according to the dogmatic Beecher, "one of the most desperate battles ever fought in the United States. It was the last struggle of the separation of church and state." [30]

If what was done in Connecticut in 1818 and in Massachusetts in 1834 was designed to cut the clergy's influence in politics, there was no noticeable decline in their political activities as the century progressed. Indeed, at times their intrusion into the political arena became bolder than ever. In a Fourth of July sermon in 1827 Ezra Stiles Ely sounded the keynote for his colleagues and gave a blueprint for political action. "Every ruler should be an avowed and a sincere friend of Christianity," he declared. His hearers should "promote Christianity by electing and supporting as public officers the friends of our blessed Saviour." To effect this end, Ely continued, "I propose, fellow-citizens, a new sort of union, or, if you please, a Christian party in politics, which I am exceedingly desirous all good men in our country should join." He asserted that the Presbyterians alone could bring half a million voters into the field against any advocate of Deism "or any species of avowed hostility to the truth of Christianity." Finally, he boasted that the five chief Protestant sects "could govern every public election in the country." [31]

The evangelists were particularly vocal during the Jacksonian era. It was not merely on moral grounds that they opposed Jackson. There were reasons that transcended his personal behavior or party affiliations. To Albert Barnes, military heroes lacked the qualifications for such an important office as the presidency. In words which have since been often echoed he declared,

In the field we will honor them. We will speak the praises of the defenders of their country. We will crown them with laurels, and record their names high on the historic page. . . . But let their voice die away on the field of battle; and let not the claim be urged by military fame, to direct the counsels of the cabinet, or the voice of legislation. Legislative

30 Lyman Beecher, *Autobiography*, I, 453.
31 Ely, *The Duty of Christian Freemen to Elect Christian Rulers*, pp. 4, 6, 8, 11. For the best rebuttal from the pen of a minister, see Fuller, *The Tree of Liberty*.

and executive counsels demand other talents than those which direct the storm of war.[32]

It was understandable that the clerics should cry out against the spoils system. Daniel Baker, who had enjoyed Washington during Adams's Administration, deplored the loss of jobs and condemned the "Hickory broom" for sweeping "so many excellent persons" out of employment. "Are all these innumerable removals right?" he asked.[33] Bushnell, in an essay on "American Politics," also condemned the "depravity of the doctrine which proposes to give the spoils of victory to the victors." [34] Lyman Beecher looked to the West as the area from which would come a concerted opposition to Jacksonian democracy. The sentiments of the Finneys and Leavitts were best expressed by their close friend Lewis Tappan, who declared, "I consider Genl Jackson a very unfit man to be at the head of the Government." [35] And as an ardent Whig and political pamphleteer, Calvin Colton's opinion of Old Hickory was only too well known.

A decade later Francis Wayland joined the ranks of ministers meddling in politics when in 1842 he headed the party of "law and order" against the Dorr Rebellion. The details of Dorr's uprising need not be mentioned here. Suffice to say that after a number of fruitless attempts to extend the suffrage in Rhode Island an association was formed in 1840 to agitate for the abolition of the property qualification for voting and for a written constitution. Dorr played a leading role in the movement which set up a People's party, held a convention, and submitted a constitution to the people who subsequently approved it. The government in power, denying the legality of such action, called its own convention and submitted a constitution which the electorate turned down. By May, 1842, two separate governments were claiming the right to represent Rhode Islanders. Dorr's appeal for Federal aid was re-

[32] Albert Barnes, *An Address, Delivered July 4, 1827 at the Presbyterian Church in Morristown*, pp. 27-28.

[33] Daniel Baker to James H. Handy, May 28, 1829, quoted in Baker, *The Life and Labors of the Rev. Daniel Baker*, p. 131.

[34] Quoted in Cheney, *Life and Letters of Horace Bushnell*, p. 94.

[35] Lewis Tappan to Benjamin Tappan, Oct. 19, 1832 (Benjamin Tappan Papers).

fused; the conservative government proclaimed martial law; a
series of minor battles between Dorr's followers and the state militia ensued; and Dorr finally gave himself up, ending what was
termed an insurrection.[36] Wayland's role in maintaining the status
quo was that of crystallizing, in his work *The Affairs of Rhode
Island*, the opposition to Dorr.

Prior to 1842 the president of Brown had the reputation of being
politically progressive. In 1825, for instance, in two addresses on
the theme of the *Duties of the American Citizen*, Wayland gave
evidence of being far ahead of his colleagues. While this work
dealt primarily with the supposed threat of monarchial, despotic,
Catholic Europe against the free, republican, Prostestant America,
it also contained an eloquent tribute to human rights:

Thanks be to God, men have at last begun to understand the rights, and
to feel for the wrongs of each other! . . . Let a voice . . . tell that the
rights of man are in danger, and it floats over valley and mountain,
across continent and ocean, until it has vibrated in the ear of the re-
motest dweller in Christendom. Let the arm of oppression be raised to
crush the feeblest nation on earth, and there will be heard everywhere, if
not the shout of defiance, the deep-toned murmur of implacable dis-
pleasure. It is the cry of aggrieved, insulted, much abused man! [37]

The publication of these addresses when he was not yet thirty put
Wayland at the forefront of Baptist leaders. His eulogy of Adams
and Jefferson in 1826 and his *Elements of Political Economy* published in 1837, also contained forward-looking political ideas.

In 1842, however, Wayland was not so concerned with the rights
of man. *The Affairs of Rhode Island* consisted of three parts.
First, Wayland described some perils from which Providence and
the rest of the state had been rescued by the rout of the rebellious
forces. Next, he considered the causes for the recent conflict.
Finally, he outlined his complete political program, injecting
through it all a strong religious overtone. He commenced his
work by calling the Dorr Rebellion a matter touching upon the

[36] Details of the Dorr Rebellion may be gleaned from King, *The Life and Times
of Thomas Wilson Dorr; Dorr, Report of the Trial of Thomas Wilson Dorr, for Treason
against the State of Rhode Island; Facts Involved in the Rhode Island Controversy*;
Mowry, *The Dorr War*.
[37] Wayland, *The Duties of an American Citizen*, p. 11.

very existence of society. He believed that the issue between law and anarchy, between the ballot box and the cannon's mouth, between constitutional government and that by "lawless soldiery" must be resolved.[38] Dorr was painted in black colors throughout the work, and the large vote piled up in favor of the new constitution was minimized. The author asserted that scores had withdrawn from the movement, leaving a determined few to organize a government. He ridiculed the mob who followed Dorr and pictured the rebellion as degenerating into lawlessness.

In the course of his argument the Brown president considered the criticisms against Rhode Island's suffrage requirements and he justified the peculiar limits to universal manhood suffrage which Rhode Island imposed. They were low enough, he felt, and citizens of the state had long been accustomed to complying with them. Besides, it was his conviction that the practical value in extending democracy may be overbalanced by other considerations. As he put it,

It should be also remembered that in any social compact, not only the rights, but also the feelings of our fellow men, should be strictly regarded, and that it is frequently better to yield in a doubtful matter, than to suffer the accusation of injustice from too strict an adherence to our own opinions.[39]

In other words, Wayland looked on suffrage more as a matter of feeling than of right, as a doubtful matter and, in the words of one critic, "a thing not worth the quarrelling about, upon the one side or the other." [40]

In his conclusion he approached the shadows of James I and Thomas Hobbes. Man, he asserted, has a right of revolution only when his government has utterly failed to accomplish its purposes. But even then his actions are limited. "We are not at liberty to enter a society and enjoy its advantages," Wayland declared, "and then conspire to overturn it; to sever allegiance, and when we please, to violate it. We have no more liberty to overturn the social compact when we will, than the marriage compact." Gov-

---

[38] Wayland, *The Affairs of Rhode Island*, p. 5.
[39] *Ibid.*, pp. 13-14.
[40] Bolles, *Review of "The Affairs of Rhode Island*," p. 15.

ernment is an ordinance of God and God enjoins obedience to that government. To break that commandment is as bad as breaking any other. To overthrow your government is a sin against God. "You do it at the peril of your souls." [41]

Wayland's work contains many misguided notions. It distorts the events in the rebellion to fit his pattern of law and order struggling against a rabble of "lawless soldiery." It was obviously hastily written and lacks the usual calm, dispassionate approach of its author. Wayland may have pioneered in education, but in politics he must be ranked among the arch conservatives.

Beecher's battle for the standing order, the Christian party in politics, and Wayland's stand in the Dorr Rebellion were all representative of the ministerial mind in the nineteenth century. Why did these men considered so advanced in other fields of endeavor lag behind in the shaping of political thought? A number of reasons might be suggested. First, in the matter of church-state relations American Protestants were at a distinct disadvantage. Their position in a republic where there was no state religion, where there was universal toleration and yet where there was a tradition of religious influence in politics led to a curious dichotomy. On the one hand, they, as leaders of evangelical sects, applauded the idea of freedom from Catholic state religions. On the other, they yearned for the control their ancestral colleagues enjoyed over the affairs of state.

A second reason stems from their idea of government. To men who ascribed to a divine Providence the governance of the world, it was logical to conclude that political institutions were divinely inspired, and should conform to the laws of God. Hence obedience to those laws was something the cleric would not question. Consequently, ideas of popular sovereignty and the social contract received short shrift from evangelists, and the right of revolution was anathema to these men. To refuse to obey the laws of the land was to disobey God. As Albert Barnes put it, "Submission to government and to law is a duty of God." [42]

[41] Wayland, *The Affairs of Rhode Island*, p. 29.
[42] Albert Barnes, "The Supremacy of the Laws," *The American National Preacher*, XII, No. 8 (1838), 113. For slightly different approaches on this theme, see Wayland, *The Duty of Obedience to the Civil Magistrate*, and Green, *Faith and Works*.

Then, too, the demands of their followers helped shape their political views. The religious community could accept innovations in doctrine but it would not brook similar political changes. The popular evangelist could preach successfully on the comparatively harmless unchartered religious courses but to veer from the narrow political conservatism of his flock was to flirt with failure. Northern evangelists, therefore, were defenders of the status quo. While they were willing to pioneer in social questions and plow new soil theologically they felt inspired to condemn innovation in the political and economic fields. That so many radical figures in these areas, such as Owen and Frances Wright, were imbued with an antireligious sentiment probably had much to do with this opposition. To eradicate prostitution or secure temperance legislation was in line with the progress of their age, but to secure universal suffrage, lend support to a man like Jackson, or engage in a rebellion were activities likely to shake the whole social fabric.

And the social fabric was not to be taken lightly. Wayland, who with Bushnell probably wrote more on political matters than any other minister of his time, looked askance at those who were "very much bent upon taking the social fabric to pieces" and who believed that they could construct a better one. "The whole history of our globe seems not yet to have convinced men," he remarked, "that it has always been found very difficult to improve an edifice, by leveling it with the dust, when you are obliged to reconstruct it out of the very same materials." [43]   George Duffield, leader of the New School Presbyterian faction in Detroit, was another who joined in making gloomy observations regarding the threat to society of revolutions, innovations, and democratic principles in general.

The ideas of the evangelists on popular sovereignty, the social contract, and democratic government are particularly worthy of close study. On no other subject do they display such uniform agreement. Lyman Beecher's *The Memory of Our Fathers* (1828), Albert Barnes's *Supremacy of the Laws* (1838), Calvin Colton's *Democracy* (1843), Bushnell's *Politics under the Law of God*

---

[43] Wayland, *The Dependence of Science upon Religion*, p. 33.

(1844), and Wayland's *The Duty of Obedience to the Civil Magistrate* (1847) reveal strikingly similar treatments of a common theme, the origin of government, and the duties of its citizens.

Indeed, as early as 1806 Lyman Beecher sounded the keynote for the cleric's political creed: "Civil government is a divine ordinance." [44] Later, in his address in 1828 eulogizing our forefathers, he called on his generation to copy the theocracy of seventeenth-century New England, "to cherish with high veneration and grateful recollection the memory of our Fathers." He told his hearers to uphold and extend the nation's religious institutions, to see to it that their civil leaders supported religion, and to "regulate the suffrage of the nation with reference to the preservation of its moral purity." [45]

Barnes echoed Beecher ten years later when he affirmed that government was instituted by God:

It has not its origin in man; and is not to be regarded merely as of human arrangement. It is the appointment of the Ruler of the nations. The necessity of government has not grown out of any conventional arrangements of society; nor may it be dispensed with by any conventional arrangements. [46]

Barnes did not stop with an affirmation of divine right in government. To him, "all our institutions are based on the gospel." [47] Even Charles Finney, who published little of a political nature, was of the opinion that "true political economy must consist in national and individual obedience to the law of God. This idea of the obligation of nations and governments to conform to the moral law . . . is becoming developed in the minds of statesmen." [48] He followed Lyman Beecher's interpretation that the American republic "in its constitution and laws, is of heavenly origin. It was not borrowed from Greece or Rome, but from the Bible." [49]

[44] Lyman Beecher, *The Remedy for Duelling*, p. 4.
[45] Lyman Beecher, *The Memory of Our Fathers*, pp. 22, 30.
[46] Albert Barnes, "The Supremacy of the Laws," *The American National Preacher*, XII, No. 8 (1838), 113.
[47] Albert Barnes, *The Literature and Science of America*, p. 27.
[48] Finney to Henry Cowles, Dec. 23, 1841 (Cowles Papers).
[49] Lyman Beecher, *Lectures on Political Atheism*, pp. 174-175.

A somewhat different implication of divine right was emphasized by Wayland, who declared that the more closely a state patterned itself after divine decrees the more successful it would be.
"God bestows his richest blessings in strict accordance with the
moral character of his creatures," he asserted.[50] The most complete
expression of Wayland's political philosophy, however, is found in
his *Elements of Moral Science*. Assuming as he did that society
was an ordinance of God, he pointed out that "it is the will of
God that man should live in a state of society." Although he
also assumed a contractual society similar to that of Locke, he
clothed it in a religious garb, denied the right of revolution, and
distinguished between the agreement forming civil society and
what he called simple or voluntary ones:

In a simple society the contract is voluntary, and is, like any other contract, dissolved at the pleasure of the parties; or it ceases to be binding
upon either party, if its conditions are violated by the other party. But,
civil society being an institution of God, specific duties are imposed upon
both parties, which remain unchanged even after the other party may, in
various respects, have violated his part of the contract. In civil society
we are under obligation to God as well as to man, and the former obligation remains even after the other has been annulled.[51]

The most detailed elaboration of this modern divine right doctrine is found in the writings of Horace Bushnell. Bushnell's long
residence in Hartford gave him the opportunity to speak forth on
many local public issues. His efforts on behalf of a water works
and a park were the more colorful of his engagements in city
politics. He never hesitated to express an opinion about national
issues, and even when he was abroad he took the opportunity to
delve into questions far removed from ecclesiastical affairs. While
he was in England, the Oregon boundary dispute was raging, and
the Hartford divine proceeded to write a pamphlet explaining the
American position. While in France, he visited the Chamber of
Deputies and, although he could understand nothing of what was
being said, thrilled with pride at the prospect of the French government gravely considering the demands and arguments of his
native state.

[50] Wayland, *The Philosophy of Analogy*, p. 30.
[51] Wayland, *Elements of Moral Science*, pp. 380-381.

Bushnell's main concern in political affairs was that principles should be adhered to. He disliked compromise, despised the political deal, and denounced the leaders to whom ends were more important than means. His major attack was made in 1844 at the height of Clay's campaign against Polk and was appropriately titled *Politics under the Law of God*. It was first delivered as a Fast Day sermon and was in the opinion of one authority "one of the most impassioned which Bushnell ever preached." [52]

A close reading of this work is illuminating. Bushnell was ill when he wrote it, and it suffers from having been hastily written. It lacks much of the polish and close reasoning which characterize his other literary efforts. At the outset he defended himself against the charge that he was speaking on issues out of his realm and denied that there was anything mischievous or dishonorable about his motives. "My ideal," he declared, "was to make a bold push for principle." [53]

As a springboard for his ideas, the Hartford preacher first considered the action of men in groups. There is a difference, he believed, in men's practices when members of associations and when they act independently. In the former instance they tend to act irresponsibly. "They yield to impulse, to party spirit and policy, without any consideration of moral constraints and principles. As public bodies they have no conscience." [54] In the selection of public officers, the discipline of parties and the methods of law-making, Bushnell believed men have become particularly insensible to Christian principles and moral obligations. Previously in history, he asserted, such was not the case, but by 1844 a serious degeneration has taken place.

Now, the whole scene . . . is reversed. The pulling of wires unseen, and a long and weary agitation, are now necessary to prepare the day. If good men are nominated, it is by the special industry and good fortune of friends. . . . It is the party that is voted for. . . . Moral considerations have little or no weight. . . . Duty and fear of God must yield to party allegience.[55]

[52] Mead, *Horace Bushnell, the Citizen*, p. 15.
[53] Bushnell, *Politics under the Law of God*, p. 3.
[54] *Ibid.*, p. 5.
[55] *Ibid.*, p. 7.

Sensitive to the criticism that will be leveled against him for meddling in politics, especially during an election year, the crusading preacher asserts his right to speak on such matters. "I cannot leave politics alone, till I am shown that politics are not under the government of God. . . . It is my duty to follow you and assert God's law." [56]

The second part of the work contains his views on specific issues in which he has found a particularly noticeable absence of a moral obligation. The Missouri Compromise is the first to receive his condemnation. He contrasted his feelings as a youth in 1820, hearing the news of the event as it echoed across the Connecticut countryside, with his reactions as a man in 1840, viewing the fruits of the deed.

In the great Missouri question, on which the personal freedom, character and happiness of so many millions of human beings, the honor and security of our liberties, and the moral well being of a great and fertile section of our territory, were pending, what were the considerations that weighed in the deliberation, and determined the final vote? Was it the immortal principles of justice and humanity?—. . . No! it was the balance of power between the slaveholding and the non-slaveholding states.[57]

It is at this point that Bushnell made his most violent attack on Henry Clay. "The man who was foremost in that transaction," he thundered, "who therein took upon his soul the sorrows of untold millions of bondmen, and the moral desolation of the fairest portion of the globe, the nation follows with its warmest plaudits, and the promise of its highest honors." [58]

In the third portion of this work Bushnell advanced his reasons why American politics were so devoid of principles. It is here that he elaborates most completely his views of government.

We have taken up, in this country, almost universally, theories of government which totally forbid the entrance of moral considerations. Government, we think, is a social compact or agreement—a mere human creation, having as little connection with God, as little of a moral quality, as a ship of war or a public road. . . . It also results that a ma-

---

[56] Bushnell, *Politics under the Law of God*, p. 6.
[57] *Ibid.*, pp. 7-8.
[58] *Ibid.*, p. 8.

jority may at any time, and in any way, rise up to change the fundamental compact. . . . The nefarious doctrine advanced to justify the
Rhode Island rebellion, is, I grieve to say, nothing but the shallow theory
of government generally prevalent in this country, carried out to its
legitimate conclusions.[59]

He proceeded to censure Locke's theories calling them atheistical in
origin and anti-Christian in practice.

The author painted a dire prospect before his nation if she continued to separate politics and moral principles. "God cannot endure a nation which cannot endure him," he avowed. He will
punish them for rejecting His laws; a fierce judgment awaits
America; the walls of the social structure will crumble. If that
were not calamitous enough, public law will disappear, the constitution will become valueless, and patriotism will wither in the
absence of a religious influence in the state. In short, it is quite
apparent, Bushnell asserted, "that the divorce of politics from
conscience and religion, which is going forward, must infallibly
end, if not arrested, in the total wreck of our institutions and
liberties." [60]

The concluding portion of his work contained the cleric's solution to the problem. First, the people must open their eyes to
what they have done, recognize their sin, "and repent of it with
shame and fasting." Second, restore conscience to public matters,
do what is well-pleasing to God, and choose no one for office who
is not wholly virtuous. "If you have an eye that will look on a
partizan without principle," the eminent doctor advises, "pluck it
out and cast it from you. If you have a hand that will vote for
wickedness, cut it off." A third way to restore morality to politics
would be to do away with slavery which, he declared, "is the curse
of this nation." His conclusion was as ominous as he could make
it. "Our politics are now our greatest immorality. . . . Let us
go to God this day, and ask him . . . to save our beloved country
from its perils and avert the doom its sins provoke!" [61]

[59] Bushnell, *Politics under the Law of God*, p. 10.
[60] *Ibid.*, pp. 12, 14, 15.
[61] *Ibid.*, pp. 15, 16, 18, 19.

Popular sovereignty and the social contract theory received ample attack from Bushnell in other articles and addresses. In one essay he expressed his dislike for the system of checks and balances in government which he called "a preposterous conceit . . . which undertakes to make bad society good enough for good government." [62] In an address extolling the *Fathers of New England* (1850), he denied the application of the social contract theory to the early colonists, asserting that they came only for religious reasons and had no intentions of laying the foundations of a great republic. "They had no schemes of democracy to execute. They were not, in fact, or in their own view, republicans in their idea of government." [63]

The Civil War served only to strengthen Bushnell in his divine right beliefs. Early in the war, prompted by the initial Northern setbacks, he wrote encouragingly of the need to profit from adversity. In considering the effect of defeat in *Reverses Needed* (1861), he admonished his readers not to look for persons to blame. After all, the war was a product of the American Revolution! "It is a remarkable, but very serious fact," he observed, "that our grand revolutionary fathers left us the legacy of this war, in the ambiguities of thought and principle which they suffered, in respect to the foundations of government itself . . . they organized a government . . . without moral or religious ideas; in one view a merely man-made compact." [64]

In the course of his argument, he scoffed at Jefferson's and Rousseau's theories of a social compact. In refutation of this political philosophy, he stated,

There was never, in the first place, any such prior man, or body of men, to make a government. We are born into government as we are into the atmosphere, and when we assume to make a government or constitution, we only draw out one that was providentially in us before.[65]

The Hartford preacher found many things wrong with the social contract theory. Popular sovereignty or democratic government

---

[62] Bushnell, "Of Bad Government," *Moral Uses of Dark Things*, p. 61.
[63] Bushnell, *The Fathers of New England*, p. 19.
[64] Bushnell, *Reverses Needed*, p. 9.
[65] *Ibid.*, p. 16.

was only one way of designating a state's ruler.   The succession of
blood was another, and, according to Bushnell, they were "both
equally good and right when the historic order makes them so."
Then, too, since the authority of government under the social contract was not sacred, it was not imbued with a morally binding
force.   Laws, according to the Hartford preacher, become laws
only when there is felt to be some divine right in them.   Bushnell
also blamed the emergence of states' rights doctrines on this theory
of government.   "We begin with a godless theorizing, and we end,
just as we should, in discovering that we have not so much as made
any nation at all." [66]   Three years later similar thoughts were expressed in another work entitled *Popular Government by Divine
Decree,* in which he questioned whether the consent of the governed was a sufficient basis for just government.   One might almost
call Horace Bushnell subversive.

There are a number of other themes that, added to this glorification of the divine right doctrine, constituted a common denominator for the political creeds of the Northern evangelists.   Varied
though these men were in their party affiliations, still they were of
one mind in placing principles over political allegiance.   No ante-
bellum evangelist, loyal Democrat or Whig, hesitated to cast his
party aside when issues dear to his standards of right and wrong
were at stake.   In politics, the evangelist was the spokesman for
morality, and, as such, practical considerations were subordinated
to matters of principle.

This can best be illustrated in the reactions of evangelists to the
problem of supporting candidates for office.   Lyman Beecher as
a loyal Federalist assumed that his party's candidates were superior
to their opponents.   Calvin Colton as a hard-working Whig normally had little difficulty indicating his choice, while Peter Cartwright, staunch Democrat that he was, rarely hesitated to throw
his weight behind that party.   But when the choice to be made
lay between two men, neither of whom was perfect in terms of
morality and personal conduct, the evangelists forsook their loyal-
ties and stood on integrity.

[66] *Ibid.,* pp. 17-18, 21.

Early in his career Beecher faced the dilemma of choosing between two political evils. In his *The Remedy for Duelling* (1809)
he declared,

But suppose the duellist in all respects, excepting this crime, is a better
man than his opponent; of two evils may we not choose the least? Yes,
of two natural evils you may. If you must lose a finger or an arm, cut
off the finger. But of two sinful things, you may choose neither—and
therefore, you may not vote for one bad man, a murderer, to keep out
another bad man, though even a worse one.[67]

A similar sentiment was voiced by Bushnell, who, though differing
from Beecher on many points, agreed wholeheartedly that one
should not choose the lesser of two evils in balloting. In *Politics
under the Law of God* (1844) Bushnell considered this subject
and answered those who, opposing the extremists of their day,
argued that if you did not choose the least evil you were in effect
voting for the greatest. To Bushnell, such an argument had little
validity. If two evil candidates are running, "That is not your
fault, but the fault of those who offer you the alternative. . . .
There was never a maxim more corrupt, more totally bereft of
principle, than this—that, between bad men, you are to choose the
least wicked of the two." Practical questions of vote garnering
little mattered to him. "A vote is by no means thrown away because it does not go into the balance of the main question," he
believed. "Give it in as a visible token of innocence and incorruptible principle—a piece of clean white paper." [68]

Finney followed his Connecticut colleague in condemning party
politics which he called "perfectly dishonest." "No man can be
an honest man," he declared, "that is committed to a party, to
go with them, let them do what they may." Christians should not
compromise with their ideals by voting for the lesser of two evils.
He believed that there were enough religious voters in any election
to turn the scale. "Now let Christians take the ground that they
will not vote for a dishonest man, or a Sabbath-breaker, or gam-
bler, or whoremonger, or duellist, for any office, and no party
could ever nominate such a character with any hope of success."

67 Lyman Beecher, *The Remedy for Duelling*, pp. 32-33.
68 Bushnell, *Politics under the Law of God*, pp. 17, 18.

If this were done, and Christians conscientiously refused to vote for "ungodly" candidates, "a blessed influence would go over the land like a wave." [69]

Such a view encouraged a profound distrust for the major political parties among ministers and their devoted followers. "I pray you think less of parties and more of your country," warned Wayland in 1825, and a year later the deaths of Jefferson and Adams prompted him to discourse on "the utter worthlessness of party distinctions." [70] His words were echoed by Lyman Beecher, who worried about "those deep-rooted and permanent divisions" which split the nation and who exhorted his listeners to banish party spirit.[71] Wayland's essay on *The Duty of Obedience to the Civil Magistrate* (1847) contains similar sentiments on the tyranny of party. Bushnell's pamphlets are filled with a marked suspicion of political parties and the discipline they demanded. "I do not complain that we have parties. . . . But, in the name of God and all that is sacred, I protest against the doctrine that every man shall do what his party appoints, and justify what his party does." And here Bushnell added his choicest form of condemnation: "It is the worst form of papacy ever invented." [72]

This inflexible stand may have had interesting repercussions on the American political scene which are worthy of speculation. By expressing suspicion of politics and minimizing the contribution of the legislator and office holder, the minister discouraged his followers from holding their political leaders and candidates in higher esteem. Then, too, by refusing to countenance compromise, the evangelist encouraged the rise of the small splinter parties that engaged in so many elections in the middle period and that added so much color to our political history. Much of the fanatical dogmatism of the third party in our history has a revivalistic ring.

Those evangelists who entered into politics actively managed quite well. Joshua Leavitt had a fine time supporting the Liberty

[69] Finney, *Lectures to Professing Christians*, pp. 103, 104, 105.

[70] Wayland, *The Duties of an American Citizen*, p. 44; "The Death of the Ex-Presidents, July 4, 1826," *Occasional Discourses*, p. 90.

[71] Beecher, *The Memory of Our Fathers*, p. 34.

[72] Bushnell, *Politics under the Law of God*, pp. 11-12.

party and aiding in the birth of the Free Soil party. Calvin Colton was high in the councils of the Whigs. His *Junius Tracts* (1844) contain some of the best examples of his party's line, and he did yeoman service in pleading for protective tariffs. On the other side of the fence, Peter Cartwright was almost as successful garnering votes as he was gathering lost souls. That he rose no higher in the political arena was not his fault. In the pulpit he had only the Devil to fight. In the hustings, he had Abraham Lincoln!

Another political common denominator among evangelists was their tendency to equate political progress with Protestantism. This, of course, was the logical continuation of the connection Protestants made between progress and the Reformation. To the nineteenth-century evangelist, when Luther hammered his ninety-five theses on the door of the Castle Church in Wittenberg, Western Civilization began to advance. Then, for the first time, "property became sacred. Laws became equal and just. The oppressed began to breathe freely. . . . A new era dawned upon the world." [73]   And, according to Wayland, the progress in the period since the Reformation has been wholly dependent upon the expansion of Protestantism. The increase in the standard of living of the lower and middle classes and the improvement of their "intellectual character" have been achieved primarily because of the "pious zeal of Protestant Christians." [74]   That the American government had advanced since the revolution went without saying, but to the evangelists, this improvement was the direct result of the Protestant stamp on the nation. It remained for Wayland to best express the ministerial view when he remarked, "It is equally evident, that popular institutions are inseparably connected with Protestant Christianity. Both rest upon the same fundamental principle, the absolute freedom of inquiry . . . the doctrines of Protestant Christianity are the sure, nay, the only bulwark of civil freedom." [75]   Bushnell developed a similar argument in his *Crisis of the Church* (1835), and Lyman Beecher recited the same for-

---

73 Wayland, *The Dependence of Science upon Religion*, p. 30.
74 Wayland, *The Duties of an American Citizen*, p. 5.
75 *Ibid.*, p. 19.

mula—Protestantism equals political progress—on many an occasion.

Although in general evangelists seemed to support the political status quo, there were notable examples of democratic leanings among these men. Lyman Beecher was no revolutionary, but at one stage in his career he declared,

To effect the moral renovation of the world, a change is required in the prevailing forms of government.

The monopoly of power must be superseded by the suffrages of freemen . . . the mass of mankind must be enlightened and qualified for self government, and must yield obedience to delegated power.[76]

For some, it required a trip to Europe to bring out their interest in political equality and liberty. Finney's two trips to England accomplished something in this direction. Francis Wayland, recording his reactions to the European political scene, wrote, "I know not how it is but all I see renders me more doggedly a democrat and Puritan." [77] Albert Barnes took the occasion of European revolutions to laud the divinely inspired republicanism of those peoples intent on overthrowing thrones. [78] Maffitt indicated his democratic leanings by speaking in New Orleans, congratulating France on the establishment of a republican government.

It is evident that some evangelists were a democratizing influence on their followers. One notable example of a change in views that was brought about in part by Beecher, Finney, and others was that of Lewis Tappan. Writing to his brother in 1849, he compared his life before he was brought under the influence of evangelists and after. "I am more democratic than I was when I lived in Boston," he concluded.[79]

The occasional democratic leanings of the evangelists and their support for the status quo made for a certain inconsistency in the

---

[76] Beecher, *The Memory of Our Fathers*, pp. 9-10.

[77] Quoted in Murray, *Francis Wayland*, p. 85.

[78] See Albert Barnes, *The Casting Down of Thrones*.

[79] Lewis Tappan to Benjamin Tappan, April 23, 1849 (Benjamin Tappan Papers). For a more detailed examination of the connections between evangelism and the democratic faith, see Gabriel, *The Course of American Democratic Thought*, pp. 37-38.

development of their political philosophy. This is no more clearly illustrated than in the writings of Francis Wayland. The Brown president's political ideas resembled a stained-glass window: many colors composed it; many conflicting views contributed to it. In one of his major works, *The Elements of Moral Science* (1835), the reader can follow a whole spectrum of ideas which, if examined in their entirety, contain an eloquent defense of liberty but which, if studied separately, contain a theory seriously limited in its application. In passages strikingly anticipatory of John Stuart Mill, Wayland applied the golden rule to personal liberty. There was, in his interpretation, a duty of reciprocity which permits every man to gratify his own interests and desires as long as his actions do not interfere "with the means of happiness which God has granted to his neighbor." [80] Man has the freedom to pursue his own happiness as long as he leaves for everyone else a similar undisturbed exercise of their common right. This universal reciprocity applies to nations as well as individuals. It pertains to man's body and mind, to his occupation, to his political activities, and to his religion. In eloquent fashion the Baptist educator defended religious toleration, denying to the individual or the state the right to dictate how anyone should worship. If the individual abuses this liberty, if he worships false gods or none at all, he is accountable not to society but "only to God." [81]

There are exceptions, however, which Wayland quickly indicated. An infant lacks this limitless liberty. There is a period in youth when parents have a right to their offspring's services. In the case of apprenticeship also there can be no such unhampered freedom. Then, too, employees may transfer their right over their own labor for a period of time in return for a satisfactory equivalent. But more important, society checks the right of personal liberty:

Society is bound to protect those rights of the individual which he has committed to its charge. . . . Society has the right to prevent its own destruction. . . . If a man uses his intellect for the purpose of destroying

80 Wayland, *Elements of Moral Science*, p. 204.
81 *Ibid.*, p. 218.

his neighbor's reputation, it is the duty of society to interfere . . . to prohibit the use of intellect for the purpose of exciting the passions of men.
. . . Hence, society has a right to prohibit obscene books, obscene pictures
. . . incendiary and seditious publications, and every thing which would
provoke the enmity or malice of men against each other.[82]

Wayland likened society to a parent guarding his children,
shielding them from harm, forbidding them certain things for their
own good. And when morals were at stake, society, like the
parent, must interfere for its own protection with individual liberties. "If anyone, therefore, is disposed to use his intellect for
the purpose of destroying, in the minds of men, the distinction
between virtue and vice, or any of those fundamental principles
on which the existence of society depends, society has a right to
interfere and prohibit him." Nor must society, for the sake of
individual liberty, try over and over again an experiment that
history has proved always ends in "licentiousness, anarchy, misery
and universal bloodshed." [83]

An additional hedge is placed on the individual's freedom. The
representatives of government—judges, prosecuting officers, lawmakers and the like—have to step in at times and check liberty in
order to preserve it, Wayland maintained:

We hear at the present time very much about the liberty of the press, the
freedom of inquiry, and the freedom of the human intellect. All these
are precious blessings. . . . But it is to be remembered, that no liberty can
exist without restraint. . . . It therefore becomes all civil and judicial officers, to act as the guardians of society . . . resolutely to defend the
people against their worst enemies.[84]

When Wayland gets through, there is little left of his limitless
liberty.

Evangelists were not, by any means, the most outspoken ex-
ponents of freedom of thought in our society. Indeed, in word
and action they were often highly intolerant and notorious in their
disregard for the opinions and freedoms of others. Charles Finney
and Jacob Knapp ran roughshod over their opponents and in scath-

[82] Ibid., pp. 233, 235, 235-236.
[83] Ibid., pp. 236, 237.
[84] Ibid., p. 239.

ing sentences denounced those who refused to believe as they. Cartwright and Beecher lashed out at Unitarians with a ferocity that rivaled medieval vituperation of heretics. Assuming so firmly the rightness of their own beliefs, they were prone to dismiss the divergent opinions of others. On the whole, they could never be used to illustrate the American ideal of tolerance.

Nonetheless, one or two gems in defense of the freedom of thought sparkle among their otherwise lusterless pages. Albert Barnes was one who occasionally defended liberty of conscience. "The most appalling danger that threatens our country," he once wrote, "is the threatened restriction of the right of free discussion." [85] We need not fear foreign armies or menacing fleets, he added, but only those checks that are put on full and free inquiry. Even Lyman Beecher espoused such sentiments at times. When he launched his attack against "political atheism," he was careful to note that he did not favor laws against atheism, infidelity, or heresy, "for free inquiry is the birth-right and the duty of man, and the only condition of all-pervading truth, and intelligent self-government." [86] It was not until he was on trial himself, however, defending his theological views, that he waxed most eloquently on this subject. In his concluding remarks, denying the charge of heresy, he exclaimed,

I have never believed that truth will triumph by the force of legislation. Decide as the court may, it will not prevent men's preaching either way. It is no doubt proper and necessary to remove convicted heretics, if such shall be in your communion. But you can never cramp the intellect of such people as dwell in this country. You cannot prevent or repress free inquiry. [87]

There was another role evangelists were intent on playing. They were energetic, vocal spokesmen for nationalism. Their nationalistic expressions can be classified in four categories. There were: first, those expressions of patriotism which reflected a pride in one's nation; second, those which were, in effect, a misinterpretation of history in favor of the United States; third, ideas that

[85] Albert Barnes, *The Literature and Science of America*, p. 24.
[86] Beecher, *Lectures on Political Atheism*, p. 117.
[87] *Trial of the Rev. Lyman Beecher*, p. 80.

equated the American federal system with perfection; and fourth, the more bellicose statements that were affirmations of manifest destiny.

Bushnell illustrated the first category when he wrote, in watching the impact of American expansion on European shores,

What a proud thing for the American, standing here as a stranger, to see his new country rising in its greatness before the world! Here he stands to hear the debate which begins to reveal the jealousy of powers and to show that thrones are quaking lest the great republic should overshadow monarchy and legitimacy.[88]

How typical that he should add, with no loss of that pride, "Would that I could have understood the words of the speakers."

In interpreting history the evangelists succeeded in whitewashing the American past quite effectively. They lacked objectivity in evaluating events and were the most flagrant perpetrators of myth and legend. Albert Barnes was perhaps the most serious offender in this respect. In writing of our history he declared, "It is more rich in incident, more fruitful in results, presenting more scenes of profound wisdom, and dangers, more magnanimity and patriotism, by far, than the early days of Egypt, or Babylonia, of Greece, and of Rome." [89]

It was in speaking of our nation's founding that the minister was most eloquent—and most inaccurate. Horace Bushnell, for instance, described the early colonization in these words:

The true increase of a nation is not that which is made by conquest and plunder, but that which is the simple development of its vital and prolific resources. Two centuries ago, there came over to these western shores a few thousand men. These were the germ of a great nation here to arise . . . and, behold, a great wealthy, powerful and free nation stalks into history with the tread of a giant, fastening the astonished gaze of the world—all in the way of simple growth! [90]

Lyman Beecher had an equally exalted opinion of the founding fathers. "They were a race of men as never before laid the founda-

[88] Quoted in Cheney, *Life and Letters of Horace Bushnell*, p. 162.
[89] Barnes, *The Literature and Science of America*, pp. 11-12.
[90] Bushnell, *Views of Christian Nurture*, p. 153. Other examples of the way Bushnell whitewashed history can be found in "The Founders Great in their Unconsciousness" and "The Age of Homespun" in *Work and Play*.

tions of an empire," he wrote—"athletic, intelligent and pious."
He was convinced that "the history of our nation is indicative of
some great design to be accomplished by it" and called upon his
generation "to cherish with high veneration and grateful recollections the memory of our Fathers." [91]

The leaders of the American Revolution received their quota of
adulation from these men. They lauded the sagacity of those who
devised the Constitution, heaped heavy praise upon the shoulders
of Washington and other Federalists who guided the young nation
through perilous days, and justified the revolution as a divinely
inspired, righteous event. Barnes, in praising the Revolutionary
heroes, remarked, "A nation's unparalleled prosperity has recorded
the magnitude of their undertaking, and sealed their claim to the
gratitude of the long ranks of coming men." He was certain that
no other people "has recorded integrity of a higher order, love of
country of a purer character, and valour more daring" than that
of the Revolutionary generation.[92]

Joshua Leavitt continued the tradition when he came to write
on the Monroe Doctrine. In his study of that portion of our foreign policy he did a remarkable job of misrepresentation. Not
only did he overemphasize the threat to American independence
in the form of the Holy Alliance, but also, in more glaring fashion,
he completely discounted any British influence in the action. The
creation of the Monroe Doctrine, Leavitt asserted, "is to be credited
in full to the wisdom and sagacity and patriotic courage of the
American administration. And any attempt in any quarter to
disparage the importance, or discredit the independence of this
proceeding, it unjust and wrongful in Englishmen, and unpatriotic
and mean in Americans." [93]

It is interesting to see how the evangelists developed the theme
of national perfection. Starting with the premise that America
was guided in her destiny by Providence, and assuming that her
beginnings were shaped by almost godlike men, the Northern

[91] Lyman Beecher, *The Memory of Our Fathers*, pp. 11, 16, 22-23.
[92] Albert Barnes, *An Address, Delivered . . . at the Presbyterian Church in Morris-town*, p. 6. Typical of his nationalism is *The Love of Country*.
[93] Leavitt, *The Monroe Doctrine*, p. 22.

evangelists concluded that the American system of government and the American way of life were the best that could be devised. Protestantism, republicanism, and progress spelled only one thing— a perfect state. As Albert Barnes put it, "The peculiar form of our political blessings is the result of the world's experience. The American constitution contains the embodied wisdom of all other nations. . . . In regard to government, it is the last hope of the world." [94] Bushnell was another who lauded the Federal constitution, calling it in one speech, "the greatest achievement of legislative wisdom in the modern history of the world" and boasting that it would some day shelter the rights and interests of two hundred million people.[95] He, of all ministers, was the most outspoken in ascribing this perfection to the supremacy of Protestantism in the nation, and in one of his earliest published sermons asked, "What nation ever did as much in fifty years, to soften the condition of man, and prove the faith of the cross? If but a hundred more such years are given us to enfold our growth, what spectacle so august! what power so commanding over the destinies of man!" [96]

In turning to the fourth type of nationalistic expression, we find many illustrations of a clerical belief in manifest destiny. Calvin Colton sounded the keynote for this faith in the divinely inspired future of the nation. In his history of revivals he wrote enthusiastically:

One grand theatre, remote from the common turmoil of the nations, has already been prepared and opened for a fresh and interesting experiment of Christianity, and scenes of bright and hopeful omen have been enacting there for many generations. Where, may it be asked, has a state of society occurred, in the providence of God, since the opening of the Christian era, so favourable to the progress and triumphs of true religion, as in the United States of America? [97]

But religion was not the only way in which America's manifest destiny expressed itself. To Edward Beecher, busy campaigning for money to build colleges, education was another:

[94] Albert Barnes, *An Address, Delivered* . . *at the Presbyterian Church in Morristown*, p. 11.
[95] Bushnell, *Speech for Connecticut*, p. 13.
[96] Bushnell, *Crisis of the Church*, pp. 14-15.
[97] Colton, *History and Character of American Revivals of Religion*, p. 31.

The great distinction of North America above every other portion of the globe, is that it was chosen by God to enjoy the honor of being the receptacle of Puritan ideas. . . . God has given to the Puritan churches, as their glorious birthright, the power to lead this nation in the great work of education not only at the East, but at the West also. His providence calls them to it. It is their manifest destiny, their great mission.[98]

Politically, these men believed there was a glorious future for America. The Irish Methodist, Maffitt, summed up the ministerial confidence that "America is destined, at no distant period, to take a more elevated and important station in controlling the destinies of the earth. . . . The Almighty seems to have determined in her favor." [99] Bushnell probably painted the most happy picture of America's destiny:

We are the grand experiment of Protestantism! Yes we—it is our most peculiar destiny—we are set to show, by a new and unheard of career of national greatness and felicity, the moral capabilities and all the beneficent fruits of Christianity and the Protestant faith. . . . God even reserved a world for its development. . . . God sent us hither to make this signal experiment.[100]

Bushnell's enthusiasm for his country sometimes approached the chauvinistic. At one point he asserted that whatever beneficent had occurred in Europe in the nineteenth century "has been instigated, more or less directly, by the great idea that is embodied and represented in the institutions of the United States." [101]

A few divines carried manifest destiny one step further and spoke in terms of American intervention in world affairs. Albert Barnes was one of those who thought "the spread of intelligence and virtue cannot fail ultimately to extend the same principles of government throughout the earth." He believed that to make our form of government adopted throughout the world required "only the silent unobtrusive course, of spreading . . . the mild sentiments of our religion, and the established maxims of our learning." He considered it even possible that the United States might be

98 Edward Beecher, *The Question at Issue*, pp. 18, 32.
99 Maffitt, *Literary and Religious Sketches*, pp. 86-87.
100 Bushnell, *Crisis of the Church*, p. 12.
101 Bushell, *Moral Uses of Dark Things*, pp. 349-350.

called on "to exert a more direct influence on the destinies of men." [102]

Distant nations shall direct their eyes for counsel to our infant Republic; and the voice of the American nation, rich in experience, though young in years, shall be heard in the chaos of revolution, and settle the troubled elements down to rest.   In the era of better things, which is about to rise in the world, our land shall be first; our counsels the guide of other nations; our countrymen everywhere the devoted advocates of the rights of men. . . . It will be sufficient honour in any nation to be known as an American.[103]

Francis Wayland did not stop there.   To him intervention was more than the silent workings of enlightened peoples.   "Should the rulers of Europe make war upon the principle of our constitution," he wrote in 1825, when Metternich and the Monroe Doctrine were current table topics, "it is manifest that we must take no secondary part in the controversy" but must breast ourselves to the shock of congregated nations:

Then, on the altar of God, let each one devote himself to the cause of the human race; and in the name of the Lord of Hosts go forth unto the battle.   If need be, let our choicest blood flow freely; for life itself is valueless, when such interests are at stake.[104]

By the outbreak of the Civil War evangelists were rivals to none in their patriotism.   The willingness with which they approached the start of hostilities is a commentary on the extent to which the slavery question and antagonism toward Southerners had carried those who normally were preachers of peace.   Even those ministers who had formerly opposed war and urged the cause of the American Peace Society were outspoken in their support of an appeal to arms in 1860.   A mild-mannered man such as Francis Wayland, who had been president of the American Peace Society, who had opposed the Mexican War, and whose *Elements of Moral Science* specifically condemned the recourse to war in the settling of disputes, wrote a friend in 1861 favoring war: "The best place

---

[102] Albert Barnes, *An Address, Delivered . . . at the Presbyterian Church in Morristown*, pp. 14-15, 25.

[103] *Ibid.*, p. 20.

[104] Wayland, *The Duties of an American Citizen*, pp. 29, 30.

to meet a difficulty is just where God put it.   If we dodge it, it will come to a worse place." [105]   Wayland supported the Northern cause with pen and tongue.   Like a Fichte unable to fight himself, he filled regiments of troops with lofty ideals of nationalism and at their embarkations sent them forth with benedictions.   Finney welcomed the coming of the war, and Bushnell as early as 1856 was willing to sacrifice a son in battle.   Joshua Leavitt's reactions to the prospect of armed conflict bordered on enthusiasm.   As spring of 1861 approached he wrote his brother, "I do not think you feel right about the boys going to war.   It seems to me, not only a duty but a privilege, and with many benefits as well as dangers. . . . There is hardly one of our boys who has not already *doubled his manhood.*" [106]

When it came to affairs of state, political issues, and the concerns of the day, the evangelists were often over their heads. Nonetheless, they never hesitated to speak out against what they felt was wrong, to support what they believed in, and to try to influence their fellow men for the general good.   While they often lacked objectivity, they were always at least sincere.   Had they all been politicians rather than ministers they would probably not have been so successful.   Had they been statesmen, American affairs might have been handled on a slightly higher plane.   That they were so dogmatic in their views was indicative of what they felt was a divinely inspired reasoning.   That they erred so often is happily evidence that they were human.

[105] Francis Wayland to Hon. Lafayette Foster (n.d.), quoted in Murray, *Francis Wayland*, p. 146.
[106] Joshua Leavitt to Hooker Leavitt, March 2, 1861 (Leavitt Papers).

VI. THE THINGS OF THIS WORLD

Wealth is no more than a peculiar form of talent which God confers upon us for the time being, and for the use of which he will hold us to a strict account.[1]

You are never to complain of your birth, your training, your employments, your hardships; never to fancy that you could be something if only you had a different lot and sphere assigned you.[2]

DURING A CRUCIAL REVIVAL in the city of Boston in the 1830's two leading ministers labored over an attentive congregation and tried to win converts to their faith. Addressing the assembled inquirers in persuasive prayerful pleas, the two alternated in their appeals, and in majestic, melodious phrases attempted to garner souls for their Lord. The first endeavored to impress upon his hearers that they had to give themselves and their all to Christ in order to be saved. The second, aware that the group contained many from the middle and upper classes, interrupted his colleague to explain that they need not be afraid to give up their all to Christ—property, money, and everything—because he would give it right back. The first thereupon rejoined, answering his fellow cleric indirectly, by pointing out that God's claim was absolute. For awhile a theological tug-of-war was waged over the bowed heads of the waiting converts until Charles Finney and Lyman Beecher reconciled their differences and returned to the matter at hand.[3]

This interlude throws into sharp focus a basic dichotomy in the economic ideas of American evangelists and, indeed, of Protestantism itself. On the one hand, there was a conscious effort to subordinate the things of this world to the things of the spirit, to put the demands of the soul above those of the body, to make religious

---

[1] Wayland, *An Appeal to the Disciples of Christ*, p. 5.
[2] Bushnell, *Sermons for the New Life*, p. 19.
[3] For an account of this bout, see Finney, *Memoirs*, pp. 315-316.

affairs of primary importance and earning a living, amassing property, and other mundane matters secondary. On the other hand, there was a strong impulse toward the protection of property, the defense of the capitalistic system, and the appeasing of the monied classes on the part of most evangelists. How these two seemingly conflicting attitudes were reconciled in the minds of some of our evangelists is a curious commentary not only on the religious figures themselves but also on their society and the age in which they lived.[4]

That evangelists should converse authoritatively on economic matters was to be expected. An understanding of spiritual affairs, they believed, gave them an insight into such questions as the sanctity of private property, the bank and tariff issues, and the ten-hour day. To men who were versed in moral laws, it was easy to comprehend the so-called economic laws. When Finney and Beecher battled over the place of wealth in the act of conversion, they were merely exercising their prerogative as men of God.

It is not surprising, therefore, to find one evangelist, Calvin Colton, devote, when his voice had failed him, the bulk of his time and energy to writing in defense of protectionism, nor to discover another, Joshua Leavitt, arguing at equal lengths in favor of free trade. Horace Bushnell's readers were not startled when he gave his estimate of "Agriculture at the East," told "How to Be a Christian in Trade," or appealed for a new water works for Hartford in a sermon he titled *Prosperity Our Duty*. Theological training did not prevent Baker and Beecher from undertaking arduous money-raising schemes, while Finney's strictures against speculation were accepted without question. And it was only natural that a Baptist divine should write a textbook on political economy. Evangelists were diversified individuals and were never

---

[4] Historians of late have addressed themselves to the role Protestantism played in sanctifying economic success and campaigning for capitalism. The classic works on this subject are, of course, Max Weber, *The Protestant Ethic and the Spirit of Capitalism*, translated by Talcott Parsons, and R. H. Tawney, *Religion and the Rise of Capitalism*. The most detailed authoritative study for nineteenth century America is Henry F. May, *Protestant Churches and Industrial America*. See also chap. xii in Perry, *Puritanism and Democracy*. Charles W. Schneider's essay, "The Puritan Tradition" in F. Ernest Johnson, ed., *Wellsprings of the American Spirit*, touches cogently on this topic.

more dogmatic than when they were expressing opinions on economic matters.

As religious leaders it is also understandable that these men should have subordinated money-making to the drama of salvation. The first step in this subordination was a profound distrust of money and material possessions. Albert Barnes spoke for the profession when he declared,

The love of gain . . . is still our besetting sin. This passion goads our countrymen, and they forget all other things . . . they go for gold, and they wander over the prairie, they fell the forest, they ascend the stream in pursuit of it, and they trample down the law of the Sabbath, and soon, too, forget the laws of honesty and fairdealing, in the insatiable love of gain.[5]

According to Charles Finney, "The whole course of business in the world is governed and regulated by the maxims of supreme and unmixed selfishness." Commercial activities as they were practiced, he held, were inconsistent with God's commands. Luther-like, he denounced the maxim, "to buy as cheap as you can, and sell as dear as you can—to look out for number one" and urged his followers not to conform to the selfish ways of the world.[6] One of his ardent followers echoed his pastor's sentiments when he wrote, "O this money that destroys a man's spirituality; and endangers his soul!"[7]

The second step in this effort to put spiritual affairs over material ones was to convert those who had great wealth. There was method behind the madness of the ladies of Rochester who, as Finney's agents during his revivals there, "would visit the stores and places of business, and use all their influence to secure the attendance . . . of the persons engaged in these establishments."[8] Finney's attitude was a practical one. While he denounced the cares of the world and heaped suspicion on the practice of making money, he recognized the need for enlisting the moneyed classes

[5] Albert Barnes, "Revivals of Religion in Cities and Large Towns," *American National Preacher*, XV, No. 1 (1841), 23.
[6] Finney, *Lectures to Professing Christians*, p. 95.
[7] Lewis Tappan to Finney, June 9, 1833 (Finney Papers).
[8] Finney, *Memoirs*, p. 438.

in his campaign to reform society. His success rested on their monetary support, and, as he put it, "the system of our trading still continues and is likely to continue until there is a radical overturning in both the world and church upon the subject of money making." [9]

Having influenced the affluent sections of society, the final step was to direct their energies and wealth into beneficial, philanthropic ventures, to energize the wealthier converts to benevolence. The evangelists thus succeeded in almost simultaneously taking three views toward money—despising it, embracing it, and putting it to use. Of the three, the importance of stewardship became a recurrent theme for the American man of God.

Typical of evangelistic schemes of stewardship was Justin Edwards's plan by which a merchant (such as his own brother-in-law) would devote from 10 to 25 per cent of his income to charitable and benevolent objects. In 1834 Edwards thought it would be well for all merchants to adopt the resolution Nathaniel R. Cobb, of Boston, had drawn up:

By the grace of God, I will never be worth more than $50,000.
By the grace of God, I will give one fourth of the net profits of my business to charitable and religious uses.[10]

Edwards went a step further and set up a sliding scale, suggesting those worth $20,000 give half their net profit, those earning $30,000 three quarters, and those who reached $50,000 to give their whole profit. It remained for Finney to stimulate benevolence on a major scale and with the aid of the Tappans carry philanthropy to new heights. The merchants who came under Finney's influence in New York engaged in stewardship with a vengeance, agreeing not to amass property for selfish reasons but to "consecrate the whole of it to the Lord." As Gilbert H. Barnes so aptly put it, "Heretofore benevolence had been their pastime; it now became their vocation." [11]

---

9 Finney to Cowles, Dec. 23, 1841 (Cowles Papers).
10 Hallock, *Light and Love, a Sketch of the Life and Labors of the Rev. Justin Edwards*, p. 390.
11 Gilbert H. Barnes, *The Antislavery Impulse*, p. 21.

Indicative of Finney's influence is the change in attitude that one can trace in Lewis Tappan.   In 1828 before he encountered Finney, Tappan wrote, "I am much engaged in business, selling gros de Naples, pins, bobbins, fans, etc., on a large scale to be sure.   Don't turn up your nose, your Honor, for I have leisure; books; pen, ink and paper, as you see. . . . As for making money, I am not insensible, of course, to that pleasure." Years later, with Finney's preaching (and a commercial panic) behind him, he wrote his brother in a different vein, "I have enough property to support my family and I am tired of laboring at the oar to acquire money, when so much can be done in moral enterprises." [12]

In applying Christianity to trade and commerce, the distrust of money and the channeling of benevolence were not the only activities evangelists emphasized.   Many of them threw an aura of respectability over wealth and economic influence.   Success and prosperity were, after all, to use the Calvinistic formula, good indications that an individual was pleasing in God's sight.   Poverty and business failure seemed poor signs of one's salvation.   The justification of prosperity, therefore, was part of the ministerial approach toward money matters.

This is no better illustrated than in Horace Bushnell's sermon, *Prosperity Our Duty* (1847), which contained his standard for measuring an individual's or a nation's success.   In this sermon the Hartford preacher quickly removed any fears his audience might have had that he was speaking on a topic foreign to him:

I regard it as a question that involved . . . the dearest interests of character and religion.   For . . . a state of prosperity is itself one of the truest evidences of character and public virtue, a reward of honor which God delights to bestow upon an upright people.[13]

Bushnell's sermon was, in effect, a nineteenth-century modernization of the Calvinistic business ethic.   Thrift, frugality, industriousness were lauded; laziness, idleness, and waste were described as deadly sins.   The dangers that spring from an unprosperous man were moral as well as economic.   According to Bushnell,

[12] Lewis Tappan to Benjamin Tappan, March 14, 1828, and Aug. 6, 1849 (Benjamin Tappan Papers).
[13] Bushnell, *Prosperity Our Duty*, p. 4.

It is the duty of every man to be a prosperous man; if by any reasonable effort he may. God calls us to industry, and tempts us to it by all manner of promises. He lays it upon us as a duty to be diligent in business. . . . He is pleased with thrift and makes it the sister of virtue. Every shiftless character, therefore, is a character so far lost to virtue.[14]

Bushnell was not as successful in sloughing off Calvin's economic prejudices as he was in rejecting old fashioned doctrine. Permeating his sermon is the old Calvinistic preference for the successful member of the middle class. "Give me," he exclaimed at one point, "a worldly, money-loving, prosperous, but strenuous and diligent hearer, and deliver me from one who has run down all his vigor, and debauched every earnest capacity, by his indolence or improvidence."[15] The same held for society as well as for the individual, he added. He favored an industrious, enterprising, successful community, alert to ways in which its prosperity might be enhanced.

This sermon told Bushnell's hearers precisely what they wanted to hear. Nor was he the only divine whose words were agreeable to the middle class. Finney's strongest following came from the professional and mercantile groups. Lyman Beecher, although occasionally radical in his economic views, gained most ground when talking to Boston businessmen, and his church in Cincinnati was the most stylish in town. His son, Henry Ward, was the darling of Brooklyn's wealthy. All these men urged conservatism and conformity. Their seemingly radical social lances were broken on the hard rock of their economic conservatism. "Let a man be a mechanic, a physician, a merchant, or what he will," Henry Ward once declared, "he will find that he must conform to the wishes and opinions of those by whom he is surrounded. . . . Men are accountable for their feelings and opinions as well as their conduct."[16] How great an impulse to reform there might have been had these evangelists taken a more progressive stand. How

---

[14] *Ibid.*, p. 6. His words were echoed by Lyman Beecher, who on one occasion wrote, "If you wish to be free indeed, you must be virtuous, temperate, well instructed, with the door of honor and profit open to you and your children." Lyman Beecher, *Political Atheism*, p. 124.

[15] Bushnell, *Prosperity Our Duty*, p. 6.

[16] Quoted in Thompson, *The History of Plymouth Church*, pp. 36, 39.

great a dent they might have made in the hardening shell of American middle-class conservatism.

Some steps were taken in that direction. Indeed, for a while it looked as though the influence of Lyman Beecher was to be thrown on the scales for economic democracy. His early works contain strong statements in favor of economic equality, the removal of privilege, and the regulation of economic activity. As late as the 1830's his interest in workingmen and their problems was still strong though a reaction, due partly to his distrust for the Owens and Fanny Wrights in society, had begun to set in. He ended his career as a conservative who almost rivaled the reaction of Bushnell or Calvin Colton.

One of the first expressions of Beecher's advanced views occurred in 1820, when he published a work entitled *The Means of National Prosperity*. The heavy cloud of gloom created by the economic panic of 1819 hung over him as he wrote and the persistent problem of finding an elusive prosperity was, he declared at the outset, one of the reasons for his discourse. According to Lyman, there are five things on which depended a nation's prosperity. They were: "the encouragement and successful prosecution of agriculture"; second, "the protection and encouragement of manufactures"; third, a similar promotion of commerce; fourth, the support of literary institutions and science; and last, the aid given to Christian institutions.[17]

In indicating how agriculture might be encouraged, the Litchfield doctor showed his democratic leanings. He favored raising the social position of agricultural workers, the formation of associations to collect and distribute agricultural knowledge, the improvement of roads, the construction of canals, and "wise acts of legislation, calculated to secure to the husbandman a steady market and a fair price."[18] Beecher later expanded on this point:

No human skill can indeed control the elements, or regulate the seasons, so as to secure the equable fruitfulness of the earth . . . or so control the family of nations as to prevent the fluctuations of demand and price, oc-

17 Lyman Beecher, *The Means of National Prosperity*, pp. 3, 7, 15, 16, 18.
18 *Ibid.*, p. 5.

casioned by the interchange of peace and war. But much may be done, by a wise policy, to check these fluctuations of the market, and especially to withold them from extremes, which are destructive to national industry. No calamity is greater than a capricious market, baffling the sober extended calculations of industry, and converting the husbandmen of a nation into a body of speculators. . . . A steady market, and a fair profit, for the product of the field, is among the greatest national blessings, and noblest objects of national policy.[19]

Lyman Beecher might be said to stand midway between Colbert and the AAA.

Beecher revealed an acquaintance with economic theory and a bias for protective tariffs, in speaking of the need for encouraging manufactures. Joining the early proponents of the American System, Lyman listed the many advantages to be gained from prosperous manufactures. He cited too the dangers to be incurred from a dependence on foreign nations for necessary finished goods. He asserted that such a panic as the one that occurred in 1819 would not have happened had there been an abundance of manufacturing establishments. Beecher envisaged a state controlling for the welfare of the people all phases of agriculture, industry, and commerce, acting as a salutary check on the extremes of wealth and poverty that were likely to occur.

There were other factors, Beecher believed, which made for national prosperity. Free public schools, a healthy people, and laws that governed the accumulation and preservation of property were also necessary. A wise, incorruptible administration of justice and a police power strong enough to preserve order were equally vital. But above all else, the man who had just lost his battle for the standing order declared defiantly, above all else was the need for state support to religion. "There is no safe way of raising a nation to wealth and power, but at the same time that you make it great, to make it good." He called for direct aid to the Protestant churches. "What should prevent legislators from favoring the institutions of religion, as a means of national prosperity?" he demanded. "May not the fear of God be promoted by legislators, without superstition?"[20]

[19] *Ibid.*, p. 7.
[20] *Ibid.*. pp. 18, 19.

Beecher devoted much of his work to a Christianization of the economic laws, to refuting various explanations of why the panic of 1819 had occurred, and to uttering pious platitudes. There were not such things as factions, he declared. Men have common interests, common objectives. There should be no animosity between individuals or groups. He maintained "there is no collision of interest, or foundation for envy, between the several classes of men, whose exertions are required to promote the general welfare of a nation." [21] There was a mutual dependence. If one suffers, all suffer.

Although he indicated his preference for the regulation of economic affairs by the state, Beecher made clear that he was looking for no easy road toward the solution of his generation's problems, no panacea for prosperity. While the state had its obligations, so did the citizens. He emphasized that "it is not in the power of government to render a nation of improvident families great and happy." [22] In the final analysis it is upon the individual himself that the means of national prosperity must rest. He concluded with an appeal for the sterner virtues of thrift, frugality, and industriousness.

The high-water mark of Beecher's democratic leanings was reached in 1828. He had been in Boston only two years, not long enough to feel comfortable among the fashionable members of his church. He had just tangled with the ultraism of the Finneyites and was still waging his lonely war against Unitarianism. In 1828 he was in a fighting mood. He considered himself a crusader, and in an address called *The Memory of Our Fathers* he gave to Boston his blueprint for a better world. It was Beecher at his best.

A great renovation was needed, he began. Reform was in the air, and vast changes were required in the civil and religious conditions of nations. The first change Beecher would make lay in land reform. "The monopoly of the soil must be abolished," he affirmed, and he continued:

[21] *Ibid.*, p. 20.
[22] *Ibid.*, p. 24.

Hitherto the majority of mankind who have tilled the earth, have been slaves or tenants. The soil has been owned by kings, and military chieftans, and nobles, and . . . landlords . . . until the majority, who paid the rent, have sustained in the sweat of their brow, not only their own families, but three or four orders of society above them; while they themselves have been crushed beneath the weight, and have lived on the borders of starvation.[23]

Man must be unshackled, the evangelist demanded. In order to accomplish this, "the earth must be owned by those who till it." [24]

A similar theme was the burden of another of Beecher's bombastic works. In his *Lectures on Political Atheism,* he attempted to incorporate for orthodox religion the tradition of reform and progress and to refute those political atheists who were offering Bibleless panaceas. The book was "dedicated to the workingmen of our nation," whose friend Beecher professed to be. In these lectures he covered a wide range, considering proofs for the existence of God, discoursing on the nature of the Deity, outlining the perils of atheism, surveying the republican elements of the Old Testament, attacking Hegelian philosophy, and touching on a variety of other matters. But the main theme of his book was land reform:

History teaches us that in all past time the earth has been owned, and knowledge and power have been monopolized, by the few; while the people, the labouring-classes, the great body of mankind, have been left to grope their way in darkness and slavery, tilling the earth they did not own, in the borders of starvation, and liable by a few days' sickness to become paupers.[25]

While there was a need for democratization of land holdings, Beecher did not believe in carrying reform too far. Indeed, some of the radical proposals for creating a utopia in the new world received more vituperation at his hands than monopolists. Communal societies were anathema, and men such as Robert Owen, "these Catilines" who "harangue their troops in the five hundred thousand grog-shops of the nation" were worse than the Devil.[26]

[23] Beecher, *The Memory of Our Fathers,* pp. 7-8.
[24] *Ibid.,* p. 9.
[25] Beecher, *Lectures on Political Atheism,* p. 1.
[26] *Ibid.,* pp. 106-107.

Any plan for the improvement of society that was not based on the sanctity of property and the authority of orthodox Protestantism was promptly branded political atheism. It was comforting to his followers to hear Beecher explain the close relationship between patriotism and Christianity, between the ownership of property and "the kind attractions of Heaven." The eminent divine was even suspicious of the so-called workingmen's parties which rose in opposition to Jackson, for Beecher disapproved of class appeals at the ballot box.[27] Beecher was radical only among conservatives. When he found himself among other social architects, he lost his enthusiasm for reform. Lyman's antidote to the disproportionate ownership of property, the inequalities of wealth, and other economic evils was simple. Let all have the opportunity to rise to the top and the resultant inequalities would be just.

Let the road to honour and influence be open alike to all classes of society, and the competition be that only of intellect, knowledge, enterprise and virtue; while ignorance, indolence, and immorality, constitute the only impediment to public favour; and the heart of national industry will be cheerful, and the arm of national industry will be strong, and the consequence will be contented families, and national wealth. . . . We shall have no mobs of discontented labourers to annoy us—and no standing armies to protect and enslave us.[28]

There was another school of thought among clerics which took a position that might be labeled Calvinistic contentment. Bushnell, Wayland, and others never hesitated to point out the joys of adversity and to strike the theme that though one is starving still can he be happy. In his *Spiritual Dislodgements* (1857), Bushnell justified adversities in this life as a means of loosening us "from our own evils" and preparing us for God's will.[29] In *Reverses Needed* (1861) he outlined the advantages to be derived from suffering losses, and in a long work entitled *Moral Uses of Dark Things* (1867) he indicated in a series of essays how good could come out of evil, beauty out of ugliness, and success out of ad-

[27] *Ibid.*, pp. 77-78, 106-107. Beecher was evidently misinformed about the objectives and supporters of the workingmen's parties in Boston, New York, and Philadelphia.

[28] Lyman Beecher, *The Means of National Prosperity*, p. 6.

[29] Bushnell, *Spiritual Dislodgements*, p. 7.

versity.[30]   Beriah Green was another who waxed poetic over the virtues of adversity. "Alas," he cried, "when shall we learn that man, as well as the vine, thrives on a lean soil? That poverty and toil and conflict are the very discipline his powers demand?" [31] Even Beecher believed that poverty had its compensations. Reflecting on a visit to a one-room cottage equipped with neither chimney nor floor he wrote, "How much happier the tenants of this obscure hut than the tenants of a palace rolling in splendor." [32] The tenants could not dispute him for they could not read.

Akin to this praise of adversity was a persistent glorification of labor. Carlyle's "gospel of work" was nothing new to American ministers who had for years been preaching such sentiments. Lyman Beecher's *The Means of National Prosperity* enthused about the joys of work and paid tribute to the American's "honourable and athletic ancestry." Francis Wayland glorified labor and called it "the toil of muscle, the tension of nerve, the obedience of the material to the spiritual" and claimed it was the way man showed "his preeminence as a creature of God." [33]

It was Beriah Green, however, who best symbolized this ministerial exaltation of work. As the head of a manual labor institute for higher learning he had ample opportunity to preach the joys of hard work. "The pulpit, the seat of learning, the chair of state should be occupied exclusively by men, who understand the dignity and rejoice in the influence of Work. . . . Lean supplies, rugged toil, coarse fare; how hard it is to look into these things and see what blessings they contain!" [34]

[30] He carried this theme too far, however, in his chapter on "Of Plagues and Pestilences."

[31] Green, *The Divine Significance of Work*, p. 16.

[32] Lyman Beecher to Roxanna Foote, June 18 (1799), in Lyman Beecher, *Autobiography*, I, 109.

[33] Lyman Beecher, *The Means of National Prosperity*, pp. 20-21; Wayland, *Address before the Rhode Island Society for the Encouragement of Domestic Industry*, p. 4.

[34] Beriah Green, *The Divine Significance of Work*, pp. 15, 16. Green (1795-1874) was a graduate of Middlebury and Andover who engaged in missionary work on Long Island before taking the pastorate of a Congregational church in Brandon, Vermont. While professor of sacred theology at Western Reserve College he became interested in the antislavery cause and was president of the convention which founded the American Anti-slavery Society in 1833. From 1833 to 1843 he was president of Oneida Institute.

The idea of a calling was another pet theme preached continuously by the Calvinistic evangelists. "Men are to be diligent in their calling," declared Charles G. Finney, who found idleness sinful, and in a sermon entitled "Every Man's Life a Plan of God" Horace Bushnell defended his colleague's belief that "God has a definite life-plan for every human person, guiding him, visibly or invisibly, for some exact thing, which it will be the true significance and glory of his life to have accomplished." If God has ordained our station in life and is preparing us to become that which is highest and best for us, then, the Hartford divine maintained, "there ought never to be a discouraged or uncheerful being in the world." [35] We must not complain, therefore, of our place in society, of our job, of our hardships. We must never wish we had a different lot in life assigned to us. We must never be dissatisfied with our calling. "Choke that devilish envy which gnaws at your heart, because you are not in the same lot with others . . . and then you shall find that your condition is never opposed to your good, but really consistent with it." [36] Lyman Beecher condemned the man who was "not contented with the useful and respectable station in society, assigned him in the providence of God," but who fostered in his heart "murmuring and envy." [37] Lyman and his proselytes reiterated their belief in a calling and justified acquiescence with God's economic decrees. As Lewis Tappan put it, "Now, although it might have been pleasant for me to have been a lawyer, yet is it not well to submit to the will of God, 'who placed me here,' and act well my part." [38] To those who were reaping profits, submitting to the will of God was not an onerous task.

Albert Barnes carried this conservative doctrine a step further in utilizing the New Testament to oppose economic change.

Christ never denounced differences of rank in life. He never engaged in the project of the dissatisfied and disorganizing Roman people, in the de-

[35] Finney, "How to Prevent Our Employment from Injuring Our Souls," *Oberlin Evangelist*, I, No. 24 (1839), 185; Bushnell, *Sermons for the New Life*, pp. 11, 16 17.
[36] *Ibid.*, p. 20.
[37] Lyman Beecher, *The Means of National Prosperity*, p. 21.
[38] Lewis Tappan to Benjamin Tappan, May 14, 1828 (Benjamin Tappan Papers).

mands for an Agrarian law, nor in the covetous schemes of modern infidelity, to break up all ranks in society, to denounce the rich, or to demand that all property should be reduced to a mass to be subject to the
arts of a cunning and unprincipled leader. He designed a scheme of religion, adapted to the existence of various orders in the community.[39]

Finally, this Calvinistic contentment and conservative view of
the status quo led the evangelist to a defense of the profit system.
The acquisition of property involved "the moral training of our
life." It was in the profit system that we learned what was to be
just and unjust. "We take part here for truth and justice and
right and faith and exact honor, because there is property at stake,
and who is indifferent to property?"[40]

The pleasures of adversity, the glorification of work, the plea for
industriousness, the idea of a calling, and the defense of property
all involved the linking of economic activities with God's will.
Success in commerce was connected with conversion; a profitable
career was linked with salvation. Wealth was a sign of Providence's pleasure, poverty an indication of God's design. The im-
mutable decrees of the Almighty fixed one's station, gave one a
calling, and placed the stamp of approval on worldly success. Here
was an unanswerable support for the economic status quo.

The minister who more than any other devoted his attention to
classical economic thought was Francis Wayland, the Ricardo of
evangelists. As a university president and lecturer on political
economy, Wayland considered himself particularly well equipped
to explore the field of economics. By the 1830's he had achieved
a sufficient reputation to guarantee him an audience for his economic ideas. Furthermore, the path had been propitiously cleared
for him by foreign authorities. The *Political Economy* of Say was
first published in this country in 1824 and his *New Principles of
Political Economy* ten years later. The major works of Adam
Smith, Ricardo, Mill, and Malthus were in circulation by then, and
all that remained for Wayland was to make them meaningful.
His function for America was to translate the classical economic

---

[39] Albert Barnes, *The Rule of Christianity in regard to Conformity to the World*,
p. 39.
[40] Bushnell, *Moral Uses of Dark Things*, pp. 41-42.

ideas into practical, simple terms. He felt that the works of Smith and the others, while they presented economic liberalism accurately, "did not present them in such order as would be most likely to render them serviceable either to the general student, or to the practical merchant." [41]

There was another reason for Wayland's interest in rewriting Ricardo. Following the lead of the British and Scotch religious figures and moralists, Wayland sought to harmonize classical economic thought with traditional religious principles. The Ricardian theory of rent and the Malthusian pessimistic view of population did not fit the American scene. Furthermore, while the wage-fund theory was accepted, its implications had to be played down in a land seething with Jacksonian democratic principles. The result was what Henry F. May calls a "cleansing of political economy" which in the end produced a "clerical laissez faire." [42] Along with the Rev. John McVickar, Henry Vethake, and others, Wayland produced what might be called hybrid classical economics. [43]

The first efforts Wayland made in this direction were taken toward the end of his weighty, pontifical *Elements of Moral Science*, which first came off the presses in 1835 and which by 1853 had gone through several editions. He best illustrated his juggling of moral and economic laws in the application of justice to questions of property which, he thought, was "founded on the will of God." The formula he devised gave to the individual absolute right limited only by the rights of others. "The absolute right of property," he asserted, "is the right to use something in such manner as I choose . . . and it imposes upon every one else the obligation to leave me unmolested in the use of it." [44] As long as the rights of his neighbors were not affected, a man may use his property as he saw fit.

Turning to the acquisition of profit, Wayland concluded that the individual was at liberty to sell at the market price, and hence

---

[41] Wayland, *The Elements of Political Economy*, p. iii.
[42] May, *The Protestant Churches and Industrial America*, pp. 13, 14.
[43] Cf. McVickar, *Outlines of Political Economy*, and Vethake, *Principles of Political Economy*.
[44] Wayland, *Elements of Moral Science*, p. 245.

any profit or loss incurred therein was completely justified. The workings of this law may cause hardship, he admitted, but it was an iron-clad canon touched with godlike blessing. "If property rises in value by the providence of God, while in my neighbor's possession, that rise of value, is as much his, as the property itself." [45] The worst violation of property rights, in his opinion, was that brought about by action of the government:

One man is rendered happy by accumulation, another by benevolence; one by promoting science, another by promoting religion. Each has a right to use what is his own, exactly as he pleases. And if society interferes by directing the manner in which he shall appropriate it, it must be by an act of injustice. It is as great a violation of property, for instance, to interfere with the purpose of the individual in the appropriation of his property for religious purposes, as it is to enact that a farmer shall keep but three cows, or a manufacturer employ but ten workmen.[46]

Wayland's *Elements of Moral Science* was so well received that two years later, in 1837, he was ready to bring out his companion work, *Elements of Political Economy*. It was immediately accepted as the standard work in its field, was used as a textbook in many college political science courses, and after twenty years its circulation had reached 50,000.[47] It was reprinted as late as 1875. Indeed, a metamorphosis occurred in 1878 when the Rev. Aaron L. Chapin, president of Beloit, revised it into a book that lived through eight more editions.

The Baptist minister borrowed heavily from the masters, at times doing little more than paraphrasing Ricardo or Carey. His illustration of division of labor was singularly unoriginal, indicating its operation with reference to pin making. His arguments in favor of free trade also have a Smithean flavor.[48] He approached closest the hard core of economic liberalism in his section on the use of capital. "It is necessary," he declared, "that every man be

[45] *Ibid.*, p. 261.

[46] *Ibid.*, p. 278.

[47] See Gladys Bryson, "The Emergence of the Social Sciences from Moral Philosophy," *International Journal of Ethics*, XLII, No. 3 (1932), 311.

[48] For Wayland's translation of Ricardo's iron law of wages, see Wayland, *The Elements of Political Economy*, pp. 126-129. For the pin-factory illustration, see pp. 76-77, and for his strongest free trade arguments, see pp. 92-93.

allowed to gain all that he can." [49] The individual's self-interest was also glorified:

Every man is more interested in his own success, than any other man can be interested in it. Hence, every man is likely to ascertain more accurately in what manner he can best employ his capital, than any other man can ascertain it for him. If every man, therefore, be allowed to invest his capital as he will, the whole capital of a country will be more profitably invested, than under any other circumstances whatsoever.[50]

Wayland's insistence on a moral-flavored economic liberalism was no better illustrated than in two addresses he made in 1837, which were published under the title *The Moral Law of Accumulation*. The commercial depression of that year, with the grave economic questions it raised, incited the Brown educator to consider the issue of amassing wealth and its implications for society. The panic of 1837 meant to the Baptist leader that some law of God had been violated. Casting about for a reason for this "memorable commercial catastrophe," he blamed the "moral tempers" of men.[51] He believed the entire community had been pervaded by an "excessive avidity for the rapid accumulation of property." Wayland did not denounce the desire for profit or the normal drive to amass property but he recommended that a limit be put to the gratification of such desires. Wealth should be recompense for doing something useful. "God intends that man should grow rich by adding something to the means of human happiness, and, just in proportion to the amount which we ourselves have added, is the amount of our lawful gain." [52]

The bulk of his discourse consisted of an attack against speculation which, he affirmed, was corrupting and constituted no real addition to the wealth of society. Indeed, the activities of speculators were wasteful to society and should be curbed. Furthermore, it was contrary to God's commands and could only bring disappointment and loss to those who broke the moral law of accumulation.

49 *Ibid.*, p. 111.
50 *Ibid.*, p. 117.
51 Wayland, *The Moral Law of Accumulation*, p. 8.
52 *Ibid.*, pp. 9, 10.

At every point in his argument Wayland took pains to indicate that he was not denying that a man may do with his property what he chose, nor that an individual knew best his own economic interest. They were, after all, cornerstones of classical economics. But while he adhered to laissez faire doctrines, the New England Baptist also believed in the ideas of stewardship. Like Finney, he felt that property was a gift of God and that man had to give an account of his wealth as well as the rest of his talents. Wealth "is not bestowed upon us, for our gratification, but as a means of rendering us happy, through the happiness which we bestow upon others." [53] Man has the right to do with his wealth that which he likes, but he is accountable to God.

Wayland's solutions to the problem of removing excessive speculation and restoring business prosperity were varied. First of all, everyone should pay his debts. With what Wayland did not say. Second, he urged his readers to cultivate "a spirit of mutual conciliation and forebearance." [54] Restore trust, friendship, and optimism where now only distrust and pessimism prevail. Third, everyone should produce more and consume less. By this means frivolous, useless expenditures would be done away with and expenses for necessities cut as much as possible. The question of who would buy the extra goods produced he failed to answer. Next, he suggested that every young person add to the income of the family. Where their jobs would come from did not seem to perturb him. Currency must be kept sound. Confidence in the country's banks must be restored. Mutual trust between the government and the electorate must once again exist. Wayland left no doubt about his dislike of Jacksonian democracy. More money should be devoted to education, he felt, so that the moral laws of economics would be learned and understood. Finally, he asserted, "the present crisis seems to render humiliation before God the appropriate moral temper for the whole community." [55] Fortunately, the nation

[53] *Ibid.*, p. 19.
[54] *Ibid.*, p. 25.
[55] *Ibid.*, p. 34.

managed to recover from the panic of 1837 without following all of Wayland's suggestions.

Francis Wayland also symbolized the clerical attitude in heralding industrialization. To many Northern evangelists the industrial revolution was another unfolding of God's plan for the human race. Bushnell called the new era the "Age of Roads" and exultantly asked who could doubt that the new epoch "has some holy purpose of God fulfilling, in its social revolution, which connects with the coming reign of Christ on earth." [56] The blessings that industrialization brought to Protestant America gave additional proof, if it were needed, that there was a divine governance of the world. Wayland expressed it in these terms:

> Our forging and planing, our spinning and weaving, our mowing and reaping, and threshing, our transportation . . . is now all done by machinery, and generally driven by steam. . . . A week since, I was passing through a cotton mill, and observed a young girl of ten or twelve years of age, attending upon five looms, and while doing what was formerly the work of ten men, she walked to and fro with an air of easy independence, which a lady at a reception might be well pleased to emulate. . . .
>
> God is thus lifting off from us that oppressive severity of toil which paralyzes intellect and benumbs the power of emotion.[57]

Evangelists had good reason initially to proclaim the advent of industrialization. Although in the long run an industrial society was less receptive to the Finneyite brand of religion than a commercial-agrarian one, nevertheless, in its first stages industrialization tended to aid the evangelist in his work. For one thing, it made available the leisure time of church women who could attend meetings, join societies, and work for moral reform. For another, it produced a surplus capital which could be siphoned off for benevolent ventures. Third, it produced a class of downtrodden that could be used by evangelists to illustrate the blessings of God's mercy and the operation of the moral law. Without industrialization the sustained revivalism of the early nineteenth century would have been improbable.

---

[56] Bushnell, *Work and Play*, pp. 434-435.
[57] Wayland, *The Education Demanded by the People of the United States*, p. 15.

Ministers recognized that this new age was bringing untold blessings to mankind, not the least of which was the opportunity it
afforded the industrial worker to improve his condition.   Here
curiously enough the "dismal science" of the old world gave way
before an unlimited clerical optimism.   In their opinion, industrialization meant greater production, a higher standard of living,
a happier laboring class, a more devout nation.   Under industrialization, it was maintained, "the laboring classes will be able to live
in comparative leisure and elegance, and find ample time for self-
improvement." [58]   A diligent laborer could acquire an education
and by virtuous, frugal living rise through the ranks.   It was the
American dream with the church's blessing.

The Northern evangelists were quick to recognize the potential
importance of the factory system in American society.   The factory could be an agent of great good to man if its workers and
owners were converted, or it could be a serious threat to Protestantism if it flourished without divine guidance.   As early as 1826
evangelists took notice of the factory as a source of supply for
conversions and in isolated instances invaded them, stopping their
operations and holding revival meetings.   At times their visits
were upon invitation of the owners and their preaching within the
factory walls was a bolstering of the capitalist system.[59]   "I
preached at Onei.[da] Factory last week," wrote Herman Norton,
one of Finney's lieutenants from Whitesboro, "a great commotion
there during the day to know what should be done.   Some wished
to be released from the Factory that day but God did not grant
the desires of the wicked.   I conversed with those uneasy ones." [60]

The facilities the factory afforded for assembling large numbers
of persons under one roof were not overlooked by the itinerant
preachers.   Especially in areas where church buildings were small
or where there were no churches at all, revivalists looked on factories as serving a religious as well as a secular purpose.   Finney,
Knapp, and Jabez Swan all utilized factory buildings whenever

---

[58] Bushnell, *A Discourse on the Moral Tendencies of Human History,* p. 29.
[59] See Loud, *Evangelized America,* p. 218.
[60] Herman Norton to Finney, April 30, 1827 (Finney Papers).

the opportunity presented itself.   Lewis Tappan recorded attendance at a factory service in 1826.   "We attended publick worship
in the second story of the new part of the Woolen Factory," he
wrote in his diary.   "The apartment was well filled." [61]

Religious services were a common practice in some mills.   It was
Nathaniel S. S. Beman's job as leading Finneyite evangelist in Troy
to secure a minister for the local establishment.   "We wish a
minister at the *Cotton Factory* and its neighborhood," Beman
wrote Finney, "and if he will come up on trial for two or three
weeks, there is but little doubt he may find work for the winter.
The Lord seems to be moving on the minds of the people in the
neighborhood of the Factory." [62]

Sometimes the spread of religious feeling interrupted production.
One of Beman's converts was so filled with a missionary zeal that
in the middle of the week she "felt constrained," as she put it, "to
converse with the females in the factory in her apartment and
those adjoining."   She was so successful in her efforts that when
the overseer returned he found "two or three rooms deserted" and
a little revival meeting going on instead.   "In less than an hour
both factories were stopped." [63]   They stayed closed the following
day, while a religious service kept the workers assembled until
eleven at night.   Jacob Knapp encountered a similar experience in
Lowell when his revival there assumed such proportions that "in
one of the cotton mills the superintendent, who was a Universalist,
found it necessary to stop operations.   The operators were nearly
all on their knees.   In fact, the entire factory was an anxious
room." [64]

The man who had most spectacular success in factory revivals
was Charles G. Finney.   In his *Memoirs* he boasted about his
effectiveness among young factory workers.   While visiting one
plant near Utica his presence so agitated a young girl that she could
not work.   Finney seized the opportunity and in an instant "nearly
all in the room were in tears."

[61] Lewis Tappan Diary, Nov. 19, 1826, p. 82 (Lewis Tappan Papers).
[62] Nathaniel S. S. Beman to Finney, Oct. 23, 1829 (Finney Papers).
[63] J. P. Cushman to Finney, Feb. 21, 1828 (Finney Papers).
[64] Knapp, *Autobiography*, p. 138.

The owner of the establishment was present and seeing the state of things, he said to the superintendent, "Stop the mill, and let the people attend to religion; for it is more important that our souls should be saved than that the factory run." The gate was immediately shut down, and the factory stopped; but where should we assemble? The superintendent suggested that the mule room was large; and, the mules being run up, we could assemble there. We did so, and a more powerful meeting I scarcely ever attended. It went on with great power . . . and in the course of a few days nearly all in the mill were hopefully converted.[65]

The recognition of the factory's growing importance led the evangelists to make a strong many-sided appeal to the industrial proletariat upon whom they stumbled on their visits to mills and foundries. Finney received support from the mercantile classes but in his preaching he emphasized his appeal to the poor. As he put it, "Among farmers and mechanics, and other classes of men, I borrowed my illustrations from their various occupations. . . . I addressed them in the language of the common people. . . . This was what we aimed to accomplish, to preach the Gospel especially to the poor." [66] Later in his career, this concern for the proletariat was still strong. "I ardently wish with you," wrote Lewis Tappan, "that the poor that have come to California could be brought under the influence of religion of Christ." [67] Justin Edwards was hardly plebian, but in 1844 at public meetings in Boston and New York he spoke "on the importance of the Sabbath to the laboring classes of the community." [68]

Although most ministers expressed anxiety for the position of the worker in society and for his low standard of living, they were reluctant to endorse specific proposals for alleviating their conditions. Their opposition to poor relief, for example, while it was logical in the light of their acceptance of economic liberalism, ran curiously counter to many of their preachments to the lower classes. Lyman Beecher, in an address on the subject of poor relief, recommended the addition of work houses to the system to render

[65] Finney, *Memoirs*, pp. 183-184.
[66] *Ibid.*, pp. 81, 324.
[67] Lewis Tappan to Finney, Jan. 26, 1864, Lewis Tappan Letterbook (Tappan Papers).
[68] Justin Edwards to Edward C. Delavan (n.d.), in Hallock, *Light and Love, a Sketch of the Life and Labors of the Rev. Justin Edwards*, p. 473.

effective penalties to those who were always in need of charity. He thought that the unemployed, who he assumed were idle of their own volition, "ought to be taken by the strong hand of law to the work-house, and made to earn their own support, and to aid in the support of their families." [69]   He also thought there was a close causal relationship between intemperance and poverty.

Francis Wayland was even more outspoken in his dislike of unlimited poor relief. He was concerned lest charity destroy the self-respect of the poor and was a primary mover in the conception of the Providence Aid Society, an organization which set about to supply work to the destitute. He objected to more generous types of charity because, for one thing, they tended to destroy property. In his textbook *The Elements of Political Economy* (1837) he listed poor relief along with other threats to the capitalist system, for, like common land or governmental restrictions, they tended to tap surplus funds and were, he believed, generally prejudicial to the best interest of society. Besides, he was certain that relief tended to foster indolence just as community of property encouraged laziness and kept a country poor. He also thought charity was contrary to moral law, removed from men the fear of want, decreased man's independence, and encouraged insubordination.[70]

By and large, the evangelists took the position that while they favored helping the proletariat improve his moral, social, and economic position, they opposed specific gains that labor itself attempted to achieve. As long as improvement was a general term, they approved. When the impetus to reform was channelized in a particular direction, that is, poor relief, a ten or eight-hour law, factory legislation, and the like, they disapproved. Even Horace Bushnell, symbolizing the middle period's equivalent for a social gospel, objected violently to such specific measures as laws limiting the hours of labor. Glorifying the past in the *Age of Homespun*, he wrote,

I hope . . . I have made some just impression on you all of the dignity of work. How great an honor it is for the times gone by, that when so

69 Lyman Beecher, *Autobiography*, I, 347.
70 Wayland, *The Elements of Political Economy*, pp. 123-124.

many schemes are on foot, as now, to raise the weak; when the friends of
the dejected classes of the world are proposing even to reorganize society
itself for their benefit, trying to humanize punishments, to kindle hope in
disability, and nurse depravity into a condition of comfort—a distinction
how magnificent! that our fathers and mothers of the century past had,
in truth, no dejected classes, no disability, only here and there a drone of
idleness, or a sporadic case of vice and poverty.[71]

Later, in recalling the days of his youth, he declared,

There is nothing in those early days that I remember with more zest than
that I did the full work of a man for at least five years before the manly
age,—this too, under no eight-hour law of protective delicacy, but holding fast the astronomical ordinance in the service of from thirteen to
fourteen hours.[72]

Charles Finney heartily approved an article written by one of his
Chatham Street Chapel converts in New York, S. T. Spears, who
maintained that the eight-hour law was "physiologically, economically and socially stupid to the last degree, working evil, only
evil, and that continuously." [73] Nor did the drive to limit child
labor gain the evangelist's support. Even Lyman Beecher who in
his *Means of National Prosperity* enunciated a number of mildly
radical ideas, asserted toward the end of this work that "it is indispensable that children be early accustomed to profitable industry." [74]

Later, when equality of the sexes in respect to wages and hours
was an issue, the evangelists again opposed the specific reforms advocated. "It is nothing that they can not get as high wages as
men," declared Horace Bushnell, "when they can not do as much,
or do it as well." He was among those who believed "there is
no such possibility as a legally appointed rate of wages; market
price is the only scale of earning possible for women as for men." [75]

[71] Bushnell, "The Age of Homespun" in *Litchfield County Centennial Celebration,
1851*, pp. 128-129.

[72] Quoted in Edwin D. Mead, *Horace Bushnell, The Citizen*, p. 4.

[73] S. T. Spears to Finney, Dec. 14, 1874 (Finney Papers). Spears was a medical
student who after conversion became a minister. He later had editorial connections
with *The Independent*.

[74] Lyman Beecher, *The Means of National Prosperity*, p. 24.

[75] Bushnell, *Women's Suffrage: the Reform against Nature*, pp. 11, 12.

Labor unions received unqualified opposition from these men. They were secular organizations operating for the advancement of secular interests and for a particular class. They channeled the worker's energies away from his primary job, producing goods, and incidentally from more devout pursuits. And they were more often than not, the evangelists believed, merely tools in the hands of "turbulent and selfish agitators." Francis Wayland sounded the keynote of evangelistic opposition to unions.

What is a Trades Union, but a voluntary association. Its avowed object is, to protect the laborer from the oppression of the capitalist. Now this object by itself, supposing the danger really to exist, would seem virtuous and honorable. . . . But who does not know, that this associated interference, by which a power of redress is created, unknown to the laws, and by which, in order to carry its purposes into effect, the rights of individuals have been remorselessly trampled upon, has wrought the most grievous mischiefs both to capitalist and to labor? [76]

Strikes, as the principal weapon of labor unions, were anathema. They were unwarranted efforts to improve one group's position at the expense of another. They were also, in a sense, acts of violence to which ministers as lovers of peace and harmony were opposed. Besides, the purpose behind most strikes, a raise in wages, was, according to clerical laissez-faire thought, economically unsound and theoretically impossible in the long run if natural law was to be followed.

There is little evidence that the evangelists were aware of the contradictions in their economic ideas. One hesitates to impute to men of obvious sincerity any hypocrisy in their concern, on the one hand, with the problems of the proletariat and their reluctance to support solutions to those problems, on the other. If any explanation serves to fathom the puzzling gap between word and deed and thought and action, it is to be found in the religiosity of these men. Religion was their life, their hope, their means of support. Every issue was translated into religious terms. Every problem was to be solved on religious grounds. In the final analysis, economic theories had to be keyed to a moralistic octave. Production, consumption, and distribution were secondary to salvation. A man's station in

[76] Wayland, *Limitations of Human Responsibility*, p. 105.

life, his recompense, and his hopes for improvement were to be subordinated to his relationship to God. Wealth and poverty were conditions less important in the minds of these men than salvation and damnation. They could not, therefore, be aroused too greatly by the hardships of the industrial worker. After all, as Bushnell explained it, "it is only religion, the great bond of love and duty to God, that makes our existence valuable or even tolerable." [77]

With a few outstanding exceptions, the evangelists were not good businessmen. Their salaries were usually small; their families were unusually large. Their habit of depending upon aid from principal laymen might have been token of their sublime faith, but it resulted in poor management. Their excursions into business or real estate often resulted in disaster. Daniel Baker attempted speculation in Western lands but the outcome "disgusted him for ever with such things." [78] Maffitt hated "the dull, insipid path of merchandise or trade" and longed as a youth to be free from the trammels of his business. Twice within five years he went bankrupt and "was struck with wonder and amazement" to discover all his property lost. His only explanation of inability in business was "Strange fatality!" [79] Lyman Beecher experienced great difficulty in balancing his accounts, and Finney, shortly after moving to Oberlin, was delinquent in his taxes for two successive years. Joshua Leavitt complained of his financial insecurity in almost every letter he ever wrote.

Part of their financial difficulty stemmed from the evangelists' own conception of their job. Justin Edwards, for instance, scrupulously refrained from all business ventures which, he thought, were inconsistent with the duties of his calling. The public expected its ministers to be paragons of poverty. As Lewis Tappan put it, "Our minister should set an example worthy of imitation in this day. Don't be afraid of meanness." [80] Finney summed up the clerical attitude toward economic activities when he wrote,

[77] Bushnell, *Sermons for the New Life*, p. 221.
[78] Baker, *The Life and Labors of the Rev. Daniel Baker*, p. 198.
[79] Maffitt, *Tears of Contrition*, pp. 121, 158, 201-202.
[80] Lewis Tappan to Finney, June 28, 1832 (Finney Papers).

"In short, do nothing, be nothing, buy nothing, sell nothing, possess nothing . . . but in a spirit of entire devotion to God." [81]

Of all the conclusions one may draw from the economic ideas and activities of these evangelists, three are especially worthy of mention. First, men such as Wayland and Finney assumed that there were economic laws just as rigid as the laws of God and that tampering with them was immoral as well as economically improper. Fixing a pseudo divinity on laws of supply and demand forced these men to oppose any attempt to break, circumvent, or question these laws. Second, in spite of an avowed concern for the lower classes, the evangelists neglected to give the proletariat a working faith. Although they could have provided leadership for the lower classes, they were not really interested in the problems of laborers and their message contained a moral solution rather than an economic one. Finally, they lulled the upper classes into an economic self-complacency and gave respectability to their activities. By so doing they failed to work, at a time in history when they were most effective, a positive secular reform which could have gone hand in hand with their hoped-for moral one.

[81] Finney, "How to Prevent Our Employment from Injuring Our Souls," *The Oberlin Evangelist*, I, No. 24 (1839), 186.

VII.   THE SLAVERY QUESTION

The abolition of slavery in the U. S. will be brought about by the agency of Christians. Depend on this.[1]

We regard it, as a well settled principle of both common and constitutional law, that no human legislation can annul, or set aside, the law or authority of God.[2]

THE ANTISLAVERY CRUSADE has been a popular theme for American historians.   Down through the decades since the Civil War, this multifaceted subject has been studied and explained to each succeeding generation.   Who is not familiar with the sorrowful story of slavery's establishment on American shores, of the rise of a sentiment in opposition to the institution, of the steps taken to exclude slavery from the territories?   Who has not traced the varied efforts of the Garrisons, Birneys, Channings, Parkers, and Welds as they worked in their separate ways to solve the slavery question?   Who has not transported himself to the halls of Congress to watch John Quincy Adams stubbornly stand his ground on the petition issue or to hear re-echoing through time Webster's seventh of March speech?   The Missouri Compromise, Prudence Crandall, Nat Turner, the Sims affair, Dred Scott, and Sumter are words each schoolboy knows.

This subject has had its quota of conflicting interpretations. Eminent scholars, such as Jesse Macy, Ralph V. Harlow, and Henry Steele Commager, have focused their attention on one figure or another in the slavery controversy.[3]   Gilbert H. Barnes, rejecting the narrow range of a study of one man, traced the religious origins of the antislavery impulse and told its story mainly in terms of

---

[1] Lewis Tappan to Benjamin Tappan, May 1, 1835 (Benjamin Tappan Papers).

[2] Charles G. Finney, quoted in *Report of the Fourth Anniversary of the Ohio Antislavery Society*, p. 16.

[3] Macy, *The Anti-slavery Crusade*, tells the story in terms of William Lloyd Garrison's career; Harlow, *Gerrit Smith, Philanthropist and Reformer*, and Commager, *Life of Theodore Parker*, study the movement from different ground.

the work of the various societies set up in the 1830's to further the abolitionist cause.[4]   One school of thought, led by Dwight L. Dumond, in restudying the movement, has applauded the work of Northern abolitionist agitators, while a second school, represented by men such as Arthur Young Lloyd, has taken a Southern defense.[5]   More recently, another group, of whom Avery Craven is a member, has looked upon the Civil War as the result chiefly of the work done by the "fanatics" on both sides who forced the issue into armed conflict.[6]

By restricting their focus to prominent figures and to the work done by the major organized societies, however, many of these historians distorted the picture of the nature of the antislavery movement in general.   Some attention must also be paid to those lesser known individuals who, though not always members of antislavery associations, leaders of Congress, or political pamphleteers, nevertheless contributed in no small way to the crystallization of a nation-wide sentiment concerning slavery and its place in American society.   It is in this respect that the part played by evangelists in the liberation of the slave can be considered.

Studying the religious elements in the movement has its merits. The works of Barnes and Dumond have amply indicated that the antislavery campaign was an appeal to the consciences of men to reform their society and that this appeal received heartiest, most sympathetic acceptance in the areas ravaged by Finneyite revivals. While it had religious elements and while religious leaders were its most outspoken proponents, we must not conclude that it was primarily or exclusively a church crusade.   It was rather, as James G. Randall has pointed out, a movement apart from the normal church activities, and church figures can be found on both sides of the controversy.[7]

---

[4] Gilbert H. Barnes, *The Antislavery Impulse, 1830-1844.*
[5] Dumond, *Anti-slavery Origins of the Civil War in the United States*; Lloyd, *The Slavery Controversy, 1831-1860.*
[6] Craven, *The Coming of the Civil War.*
[7] See Randall, *Civil War and Reconstruction*, p. 105; Lyons, "Religious Defense of Slavery in the North," *Historical Papers, Trinity College Historical Society.*

This interpretation is by no means a new one. As early as 1888, Dorchester in his history of American religion spoke of the crusade as having emerged from the religious sentiment of the churches and pointed out, for instance, that all twelve persons who organized the New England Anti-slavery Society in 1832 were members of evangelical churches.[8] Even earlier, Philemon Fowler, religious historian, concluded that the crusade formed a principal chapter in the development of Presbyterianism in central New York. It was in Oneida County, heart of the new revivals, that the strongest abolitionist conviction was found.[9]

During the ante-bellum period itself there was ample evidence of the religious nature of the antislavery drive. As Charles Whipple put it in one of his innumerable tracts, "The Anti-Slavery movement . . . was at its commencement, and has ever since been, thoroughly and emphatically a religious enterprise." [10] Calvin Colton, partisan though he was, summed up this coincidence of religious endeavor and the freeing of the slaves in his work *Political Abolition* (1844):

Men, making the highest religious pretensions, have taken lead, and are at the head of the movement; numerous religious papers are employed to advocate it; a large corps of religious missionaries are in the field to preach it; numerous churches and pulpits are chiefly devoted to it. . . . Nearly all the political Abolitionists, and with scarcely an exception, all the abolition preachers, lecturers, and missionaries, are religious men. It is, indeed, a proper religious enterprise.[11]

Even Webster admitted that hostility to slavery "was born in the religion of his constituents," and Lewis Tappan, fighting on the firing line throughout the encounter, observed, "It is true a portion of the Methodists are out against the abolition cause. But in New England large portions of that denomination are in favor of it.

[8] Dorchester, *Christianity in the United States*, p. 455.
[9] Fowler, *Historical Sketch of Presbyterianism within the Bounds of the Synod of Central New York*, pp. 154, 160.
[10] Whipple, *Relations of Anti-slavery to Religion*, p. 1.
[11] Colton, *Political Abolition*, p. 13.

. . . The largest part of abolitionists are christians—men devotedly pious." [12]

Many antislavery leaders were closely identified with the Great Revival. The methods used were revivalistic, and the doctrine preached focused on the sinfulness of the institution. The new measures were easily adapted to the new reform. The fanaticism of the reformer which Marryat observed and Harriet Martineau commended was typical of the religious zealot. Revivalistic lectures were a popular form of winning followers and made much more forceful impressions than pamphlets. Personal persuasion, which the evangelist had utilized in reaping souls, was taken over by the antislavery reformers. Indeed, even hymns had their part to play in the conversion to abolitionism.[13] Finally, it was in the rural towns and countryside where revivals were most frequent that the antislavery societies flourished.

Perhaps the most illuminating connection between religion and antislavery is revealed in the operation of the tract and cent societies. The tract societies were originally set up to disseminate the Gospel. Gradually temporal reforms became the subject of pamphlets distributed by the groups until finally the slavery issue was more important in its operations than the books of the Bible. The Rev. George B. Cheever, rabid abolitionist, paid high tribute to the activities of the tract societies in whipping up antislavery feeling in his New York church. "The conflict here against slavery, and all other sin, waxes hotter in consequence of the preaching of the Tract Society. We will strike up the 44th Psalm, and set forward in another campaign, depending not on man, nor man's sneaking management, but on God." [14]

Similarly, in the cent societies a religious and benevolent organization was turned into an antislavery force. Cent societies, originating as missionary groups, were formed in churches by women

[12] Addison, *The Clergy in American Life and Letters*, p. 34; Lewis Tappan to Benjamin Tappan, Nov. 13, 1835 (Benjamin Tappan Papers).

[13] For one of the popular abolition hymns, see Siebert, *The Underground Railroad from Slavery to Freedom*, p. 90.

[14] George B. Cheever to Finney, May 24, 1858 (Finney Papers).

devoted to the abolition cause. Their object was to solicit members of the congregation and obtain pledges from those who would contribute a cent a week for the movement. The societies had only one officer, a treasurer, who besides collecting the funds had to provide the meetings of the groups with "interesting information" and help distribute antislavery tracts and papers.[15] This way, it was felt, the subject of slavery could be brought to the attention of the individual periodically and at the same time habits of economy and systematic benevolence could be promoted.

In the interests of efficiency, the collectors in cent societies were usually all members of the same Sunday School or congregation so that meetings could be announced and attended with little difficulty. In some societies whole families were enrolled on the cent a week plan. "It is almost a matter of course, in religious families, to enter the name of each child, as a contributor, from its birth. . . . The associations are usually connected with a church, and have their meetings in some room connected with it." [16] This type of organization, which was copied from England, could not raise much money in behalf of abolition but the support it crystallized among the religious rank and file was important. In one Massachusetts church, $271.05 was raised in one year.[17] The attention those pennies brought to the slavery question is incalculable.

Another way in which the religious character of the antislavery crusade can be traced is in the incidence of ministers among those who pled its cause. The tradition of ministerial responsibility for antislavery agitation was well rooted. John Woolman, Charles Osborn, John Wesley, and others set a high standard for the nineteenth century to follow. Wesley's last letter was an antislavery paean. For one thing, a large number of the agents who toured the country preaching against slavery came from the ministry. Some forty-three of the fifty-six agents employed by the American Anti-slavery Society prior to 1837 were clergymen. In that year A. A. Phelps observed that two thirds of the Methodist and

15 Southard, *Why Work for the Slave?*, inside front cover.
16 *Ibid.*, back cover.
17 *Right and Wrong in Massachusetts*, p. 120.

Baptist ministers in Massachusetts were members of antislavery societies, while one out of every three orthodox pastors had joined the cause.[18]

Similar figures were advanced by Dorchester to point up this ministerial participation. He asserted that one third of those in the American Anti-slavery Society and its auxiliaries were ministers, while more than half of the others were church communicants, and he concluded that the clergy and their church followers constituted seven eighths of the working force in the crusade.[19] Many were the appeals made to ministers to enlist in the fight to free the slave. "I charge you, affectionately yet solemnly," wrote one minister to his colleagues, "plead the cause of the oppressed. . . . Enlist the church in the cause of holy freedom." [20]

But while many responded, other ministers defended slavery on religious, political, or economic grounds. Indeed, just as strong a case may be made for the argument that if ministers were the most outspoken champions of abolition they were also the staunchest defenders of bondage. The "South-side" view was preached in leading pulpits, and even some of the benevolent institutions, nurtured by revivalism, hesitated to join the antislavery forces.[21] Although she was hardly objective in her views, Harriet Martineau described the picture fairly accurately when she observed, "the most guilty class of the community in regard to the slavery question at present is, not the slave-holding, nor even the mercantile, but the clerical." [22]

In their slavery views, the Northern evangelists varied greatly, ranging from the fiercest of fire-eaters to the most cautious of conservatives. Indeed, almost each one had his own approach to the problem. While many modified their positions in the face of changing events, some were contradictory in their attitudes. Illus-

---

[18] *The True History of the Late Division in the Anti-slavery Societies*, p. 34 n.; *The Liberator*, Nov. 3, 1837.

[19] Dorchester, *Christianity in the United States*, pp. 460-469.

[20] *The Relation of the Pulpit to Slavery*, p. 1

[21] See Mears, *Life of Edward Norris Kirk*, p. 247.

[22] Martineau, *Society in America*, II, 356.

trative of the latter was Lyman Beecher's stand in the famous Lane Debate, religious landmark of the antislavery movement.

Lane Theological Seminary at-Cincinnati had among its student body a number of devout, serious-minded, would-be evangelists to whom the slavery question, like original sin or pastoral theology, was a matter of academic interest and worthy of discussion at an educational institution. Some of its students were Southerners, seven were sons of slaveholders, and one had been a slave himself. Only a few were avowed abolitionists. It seemed appropriate to these theological students in 1833 to discuss openly the merits of the colonization and abolition proposals.[23]

Two questions were debated, each for nine evenings. First, "Ought the people of the Slaveholding States to abolish slavery immediately?" Second, "Are the doctrines, tendencies, and measures of the American Colonization Society, and the influence of its principal supporters, such as render it worthy of the patronage of the Christian public?"[24] The faculty and trustees, fearing the effect such a discussion would have on the seminary, strongly advised indefinite postponement of the debate. The students resolved to go ahead; the debate was held; and at the end of the sessions all but four or five voted in the affirmative on the first question and all but one in the negative on the second. An antislavery society was immediately organized and the students set about to improve conditions of Negroes in Cincinnati, opening schools, Sunday Schools, and Bible classes.[25]

Lyman Beecher tried to caution his enthusiastic crusaders. He considered himself both a colonizationist and an abolitionist without perceiving any inconsistency. He claimed that he was op-

[23] The most detailed report of the debate and of the students' withdrawal in the face of faculty pressure is found in *Debate at the Lane Seminary*. A shorter account, more critical of Beecher's role in the proceedings, occurs in Gilbert H. Barnes, *The Antislavery Impulse*, pp. 72-78. For Beecher's side of the story, see Lyman Beecher, *Autobiography*, II, 320ff. See also Martineau, *Society in America*, II, 371-373.

[24] Henry B. Stanton to Joshua Leavitt, March 10, 1834, quoted in *Debate at the Lane Seminary*, p. 3.

[25] "We have formed a large and efficient organization for elevating the colored people in Cincinnati." Theodore Weld to Arthur Tappan, April 12, 1833, quoted in Lyman Beecher, *Autobiography*, II, 324.

posed to slavery, but that it existed and, he felt, there was nothing he could do to remove it. "You are taking just the course to defeat your own objects," he told Theodore Weld, one of his more ardent students. "If you want to teach colored schools I can fill your pockets with money; but if you will visit in colored families, and walk with them in the streets, you will be overwhelmed." [26] Thereupon the Lane president left for the East for the summer anticipating no serious consequences. On August 20th, however, the trustees prohibited societies in the seminary as well as public meetings and discussions among students. A storm of protest broke immediately. The students, almost to a man, withdrew, and the enterprising leaders of Oberlin, recently opened, invited them to their campus, where a more progressive attitude toward the Negro and abolition was practiced. Reaction against the trustee's decree spread throughout Northern abolitionist ranks.

The place of the Lane Debate in the history of antislavery cannot be minimized. The discussions dramatized the abolitionist cause, indicated the logical forcefulness of their arguments, and showed the futility of a defense of the "peculiar institution." It showed the close connection between Finney's Great Revival and the coming of the Civil War. Indeed, Beecher himself gave witness to the relationship between evangelism and the antislavery battle. Abolitionists, he declared, were "the offspring of the Oneida denunciatory revivals." [27]

Beecher was nowhere more the reluctant radical than in his antislavery views. In terms of what he preached it would have been logical for him to turn against slavery, just as he denounced dueling or intemperance. So thought Garrison, who called for Beecher's help in founding a society to fight the institution. Lyman's reply could not have been more blunt. "I have too many irons in the fire already. . . . Your zeal is commendable; but you are misguided. If you will give up your fanatical notions and be guided by us [the clergy] we will make you the Wilberforce of

[26] *Ibid.*, II, 323.
[27] Lyman Beecher to William Beecher, July 15, 1835, in Lyman Beecher, *Autobiography*, II, 345.

America." [28]   If America needed a Wilberforce, Garrison was hardly the candidate!

Beecher lacked the stamina of a Weld or the conviction of a Garrison. He called ardent abolitionists "he-goat men who think they do God service by butting everything in the line of their march." [29]   In 1838 he summed up his attitude in these words: "I regard the whole Abolition movement, under its most influential leaders, with its distinctive maxims and modes of feeling, and also the whole temper, principles and action of the South in the justification of slavery, as a singular instance of infatuation permitted by Heaven for purposes of national retribution." [30]

Strikingly different was the attitude of Albert Barnes. Early in his career he supported the Colonization Society. In an address on slavery in 1827 he asked his audience not to interfere with the rights of slaveholders but to "aid your fellow freemen to go to the land of their fathers, and to find a grave in their own native land." [31]   In the 1830's he joined the many others who, disillusioned with its operations, castigated the Colonization Society. For twenty years he served as a pamphleteer for the cause and as late as 1850 was still supplying Lewis Tappan with antislavery material. [32]   His major works in this field were *An Inquiry into the Scriptural Views of Slavery*, published in 1846, which ran through a number of editions, and *The Church and Slavery*, published in 1856. The former refuted the scriptural defense of slavery. Barnes maintained that the institution had no defense nor was Christianity designed to uphold and protect it. All that was needed to abolish it was the action of the Christian church. As he put it in a short piece called "Slavery Unchristian,"

There is not vital energy enough; there is not power of numbers and influence enough out of the church to sustain slavery. . . . Not a blow

[28] Lyman Beecher to William Lloyd Garrison (n.d), quoted in Johnson, *William Lloyd Garrison and His Times*, pp. 44-45.
[29] Lyman Beecher to William Beecher, July 15, 1835, in Lyman Beecher, *Autobiography*, II, 345.
[30] Quoted in Charles E. and Lyman B. Stowe, *Harriet Beecher Stowe*, p. 140.
[31] Barnes, *An Address, Delivered . . . at the Presbyterian Church at Morristown*, p. 29.
[32] Albert Barnes to Lewis Tappan, Jan. 25, 1850 (Lewis Tappan Papers).

need be struck. . . . All that is needful is, for each Christian man, and for
every Christian church . . . to free themselves from all connections with
the evil . . . and the work will be done.[33]

Throughout his writings, but particularly in *The Church and
Slavery*, Barnes called for discussion of the subject in the churches
and for agitation to free the slave.   It was not merely a political
subject to him but a moral one as well.   Barnes wanted slavery
treated like every other sin.   To remove it from the realm of politics, he believed, would permit the issue to be considered in proper
perspective, free from the embroilments of political prestige and
free from the diplomatic undercurrents of sectional jealousies.

Such a treatment required, in Barnes's opinion, the work of an
individual rather than the society.   It demanded a less hysterical
approach than that of a Garrison, a Birney, or a Gerrit Smith.   It
minimized legislation, avoided open controversy, and condemned
violent action.   As he saw it,

By prayer, by patience, by exhortation, by testimony, by the exercise of
charity and forbearance mingled with christian fidelity, by a growing
conviction of the evil, by free discussion, by a deeper spirit of piety, the
work may be done,—done by each denomination for itself; done by each
family for itself; done by each individual for himself.[34]

Barnes interpreted his role to be exhorting when the occasion
arose, writing for an audience already converted.   To him, slavery's
overthrow was a simple matter if the churches would take action.
Few, however, followed Barnes's solution of a quiet, patient "detachment" from the institution.   Indeed, a lack of detachment
was more characteristic of the ante-bellum American.[35]

Joshua Leavitt's contributions to the cause were many and
varied.   He did yeoman service preaching abolition in the columns
of *The Evangelist*, *The Emancipator*, and after 1848 *The Independent*.   He wrote and lectured on its behalf, electioneered during
presidential campaigns, attended political conventions, lobbied in

---

[33] Quoted in Thome, *Prayer for the Oppressed*, p. 3.

[34] Albert Barnes, *The Church and Slavery*, pp. 166-167.   Horace Bushnell held a
similar view of antislavery societies.   For his position, see "Horace Bushnell and the
Slavery Question," *New England Quarterly*, XXIII, No. 1 (1950), 19-30.

[35] For his other antislavery sentiments, see Albert Barnes, *The Casting Down of
Thrones*, *The Love of Country*, and *The Conditions of Peace*.

Washington, and, in general, dedicated a sizable portion of his energies to freeing the slaves. He was considered by Theodore Weld as the most important member of the American Anti-slavery Society's executive committee.[36]

Leavitt belonged to the moderate faction of the antislavery group which in 1839 broke away from the more radical Garrisonian wing. Joshua believed that the institution could be done away with through the Constitution. He early turned to political action to accomplish abolition and was an enthusiastic devotee of the Liberty and Free Soil parties. An ardent free trader, he even tried to get fellow abolitionists interested in the bearing of the Corn Laws on the question of slavery.[37] He represented that rare blend of high idealism and practical realism that served constantly to reinvigorate the abolitionist movement. Ever sincere, he desired to persuade the public that abolitionism was a logical, sensible, respectable idea, and felt the cause would not be helped "by twaddle." His aim was simple: "I want to write so that *honest* men will feel that I write honestly."[38] Although it was by his pen that he was best known, his ideas were not original, his point of view not unique. He was rather the popularizer of the crusade.

Leavitt's chief defect was a lack of tact. He was too blunt, prone to get too far ahead of the crowd in his enthusiasm. He almost ruined *The Evangelist* by preaching emancipation until his reluctant subscribers were sick of it. It took a series of revival lectures by Finney to restore the paper's circulation in 1834. Later when public opinion had caught up with him, his *Evangelist* was one of the more popular antislavery organs, reaching 10,000 subscribers by 1837.[39] He contributed no small part to crystallizing

---

[36] See Theodore Weld to James G. Birney, June 26, 1837, in Dumond, *Letters of James Gillespie Birney, 1831-1857*, p. 390. Joshua's letters to his family in the Leavitt Papers contain his thoughts on the antislavery campaign. For an account of the favorable impression Leavitt's lectures made, see Lewis Tappan to Jedidiah Burchard, Jan. 18, 1840, *Lewis Tappan Letterbook 1839-1840* (Lewis Tappan Papers).

[37] See Joshua Leavitt to James G. Birney, May 19, 1840, in Dumond, ed., *Letters of James Gillespie Birney, 1831-1857*, I, 574.

[38] Joshua Leavitt to Benjamin Tappan, Sept. 25, 1848 (Benjamin Tappan Papers).

[39] Henry S. Hutchinson to Mrs. Finney, April 7, 1835 (Finney Papers). For a description of *The Evangelist's* fluctuating fortunes and of Finney's efforts to save it, see Finney, *Memoirs*, pp. 329-330.

in the public mind a sentiment that made civil conflict when it came not only acceptable but desirable.

How different were the views of Henry Ward Beecher. Where Leavitt was consistent, he was inconsistent; where Joshua was idealistic, he was opportunistic. While both contributed to *The Independent*, the similarity stopped there. Henry Ward was twenty years younger than Joshua Leavitt, but the latter's ideas were more clearly defined, more courageously taken. Early in his career slavery was a subject he avoided. There were too many pitfalls; it was not sufficiently popular; he found more unanimity among his flock on such matters as prostitutes and prohibition. Abolitionists engaged in too many "ruinous absurdities." When he finally came over, the slavery issue was something to be exploited for his own benefit, something to be spoken of emotionally rather than rationally, hysterically rather than calmly. No better illustration of this can be seen than in the theatrical auction of the Edmunson sisters or in the ballyhoo that accompanied "Beecher's Bibles." [40]

Basically Henry Ward's plan of action was no plan at all. He did not believe in denouncing slaveholding as sinful but at times he spoke of its sinful nature; he rejected legislative action but he later favored prohibiting slavery in the territories. He refused in his articles to join in any organized attack on the institution. "Our policy for the future is plain. All the natural laws of God are warring upon slavery. We have only to let the process go on. Let slavery alone." [41] It will die a natural death. Indeed, given the choice between emancipation in fifty years "by selfish commercial influences" or in seventy-five years by the work of God's hand, Henry Ward preferred the latter, "that God may be honored, and not mammon, in the destruction of it." [42]

[40] Henry Ward's comment on abolitionists is taken from the New York *Journal of Commerce*, June 17, 1846. For a critical account of his conversion to antislavery, see Hibben, *Henry Ward Beecher: an American Portrait*, pp. 131 ff. A more sympathetic picture is given in Abbott, *Henry Ward Beecher*, pp. 151-222. His wavering slavery views can be traced in his articles in *The Independent*, three of which are included in *Patriotic Addresses*.

[41] *The Independent*, II, No. 103 (1850), 2.

[42] *Ibid.*, V, No. 235 (1853), 2.

Much has been written regarding Henry Ward Beecher's contribution to the "higher law" doctrine, most of which has overemphasized his role. Arguments on the higher law formed the basis of an article in *The Independent* at the height of the great debate in Congress on the Compromise of 1850. In this article Henry Ward also advanced the idea that there was an irreconcilable conflict between slavery and liberty. "One or the other must die," he warned. After considering the issues involved in the projected compromise, he expressed his variation of the higher law doctrine.

Not even the Constitution shall make me unjust. . . . I put constitution against constitution—God's against man's. When they agree, they are doubly sacred; when they differ, my reply to all questions . . . is in the language of Peter: "Whether it be right in the sight of God, judge ye." [43]

Henry Ward can claim little credit for having uttered such sentiments three weeks before Seward. By 1850 they were far from original anyway.

Finney's antislavery position illustrates how difficult it is to "type" individuals in one camp or another. No one was more influential, directly or indirectly, in winning converts to abolitionism than the Oberlin evangelist. Yet no one was more reluctant to call himself an antislavery agitator than he. He avoided formal mention of the subject but his sermons are filled with casual references to the sin of slavery. No evil was in greater need of remedying than bondage but he considered emancipation secondary to the religious conversion of mankind. Finney himself best described his own attitude.

When I first went to New York, I had made up my mind on the question of slavery, and was exceedingly anxious to arouse public attention to the subject. I did not, however, turn aside to make it a hobby, or divert the attention of the people from the work of converting souls. Nevertheless, in my prayers and preaching, I so often alluded to slavery, and denounced it, that a considerable excitement came to exist among the people.[44]

In spite of making abolition subservient to the saving of souls, Finney in his preaching stressed the need for the devout to engage

[43] Henry Ward Beecher, "Shall We Compromise," *ibid.*, II, No. 64, (1850), 2.
[44] Finney, *Memoirs*, p. 324. See also Wright, *Charles Grandison Finney*, pp. 138-141.

in benevolence and social reform. He believed his converts "should set out with determination to aim at being useful in the highest degree possible." [45] Social reform eventually meant the abolition of slavery since it was one of the more sinful of institutions. In a lecture to his New York congregation the evangelist said,

Are we to hold our peace and be partakers by connivance as we have been in the sin of slavery? God forbid. We will speak of it and bear our testimony against it and pray over it and complain of it to God and man. Heaven shall know and the world shall know and hell shall know that we protest against the sin and will continue to rebuke it till it is broken up.[46]

Not only should the church speak on the subject; there was a part for the individual to play. "Christians can no more take neutral ground on this subject, since it has come up for discussion, than they can take neutral ground on the subject of the sanctification of the Sabbath. It is a great national sin." [47]

Two years later the Oberlin divine urged that the crime of slavery which, he believed, was undermining society be fought through reproof, through personal expressions of disapproval:

What! shall men be suffered to commit one of the most God-dishonoring and most heaven-daring sins on earth, and not be reproved? It is a sin against which all men should bear testimony, and lift up their voice like a trumpet, till this giant iniquity is banished from the land and from the world.[48]

What was unique about Finney was the way in which he implemented his ideas. He was one of the first to exclude slaveholders from his church's communion, taking the stand while at Chatham Street Chapel that those who owned slaves were not Christians. Excluding such persons from the church was the sort of action Finney believed should be taken to bring about slavery's downfall.[49]

[45] Finney, *Lectures on Revivals*, p. 375.

[46] Quoted in McGiffert, "Charles Grandison Finney," *Christendom, an Ecumenical Review*, VII, No. 4 (1942), 503.

[47] Finney, *Lectures on Revivals*, p. 275.

[48] Finney, *Lectures to Professing Christians*, p. 55.

[49] See the New York *Evangelist*, Nov. 8, 1834; Ward, *The History of the Broadway Tabernacle Church*, pp. 26-27.

Finney was not as courageous as Leavitt, Garrison, or the Tappans in facing the raging storm of public opinion. When he returned to New York City from a trip abroad just at the height of the antislavery rioting in 1834, he remained but a day or two and hastened to the country. There were times when he even considered leaving his church because of the abolition movement. And he constantly cautioned his wife to guard her tongue on the subject. "I don't believe that it would do to say much about abolition here in publick," he once wrote.[50]

There were other occasions when Finney urged moderation. When the Lane rebels invaded Oberlin, he greeted their arrival with only mild enthusiasm. He thought the question of admitting students without distinction of color should be left with the faculty. He saw what had happened when the Lane trustees tried to formulate policy, and he pointed out, "We do not wish the Trustees to hold out an Abolition or an Anti-abolition flag." [51] He was concerned about public reaction to the indiscriminate seating of colored and white in the churches and felt that electing a Negro trustee of a church was inexpedient.[52] An unguarded remark even brought upon him the charge of being in favor of the fugitive slave law.[53] His second trip to England was the occasion of a sharp attack on him by the more rabid abolitionists.[54]

There is equally convincing evidence, however, that Finney was active in his abolitionism. In 1835, when private citizens were being attacked, homes broken into, and churches razed, Finney "exhorted the church to remain firm in the cause of Emancipation while the present storm is raging." [55] He appeared at anniversary meetings of the national antislavery organization, took an active part in the Ohio auxiliary, spoke at political meetings in Oberlin,

[50] Finney, *Memoirs*, p. 329; Finney to Mrs. Finney, Oct. 10, 1834; Nov. 24, 1834 (Finney Papers).

[51] Finney to Stanton and Whipple, Jan. 18, 1835 (Finney Papers).

[52] See *Lewis Tappan Diary Feb. 23, 1836 to Aug. 30, 1838*, Feb. 25, 1836, pp. 2-3 (Lewis Tappan Papers).

[53] See F. W. Chesson to Finney, Sept. 7, 1853 (Finney Papers).

[54] See the *National Anti-slavery Standard*, Feb. 2, 1859.

[55] R. M. Seeley to Finney, Oct. 6, 1835 (Finney Papers).

and was high in the circles of those who formed the nucleus of the crusade. In 1842 he preached in Boston at the newly opened Marlborough Chapel which was designed to permit free discussion of such reform movements as abolition. His significance in linking evangelism with antislavery cannot be overemphasized.

Finney's antislavery stand was often misunderstood. Even his good friend Lewis Tappan thought he was shirking in 1835 and told him so. Weld rushed to his defense, pointed out he had seen more frequent and striking examples of courage in the Oberlin evangelist than in any one else and explained Finney's attitude toward all reform, placing it secondary to the conversion of sinners:

The truth is Finney has always been in revivals of religion. It is his great business, aim and absorbing passion to promote them. . . . Finney feels about revivals of religion and the promotion of the church and ministry in doctrines and measures, just as you and I do about slavery. . . . You certainly underrate the amount of interest which he takes in the cause of abolition.[56]

Despite Weld's efforts, the Tappans were sufficiently irked with Finney's attitude that financial support was withdrawn from Oberlin. "It is a lamentable thing to have a falling out with so good a man as Brother Finney," Lewis recorded, "and I hope I did not do wrong."[57] Finney rushed East, called at the brothers' store, attempted to persuade them differently, lost his temper, and said he would not be influenced by threats. Others from Oberlin, including Shipherd, tried to appease the wealthy brothers, but they were reluctant to support Oberlin as long as Finney had ideas they considered "unsound" and injurious to the students.[58]

One must remember, however, that the Tappans were particularly rabid abolitionists. Their attack on Finney revealed more their own extreme position than a criticism of the Oberlin divine. Finney deplored the Tappans's willingness to bring subordinate

[56] Theodore Weld to Lewis Tappan, Nov. 17, 1835, in Barnes and Dumond, *Letters of Theodore Dwight Weld, Angelina Grimké Weld and Sarah Grimké, 1822-1844*, I, 243, 245.

[57] Lewis Tappan Diary, March 19, 1836, pp. 17-18 (Lewis Tappan Papers).

[58] *Ibid.*, April 26, May 6, 1836; William Green, Jr. to Finney, Sept. 20, 1836 (Finney Papers).

issues into the antislavery crusade, to antagonize people, to create controversies. "You err in supposing that the principle of abolition and amalgamation are identical," he wrote Arthur Tappan at the height of their dispute. "Abolition is a question of flagrant and unblushing wrong. A direct and outrageous violation of fundamental right. The other is a question of prejudice that does not necessarily deprive any man of any positive right." [59] What Finney wanted was to keep subordinate and collateral points out of the public mind until the major campaign was won. Although this disagreement was patched up, the Tappans were never as close to Finney as they had been before.

Others criticized Finney for his point of view. He deplored the fact that the antislavery crusade was running ahead of the evangelizing of America and believed that abolition should be made "an appendage of a general revival of religion." Nothing else would save the country, he felt. As early as 1836 he warned against extremist sentiment "that will roll a wave of blood over the land."

Br. Weld, is it not true, at least do you not fear it is, that we are in our present course going fast into a civil war? Will not our present movements in abolition result in that? Shall we not ere long be obliged to take refuge in a military despotism? [60]

Even his students objected to his attempts to get them to preach evangelism rather than abolition and disagreed with his moderate stand regarding Negro seats in the college chapel.[61]

Finney's place in the movement has tended to be minimized over the years, not only because the radical abolitionists who wrote histories of the crusade slighted him, but also because one of his chief contributions to the cause has been overlooked. Few have ever linked Finney's name with the development of the higher law doctrine. Yet years before Theodore Parker, Seward, or Henry Ward

---

[59] Finney to Arthur Tappan, April 30, 1836 (Finney Papers).

[60] Charles G. Finney to Theodore Weld, July 21, 1836, in Barnes and Dumond, *Letters of Theodore Dwight Weld, Angelina Grimké Weld and Sarah Grimké, 1822-1844,* I, 318-319.

[61] "Br. Finney has used his heart and head and influence to convince us that it is our duty to preach." William T. Allan to Theodore Weld, Aug. 9, 1836, Barnes and Dumond, *ibid.,* I, 323-329.

Beecher, Charles G. Finney was preaching that no human legislation could set aside the law of God.

Finney was elected one of the vice presidents of the Ohio Anti-slavery Society at its first annual meeting in 1835. This appointment pleased the four hundred society members in the three Oberlin auxiliaries and during the next few years their professor of pastoral theology worked with them, attended their meetings and was high in the counsels of the state organization.[62]

In 1839 upon the occasion of the fourth anniversary meeting of the Ohio Anti-slavery Society, Finney was elected chairman by the two hundred and eighty-six delegates, including such distinguished standard bearers as Birney, Gamaliel Bailey, Weld, and Henry Cowles, and presided during the sessions. In characteristic fashion Finney "opened the meeting with prayer." Early in the session he submitted nine resolutions and spoke on each one of them. His presiding did not prevent him from discussing other matters before the group as well.[63] Finney's first resolution asserted the right of the group to discuss freely the political character and influence of slavery. "Religion cannot be separated from politics," announced the Oberlin divine, "and government . . . must have a moral and religious character." Inasmuch as the government has undertaken to frame laws on the subject, we are justified in looking into the moral character of these laws, he added. His second resolution must be read in full.

Resolved, That for the following obvious reasons, we regard it, as a well settled principle of both common and constitutional law, that no human legislation can annul, or set aside the law or authority of God.

a. The most able writers on elementary law, have laid it down as a first principle, that whatever is contrary to the law of God, is not law.

b. Where a bond, or other written instrument, or anything else, is of immoral tendency, courts of law have refused to recognize it as legal and obligatory.

c. The administration of oaths, or affirmations, in courts of justice, is a recognition of the existence and supreme authority of God.

[62] See Price, "The Ohio Anti-slavery Convention of 1836," *Ohio State Archeological and Historical Quarterly*, XLV, No. 2 (1936), 182, 186.

[63] For a detailed summary of the meetings, see *Report of the Fourth Anniversary of the Ohio Anti-slavery Society*.

d. The Constitution of this State expressly recognizes the axiom, that no human enactment can bend the conscience, or set aside our obligations to God.

e. The general instrument on which the federal Government is founded, recognizes the same truth—that rights conferred by our Creator as inalienable, can never be cancelled, or set aside by human enactments.

f. The administration of oaths, or affirmations in all departments of the general and state governments, is a recognition of the truth, that God's authority is supreme.[64]

The succeeding resolutions implemented his assertion of the higher law. The third denied that the "Black Laws of Ohio" (fugitive slave laws) were obligatory upon the citizens of the state because they were "a palpable violation of the Constitution of this State, and of the United States, of the common law and of the law of God." The next asserted that obedience to these laws was "highly immoral." The fifth declared that "no man, by any promise or oath, or resolution, can make it right, or lawful, for him to do that which is contrary to the law of God."[65] The sixth maintained that any oath to support a human constitution was no more obligatory than the principles of that constitution were in accordance with the law of God. The seventh restated the sixth resolution but applied it specifically to the United States Constitution. The next deemed it imperative of all citizens to inquire into the moral character of Federal and state laws on the subject of slavery. The last resolution read:

Resolved, That we deem it highly improper, for Christians to decline acting on the subject of slavery and emancipation, on account of the political character and bearings of these questions, because we cannot innocently suffer legal enactments to crush our brother, when the means of prevention are peaceable, and within our power.[66]

Finney's resolutions were the highlight of the sessions. After thirty-eight other motions were passed, the presiding officer offered a prayer and the group adjourned,—"a most active, harmonious and deeply interesting session."[67] His nine resolutions provide the

64 *Ibid.*, p. 16.
65 *Ibid.*, pp. 17-18.
66 *Ibid.*, p. 19.
67 *Ibid.*, p. 9.

foundation for the higher law doctrine as it was applied to the slavery question.

Seven years later Finney carried his higher law doctrine a step further. Asserting in his *Lectures on Systematic Theology* that human government must be based on moral government and that civil laws must follow moral laws, the Oberlin divine considered the question of when human legislation was valid and when it was null and void. "The moral law or the law of nature . . . is the only law that can be obligatory on human beings," he affirmed. "No human constitution or law can be obligatory upon human beings any farther than it is in accordance with and declaratory of moral law." There were times, he asserted, when the individual was impelled to disobey human governments. "We are bound in all cases to disobey, when human legislation contravenes moral law, or invades the rights of conscience." As far as laws governing slavery were concerned, the issue was clear. "No human constitution or enactment can, by any possibility, be law that recognizes the right of one human being to enslave another." [68]

Francis Wayland's views on slavery changed considerably through the years. Normally, the Providence minister-educator was consistent in his views, inflexible in his opinions, and unyielding to the passions of each passing hour. During the first part of his career he was an outspoken opponent of abolition. He classed abolitionists with other lawless persons and as a defender of the status quo objected to antislavery societies. He did not hesitate to assert his independence of all factions, slavery and antislavery alike:

I speak as the organ of no party and of no sect. I belong to none. I am not and I never have been connected with any abolition society, and I believe that I have read as much on one side of this question as on the other. I write what seems to me the simple dictates of my individual understanding and conscience; enlightened I hope by the teachings of the Holy Scripture. [69]

Wayland's position prior to 1840 was no more clearly stated than in a chapter of his popular book *Limitations of Human Respon-*

[68] Finney, *Lectures on Systematic Theology*, pp. 434-435, 440, 446.
[69] Wayland, *Domestic Slavery Considered as a Scriptural Institution*, p. 33.

sibility (1838), that critique of limitless humanitarianism and misguided benevolence. In this work Wayland took the view that, regardless of slavery's moral evil, of its violation of God's law, individuals had no power whatsoever to abolish or try to abolish it in the Southern states. The Federal Constitution did not confer that power upon citizens of the United States and the attempt to do away with slavery, to legislate against it, and to form societies to preach emancipation were infringements of the rights of states. With an argument that anticipated the one used by John Stuart Mill in *On Liberty,* Wayland defended the right of the state, of a minority, to preserve slavery if it should so desire:

> Should all the States in the Union but one, and that one the very smallest, abolish slavery; should the majority of one hundred to one, of the people of the United States, be in favor of its abolition, still it would not alter the case. That one State would be as free to abolish it or not to abolish it, as it is now.[70]

In addition, he believed that individuals had no responsibility in the matter. "The guilt, if guilt exists, will not rest upon us as citizens of the United States," the Brown president declared. "Whether slavery be bad or good, we wash our hands of it, inasmuch as it is a matter which the providence of God has never placed within our jurisdiction."[71] Furthermore, as citizens we have solemnly promised to let it alone. Such procedure is written into the Constitution; all parties to the agreement assented to it; all parties must therefore abide by it.

The Baptist evangelist did not hesitate to indicate in his *Limitations of Human Responsibility* his impressions of Northern anti-slavery societies. He questioned the usefulness of organizations whose main purpose was to stir up feeling in the North. The only advantage to be gained from such agitation was the increase in abolition votes. But the slavery question, Wayland maintained, is a matter with which votes have nothing to do. Of abolition societies he wrote,

[70] Wayland, *Limitations of Human Responsibility,* p. 164.
[71] *Ibid.,* p. 167.

They have already become the tools of third rate politicians. They have raised a violent agitation. . . . They have, for the present, rendered any open and calm discussion of this subject in the slave-holding States utterly impossible. They have rivetted, indefinitely the bonds of the slave, in those very States in which they were a few years since, falling off.[72]

In the final analysis, Wayland concluded, the South had the right either to accept or reject Northern ideas. His summation was an interesting mixture of freedom of thought and Protestant fatalism:

They have as good a right to their ears, as we have to our tongues. . . . We have no right to force our instructions upon them, either by conversation, or by lectures, or by the mail. . . . If they will not hear us, the indication is plain, that God does not mean to use our instrumentality in the affair. We must retire and leave the case in his hands.[73]

Although he defended the rights of Southerners, nevertheless Wayland attacked slavery as a violation of personal liberty. In his *Elements of Moral Science* (1835) he asserted, "Slavery . . . violates the personal liberty of man as a physical, intellectual, and moral being." Its existence, he believed, was deleterious to the South in limiting its capital, in restricting its industrial development, in making for too great a reliance on a one-crop system. He was sure that the South would have been wealthier had it been inhabited from the beginning by an industrious yeomanry. He was also convinced that "the precepts of the gospel in no matter countenance, but are directly opposed to the institution of domestic slavery," and if the system was wrong, he continued, it ought to be abandoned immediately.[74]

The most marked change in Francis Wayland's views came in 1842. Prior to that time he had opposed slavery but would do nothing to bring about its removal. He clung tenaciously to his ivy tower in Providence and, like many an academician, taught one thing in the classroom and lived another. After 1842, however, because of the growing seriousness of the issue, because of the

[72] *Ibid.*, p. 184.
[73] *Ibid.*, p. 185. For a critique of Wayland's argument, see "Moderatus," *Review of President Wayland's . . . Limitations of Human Responsibility.*
[74] Wayland, *Elements of Moral Science*, pp. 220, 227.

increasing stubbornness of the Southern defense, and because of
the realization that his old position was untenable, he took a more
active interest in abolition.   Charles Sumner was one of the first
to note the change.   "I was in Providence yesterday, when I saw
President Wayland," he wrote to William E. Channing.   "His
views on slavery, and with regard to the South have materially
changed lately." [75]

Some indication of Wayland's change of heart is found two years
later when he debated the issue with the Rev. Richard Fuller,
Baltimore editor of the *Christian Reflector*.   The debate took the
form of letters exchanged between the two ministers through the
columns of Fuller's journal and later published in book form under
the title *Domestic Slavery Considered as a Scriptural Institution*
(1845).   Condemning the extremists on both sides, Wayland demanded the right to examine the question completely.   "There
is no subject whatever which I have not a perfect right to discuss,
in the freest and fullest manner, in public or in private, provided
I act with an honest intention," he declared.[76]

After considering the meaning of slavery, the Brown president
concluded that the holding of slaves did not necessarily involve
guilt.   He saw in slaveholding wide ground for the exercise of
Christian charity.   Some slaveholders were guilty; others were not.
Wayland could not link them all in a single condemnation.   To
the slaveholder who was convinced of slavery's wrong but who
believed that the law did not permit him to free his slaves on any
satisfactory conditions, Wayland suggested, "I answer, he may,
from the moment that he is thus convinced, hold them not for his
benefit but for theirs." [77]

Wayland's examination of the proslavery arguments from the
Old Testament was also unique.   He dismissed the extravagant
scriptural defense and the inaccurate antislavery appeals to the
Gospel, admitted slavery's existence in Old Testament times, but

[75] Charles Sumner to William E. Channing, June 23, 1842, quoted in Pierce, *Memoir
and Letters of Charles Sumner*, II, 211.
[76] Wayland, *Domestic Slavery Considered as a Scriptural Institution*, p. 14.
[77] *Ibid.*, p. 43.

defended slaveholders then on the grounds that, since God had not revealed the sinfulness of the institution, Biblical slaveholders were not guilty. From his examination of the New Testament, however, Wayland drew conclusive proof that slavery was forbidden by God's word.

Wayland's entire argument was based on grounds of expediency, a position which by 1844 such abolitionists as Leavitt, Weld, and Birney had long since rejected. When it was not feasible for an evil such as slavery to be removed without upsetting society, he felt that reform was unwise:

Thus, suppose a particular wrong to have become a social evil, to have become interwoven with the whole framework of society, and to be established by positive enactment and immemorial usage . . . suppose also the whole community to be ignorant of the moral principles by which both the wrong is condemned and the right established. In such a case, the wrong could only be abolished by changing the sentiments and enlightening the consciences of the whole community. Here it seems to me that it would be . . . a matter of imperative duty, to inculcate the principles on which the duty rested, rather than the duty itself.[78]

Wayland concluded his thoughts on slavery's abolition by observing, "In my judgment, it would be a great calamity were it to terminate by violence, or without previous moral and social preparation." [79]

It was the fugitive slave law that most provoked Wayland. Initially he tried to ignore it but during a sermon in June, 1850, he departed from his prepared address, pushed his glasses back on his forehead, and with flashing eyes and trembling voice poured forth an extemporaneous volley on human oppression and its injustices. His congregation sat spellbound.[80]

As the 1850's passed, one crisis gave way to another and Wayland became more and more outspoken. Finally, as if designed to unite the North once and for all, the Kansas-Nebraska Bill pro-

[78] *Ibid.*, p. 73.
[79] *Ibid.*, p. 252.
[80] See Murray, *Francis Wayland*, pp. 238-239. During the Civil War Albert Barnes, assessing the importance of the fugitive slave act, declared, "More than any other enactment . . . this law . . . has been the cause of the alienation of the North from the South." Albert Barnes, *The Conditions of Peace*, p. 41.

voked a storm of opposition. Voices of protest came from almost every pulpit. The leading religious periodicals joined in whipping up public anger, and it was not long before religious groups passed resolutions and sent petitions condemning the measure.[81] It was this bill that led Horace Bushnell to deliver one of his strongest antislavery addresses on *The Northern Iron* (1854). The effect of this crisis on Henry Ward Beecher is only too well known. Even Finney, who by this time was devoting almost all of his attention to Oberlin, attended a National Kansas Committee convention held in Buffalo in July, 1856, and represented the bleeding state.[82]

The Kansas-Nebraska crisis provoked Francis Wayland to compose one of his most vitriolic pieces. Speaking before a meeting held to protest against the bill, Wayland outlined his opposition on religious, patriotic, practical, and ethical grounds. Since slavery was sinful, any extension of it into new territory would be a further violation of moral law, he maintained. He saw in the bill's design a more revolutionary action than even the Dorr Rebellion. Extending slavery over this domain would tend to "dissolve the government itself, for when the essential element of a compact is reversed, every contracting party is released from his obligations in respect to it. I therefore protest against this bill," he continued, "as revolutionary and giving just cause for a dissolution of the Union." [83]

To Wayland, the prospect of slavery in Nebraska was the last straw. Not even the preservation of the Union was worth such a calamity. "I value the Union as much as any man," he declared. "I would cheerfully sacrifice to it everything but truth and justice and liberty. When I must surrender these as the price of the union, the union becomes at once a thing which I abhor." [84] That a man of Wayland's moderation should go so far in his denunciation is indicative of the import of Douglas's project in the

[81] See Nevins, *Ordeal of the Union*, II, 129-130.

[82] See Harlow, *Gerrit Smith, Philanthropist and Reformer*, p. 351.

[83] Wayland, *Dr. Wayland on the Moral and Religious Aspects of the Nebraska Bill*, p. 15.

[84] *Ibid.*, p. 16.

minds of the religious community. Wayland's concluding remarks illustrate how charged were men's emotions by 1856. In summing up, he turned upon his Southern friends and warned them against continuing in their course. His last words are a sort of benediction for the North:

Come what will, it will ever be to us unspeakable satisfaction that to the utmost of our power, we have washed our hands of this iniquity. Let us cease not to beseech the God of our fathers, to defeat the counsels of misguided men, and, if the worst shall come that he will grant to the free States the wisdom, temper, patriotism and union, which may be needed in this grave emergency.[85]

The Southern attitude toward Wayland naturally changed during these years. Where formerly he was listened to in the South, after the 1840's he was denounced. His textbooks were banned in Southern schools and, whether he liked it or not, he was thrown into the active antislavery camp. He cast his lot with the young Republican party, lauding its appearance, and in 1860 supported the nomination of Lincoln. When war broke out, he rallied his followers with pious patriotic appeals.[86]

Several conclusions can be drawn about the antislavery attitudes of the evangelists. Generally speaking, those ministers who rejected or modified orthodox doctrines, who espoused the New School theology, and who favored new measures were more receptive to antislavery views. That Finney, Joshua Leavitt, and Albert Barnes should stand in the front ranks of those who fought the good fight early in the 1830's was no accident. Their religion encouraged excursions in reform. Conversely, a conservative theologian, a believer in the Old School approach was more likely to resist abolition or to take a proslavery defense. Charles Hodge, Asahel Nettleton, and Daniel Baker were too conservative in their religion to be emotionally prepared in the 1830's for something as radical as abolition.[87]

85 *Ibid.*, p. 19.

86 See Wayland, *Appeal to the Disciples of Christ of Every Denomination.*

87 There was also a reciprocal effect. Ministers and laymen who engaged in reform activities became more receptive to changing social and religious ideas. As Lewis Tappan put it, "Abolitionism has inclined me to democracy." Lewis Tappan to Benjamin Tappan, Oct. 28, 1839 (Benjamin Tappan Papers).

Second, the activities and ideas of the evangelists during the ante-bellum era bear out the statement that antislavery swallowed up other benevolent movements, dwarfing the drives for temperance, education, and moral reform. Finney as early as 1836 exclaimed, "One most alarming fact is that the absorbing abolitionism has drunk up the spirit of some of the most efficient moral men and is fast doing so [to] the rest." [88] Abolitionism enlisted energies that might have gone into other more specific channels of economic and social betterment. Its success meant a deterioration among religious groups of reform in areas other than slavery and spelled the defeat of such other efforts to improve society, misguided or otherwise, as the American Peace Society, the various temperance organizations, the attack on vice and prostitution, and the variety of attempts to keep the Puritan Sabbath. In this respect, the antislavery movement proved eminently beneficial, for it weakened some unfortunate, intolerant enterprises whose success would have been a blotch on American social history. Abolitionism, for instance, weakened the props of the anti-Catholic movement, whose roots were sunk deep in American Protestantism. [89]

Third, the slavery issue was so important and its effect on the thinking of evangelists so far-reaching that by 1850 men who were usually peaceful and peace-loving were ready for war as a means of settling the question. When ministers of the gospel were willing to see a civil conflict engulf the Union, when men of God lashed the South with vindictive phrases and called upon their Providence to lead them through bloody battle, it is no wonder that public opinion so readily accepted the coming of the war. How less avoidable did Beriah Green make the struggle when in 1835 he wrote:

Men may say what they will of the value of the Union: but where is the Union when the mail is robbed in open day with impunity; and such men as Dr. Beman dare not attend a missionary meeting in Baltimore, for fear

[88] Finney to Weld, July 21, 1836, in Barnes and Dumond, *Letters of Theodore Dwight Weld, Angelina Grimké Weld and Sarah Grimké, 1822-1844,* I, 319.
[89] See Billington, *The Protestant Crusade,* p. 430.

of being murdered? Nothing remains but a mortified body, the breath just ready to depart.[90]

Or, for that matter, how incendiary were the words of one of Finney's friends who announced:

Ungodly prejudice cannot preserve it, the threats, money, nor deep laid plots of the oppressor cannot do it, *fall it must,* and if like Sampson, some of the friends of the slave perish under the ruins of this strong built throne of the Devil, nevertheless, it must go down, and there are others coming forward to take their places, and fill the ranks, who will neither retreat from the field, or hold their peace while a shackle remains unbroken.[91]

Even Finney's statements became more bellicose as the years passed. In 1846 he declared, "To adopt the maxim 'Our Union even with perpetual slavery' is an abomination so execrable as not to be named by a just mind without indignation." [92] When mild-mannered men such as Francis Wayland began talking in similar vein, it is no wonder the Civil War came. By 1856 Wayland was ready:

The iron already enters my soul. I feel that we are governed, not by law and the expression of the universal conscience of the nation, but by bowie-knives, bludgeons, and the lash. I hope that the conscience and love of liberty in this people will be roused.

. . . We must have concert, and act upon a plan. It may require some time and labor and sacrifice, but it is worth them all.[93]

A fourth observation must be considered. To be leaders of a movement as important as antislavery is one thing, but to be swept along toward war as a means of attaining their objective is another. The Finneys, Bushnells, Leavitts, and Waylands must be criticized for not providing more effective leadership and bringing about a better solution to the nation's difficulties. The evangelists and the Protestant churches they represented were incapable of coping with the problem of slavery and its peaceful solution. That the Civil

---

[90] Beriah Green to Gerrit Smith, Sept. 24, 1835, quoted in Harlow, *Gerrit Smith, Philanthropist and Reformer,* p. 121.

[91] R. M. Seeley to Finney, Oct. 6, 1835 (Finney Papers).

[92] Finney, *Lectures on Systematic Theology,* p. 445.

[93] Francis Wayland to Hon. C. G. Loring, June, 1856, quoted in Murray, *Francis Wayland,* p. 143.

War came indicated a failure in leadership on the part of the clergy just as much as on the part of statesmen and politicians. Prior to the 1830's the minister was a decisive figure in molding public opinion, in persuading his flock to follow his beliefs. After 1840, however, the minister, by and large, followed, rather than shaped, public opinion. Just as the control of benevolence, missions, temperance, and antislavery shifted from ministerial command to lay hands, so too did the dominant influence over the public mind. The clergy on the eve of the Civil War still were an influence in public affairs, but their relative hold over such matters had declined.

Finally, we must conclude that the "irrepressibility" of the Civil War was helped along by the evangelists. We can find clues to the irrepressibility, if it existed, in the unyielding attitudes of religious leaders on other subjects. We find it, for instance, in the Old School-New School schism in 1837, in the Methodist Church split in 1844, in the dogmatic stand of the evangelists in the Sabbatarian movement, in temperance and moral reform. It existed in the uncompromising animosity toward Catholicism that characterized nineteenth-century Protestants. And we see it in the fervent belief each minister held that he was right, that God was on his side.

In such an atmosphere conciliation on the slavery question and compromise between the sections, while not impossible under proper political leadership, became highly improbable in the face of rabid ministerial dogmatism. At the same time, we must recognize the debt owed to the courageous persistent fanatics without whose efforts emancipation would have been unlikely. Thus the American people became accustomed in the pulpit and religious press to the stand of the extremist and thus the American evangelist contributed in no small way to that state of mind which helped bring on the Civil War.

VIII.   CONCLUSION

All that is worth living for is to glorify God and to do good to all as we have opportunity.[1]

It has been a great thing for us to live.[2]

THE CIVIL WAR has long been used as a convenient dividing line in American history.   Like a great terminal morain, it divides the nineteenth century into two almost equal parts.   It separates the brash, energetic, romantic, commercial adolescence of our country from the more mature, materialistic, industrialized adulthood that characterizes the postwar years.   The historian who moves from the 1830's to the 1870's cannot help but note one of the most marked changes ever to take place in a people's development.   No other forty years, if we except our own age, produced more momentous innovations, more far-reaching transformations than this period.   Nowhere is this revolution more apparent than in the field of religion and in the evangelistic profession.

By 1860 the men who dominated the religious scene in 1826 were growing old.   Some of them, Emmons, Nettleton, Maffitt, had already died, their places filled by younger, less colorful men.   Others had retired from the limelight.   Lyman Beecher, growing more conservative as he aged, had come East and settled in the reflected glory of his son, Henry Ward, who was just reaching his prime in Brooklyn.   Finney found it necessary to resign from the presidency of Oberlin in 1865, and although he still conducted revivals it was not with the same old spirit.   He was forced to refuse many invitations to preach.   "I have been sick for about two years," he explained to one of his devotees.   In 1864 his third wife

---

[1] Justin Edwards to his brother-in-law, July 6, 1824, quoted in Hallock, *Light and Love, a Sketch of the Life and Labors of the Rev. Justin Edwards*, p. 178.
[2] Horace Bushnell to Ralph Burkett, July 25, 1873, in Cheney, *Life and Letters of Horace Bushnell*, p. 510.

died, and in 1866 and 1867 he broke down in the midst of revivals
he was leading.[3]

Ever conscious of life's impermanence, the evangelists were quick
to realize that age was creeping on, that the Civil War marked
the end of their era. "My locks are whitening, and eternity is
coming on," wrote Daniel Baker to his wife. "O be more gentle,
and mild, and even-tempered, and heavenly-minded! . . . . I am
in the midst of posterity . . . the shades of evening are gathering
around me . . . my sun must soon go down."[4] "It is hard to
realize how old we are," Joshua Leavitt confessed. "With the exception of clumsiness of motion I hardly feel more of decay than
I did at 25, although my eyes are a little dim, and I wear false
teeth and false hair."[5] "I am now an old man," reflected Jacob
Knapp in 1867. "I have outlived the generation of my early
associates."[6]

In spite of their aging the evangelists still held on to life and to
their role in it. In the same breath in which he spoke of his age,
Knapp boasted that his life had been burdened with "fearful re-
sponsibilities" and that he still was needed to influence mankind.
Albert Barnes was particularly reluctant to leave the scene of action. Thanking an admirer in 1863 for a gift she had sent him,
he confessed, "I *have* desired greatly to live a thousand years. . . .
I shall not live that long—but I shall try to live as long as I can.
How far this bottle of wine will carry me on that journey, I know
not; but I shall make it go as far as I can."[7]

The approach of old age incited the evangelists to write their
memoirs. Finney completed his in 1868. Lyman Beecher gathered
his children around him at his home to relive old memories and to
commit to paper his interpretation of past events. Baker, Cartwright, Finley, and Knapp concerned themselves with recording
their careers. Wayland ended his days revising some of his works

---

[3] Finney to F. J. Tytus, Jan. 15, 1863 (Finney Papers); Finney, *Memoirs*, p. 475.
[4] Daniel Baker to Mrs. Baker, Feb. 27, 1852, quoted in Baker, *The Life and Labors of the Rev. Daniel Baker*, pp. 450, 452.
[5] Joshua Leavitt to his mother, March 10, 1849 (Leavitt Papers).
[6] Knapp, *Autobiography*, p. 188.
[7] Albert Barnes to Miss Elizabeth Fox, Dec. 2, 1863 (Albert Barnes Papers).

to bring them up to date, while Barnes lived long enough to give two autobiographical benedictory addresses, one at sixty and the other at seventy.

Nevertheless, after 1860 the evangelist was a less important figure. His followers had dwindled; his words were less closely heeded. Politicians and generals, newspaper editors and businessmen replaced him in shaping society and influencing public opinion. He still preached, conducted revivals, issued decrees on current affairs, and engaged in typical crusades. Some of the latter were curious—for example, Edward Beecher's attack on the First International and Bushnell's diatribe against women's suffrage.[8] Some were pathetic—as Finney's fight against the Masons. Some were to be expected—as Wayland's tardy interest in Herbert Spencer. But the intellectual and religious center of gravity had shifted. The evangelist was out of step with the times. Some of them recognized their weakness. "My expectations . . . are not realized," wrote the fiery Joshua Leavitt as he contemplated returning to New England after an abortive trip to St. Louis. "Instead of success, utter failure . . . with little strength and less courage."[9] Others failed to see the new age about them. When in 1869, for instance, the Old and New School factions came together and patched up their old quarrels, Albert Barnes was considered "an unvenerable relic of an abandoned past."[10]

The reasons why the evangelist after 1860 was antiquated are obvious. The outbreak of war brought a condition for which the minister was ill-prepared. Military battles and campaigns are not the stuff of a Protestant ethic. Brotherly love has an uneasy place in civil conflict. The evangelists, in fostering the sentiment which made war acceptable, brought on their own decline.

Second, the publication of Darwin's theories in 1859, although not an important immediate factor, meant eventually and inevitably the downfall of the evangelist's universe, of his God, and of

---

[8] See Edward Beecher, "The International," *Christian Union*, Feb. 14, 1872, p. 155; Bushnell, *Women's Suffrage: the Reform against Nature*.

[9] Joshua Leavitt to Rev. A. Foster, July 27, 1866 (Leavitt Papers).

[10] Robert E. Thompson, *A History of the Presbyterian Church in the United States*, p. 179.

his style of preaching. Charles Finney spoke a different language from Charles Darwin. And the grandchildren of Finney's followers were to find evolution more convincing than original sin, the test tube more efficacious than the anxious seat, and the search for knowledge more satisfactory than conversion. Although Dwight L. Moody, Ira David Sankey, and Billy Sunday continued the tradition of Finney and Beecher, they were voices crying in the wilderness and their work was perhaps even more transitory than that of their predecessors.

Third, the coming of the railroad age contributed to their decline. Industrialization created a new society that no longer considered "sin" so important and that had little interest in the Wednesday evening meeting, in the Puritanical Sabbath, in the protracted sessions of a revival. Industrialism brought an increase in material prosperity, greater mobility, greater variety, and greater attractions. It meant improved communications, more widespread public education, new institutions competing for man's attentions. Industrialism brought also poverty, industrial strife, and the new immigration, for none of which the nineteenth-century evangelist had a solution. The Finneys, Beechers, and Cartwrights were fighting a losing battle. They no longer had the social prestige or influence a minister of the previous century had possessed, and, with few exceptions, they used unchanged blueprints in a changing world.[11]

In religious thought the rigidity of orthodoxy, even in New School packages, prevented Protestantism from changing with sufficient swiftness to keep abreast of the times. "I find plenty of good people who have quite given up the old notion of the millenium," wrote Finney's niece sadly.[12] The methods used to convert people were out of date by 1860; the techniques employed in saving souls were outmoded. "The style of preaching has so far altered the past 10 or 20 years," wrote Lewis Tappan to Finney,

---

[11] For a consideration of the impact of industrialization on orthodox religion, see Davenport, *Primitive Traits in Religious Revivals*, pp. 209-213; McComas, *The Psychology of Religious Sects*, p. 152; May, *Protestant Churches and Industrial America*, pp. 39-63; Ernest T. Thompson, *Changing Emphases in American Preaching*, p. 170.

[12] Mary A. Parker to Finney (n.d.) (Finney Papers).

"that your peculiar style . . . would not be so attractive as it once was." [13]   The "gospel on horseback" was out of place in the railroad age.

The decline of the evangelists did not come unspectacularly, however. During the winter of 1857-1858 there occurred the last of the great religious phenomena of the ante-bellum period.[14] A religious fervor swept the Northern states, bringing an "awakening" to New York, Philadelphia, Boston, Cleveland, Detroit, Chicago, and St. Louis as well as to rural districts. The nation's press devoted considerable attention to the revival. The *Independent* called it "a general outpouring of the spirit"; the *Tribune* ran several extras filled with accounts of the revival's progress.[15] By spring, 1858, there were more than twenty places in New York where a daily prayer meeting was being held. Wherever one went there were "placards, inviting young men to prayer meetings in the very heart of business places, in the principal stores and upon church doors." [16]   In the course of a year it was estimated that some five hundred thousand persons had been converted. To use Finney's words, "A divine influence seemed to pervade the whole land." [17]

Finney, Knapp, Wayland, and Henry Ward Beecher were in the thick of the revival. Finney spent that winter laboring in Boston. Henry Ward had Brooklyn at his feet. In spite of the old faces there were new techniques, innovations that marked a new era. The preaching was not of the haranguing, hypnotic style that char-

[13] Tappan continued, "Dr. Beecher's logical sermons, were he here, would not attract a quarter as many hearers as does his son Henry whose gold is not in ingots but in gold leaf." Lewis Tappan to Finney, Oct. 15, 1866 (Finney Papers).

[14] For different accounts of the 1857 revival, see Beardsley, *A History of American Revivals*, pp. 213 ff.; Arthur C. Cole, *The Irrepressible Conflict, 1850-1865*, pp. 252 ff.; Loud, *Evangelized America*, pp. 216 ff. For Finney's part in the revival, see Finney, *Memoirs*, pp. 444-447. A more analytical treatment is found in Greenblatt, *Some Social Aspects of the Panic of 1857*; Spicer, "The Great Awakening of 1857 and 1858," *Ohio State University: Abstracts of Dissertations, Summer Quarter, 1935*. See also Francis, "The Religious Revival of 1858 in Philadelphia," *The Pennsylvania Magazine of History and Biography*, LXX, No. 1 (1946), 52-77.

[15] *The Independent*, March 11, 1858.

[16] H. H. G. to Finney (n.d.) (Finney Papers).

[17] Finney, *Memoirs*, p. 444.

acterized earlier revivals. The planning and executing of the revival were in lay hands, not ministerial ones. As Finney put it, "it was carried on very much through the instrumentality of prayer-meetings, personal visitation and conversation, by the distribution of tracts, and by the energetic efforts of the laity, men and women." [18] There was less enthusiasm, less fiery emotion, less emphasis on doctrinal theorizing in 1857 than there had been in earlier revivals. Furthermore, it was more closely linked with economic affairs than any other that preceded it. The financial panic in the fall of 1857 and the subsequent economic pressure turned men's minds toward religion. It was instrumental in bringing about co-operation among sects, in laying the foundations for the religious organizations that were to blossom after the Civil War. It also did much to prepare the North emotionally for the Civil War.[19] Finally it seems apparent that it contributed in part to the 1859 revival in Ireland which extended to England and Scotland.

Nowhere was the evangelist more outmoded than in the realm of science. The eventual acceptance of biological evolution overturned the foundations on which revivalism was based and the spirit out of which emerged so many of the reform movements of the 1830's. For the most part the evangelists were innocent of evolutionary ideas. Although Horace Bushnell's *Nature and the Supernatural* (1858) and *Moral Uses of Dark Things* (1867) contain passages that seem on the threshold of evolution, few other ministers came even close to incorporating the discoveries of science into their philosophy.

A representative view of the clerical position on science can be seen in Albert Barnes's *Lectures on the Evidence of Christianity*, a collection published in 1868. His thesis was that science, like Christianity, is really fixed and unchangeable:

[18] *Ibid.*

[19] Beardsley's estimate of the revival's importance in this respect is rather exaggerated: "It was the religious influences generated by this revival which served to give strength to the wearied soldier on his long forced marches; which inspired him with courage amid the perils and carnage of battle." Beardsley, *A History of American Revivals*, p. 239.

There are no new truths; no new facts; no new principles that have been introduced in the one case any more than in the other. . . . The worlds are the same, the laws of their movements are the same. . . . There have been no changes in the structure of man that would demand a revision or a modification of the system. Not one new bone has been added to the human frame; not one new muscle, nerve, or tendon has been laid down; not one new channel has been grooved out for the flowing of the blood.[20]

Barnes went into the history of previous controversies between religion and science in an effort to maintain the correctness of his own position. He outlined four points on which, as he put it, Christianity was, in his age, in collision with the world. These included the question of the Bible's infallibility as a revelation of truth, the issue of the human race's antiquity, the origin of man, and the matter of miracles and their place in a universe of law and order. On the first point, Barnes unyieldingly defended the Bible as "a supernatural revelation of God." When it came to fixing the age of man he was willing to compromise. Six thousand years was admittedly a short time. But, "beyond all question, there is a limit, probably much within the twenty thousand years of man's residence upon the earth, according to the Bible." As for man's origin there was but one answer. "The Bible records the creation of a single pair, and no other." Miracles were defended stubbornly by Barnes, and he concluded his lecture with an appeal to ward off the influence of Rationalism, Positivism, and Pantheism.[21]

In spite of their sparse political training they continued to pass judgment on men and events of the day. Charles Finney, for instance, came out in favor of Benjamin Butler, of all men, for President in 1864. Horace Bushnell earnestly defended Grant during the unsavory years of his presidency, believing that the general had had "a wise, sagacious, and firm political administration."[22] Throughout the war Bushnell, along with others, continued to

[20] Albert Barnes, *Lectures on the Evidence of Christianity in the Nineteenth Century*, pp. 358-359.

[21] *Ibid.*, pp. 376-377, 401-402.

[22] Cheney, *Life and Letters of Horace Bushnell*, p. 482.

give the public the benefit of his opinions of the military fortunes of the North.

Just as the evangelists were behind the times in science and politics so too were they in social and moral reform. The old patterns were adhered to; the 1830 methods were followed. The moral reform societies had an abortive rebirth during the war years in the Citizen's Association which was "a sort of vigilance committee" and in which prominent laymen and clergy worked "reforming abuses, watching the health, business, the schools and things generally." [23] In the late 1860's Finney led a crusade against Masonry which rekindled some of the fires that had been banked for thirty years. Popular amusements and the theater were still anathema and revivalists still worried about the threats to morality in the form of prostitution, intemperance, and Catholicism. Some of Finney's last articles outlined the dangers of worldly amusements which by 1870 included, he discovered, sports, the theater, ball games, and church socials. "Nothing is right," he maintained to the last, "unless it is done with ultimate reference to the glory of God, and the interests of His kingdom." [24]

It is appropriate to consider whether among this group of figures, amid the variety of viewpoints and the differences of aims and methods, any stereotype emerges which we can call the early nineteenth-century Northern evangelist. Out of the morass of diversity, disagreement, and dispute there emerge a number of common characteristics. These may be classified in three groups; first, similarities in personality; second, uniform beliefs; and third, homogeneity in their activities.

The briefest survey of the personalities of these ministers indicates that they were all colorful individuals, with unique mannerisms. They cut a distinctive figure as they rode across the countryside, pounded pulpits, or struggled with Satan to save men's souls. Beecher's flowing locks, Finney's flashing eye, Cartwright's flying

---

[23] Mary A. Parker to Finney, June 27, 1864 (Finney Papers).

[24] Finney, A More Excellent Way, MS dated Jan. 22, 1873, p. 10. See also his Innocent Amusements, MS dated Jan. 16, 1873. For an example of public support, see H. C. Dickinson to Finney, Feb. 25, 1873 (Finney Papers). For Finney's last crusade, see "Finney's Fight against the Masons," Ohio State Archaeological and Historical Quarterly, LIX, No. 3 (1950), 270-286.

coat tails—all blend into one picture. If we were to generalize, we could describe the Northern evangelist as a tall, handsome, melodic-voiced individual, somewhat eccentric and strongly emotional—to whom every incident was an opportunity to serve his Lord. He loved a fight, whether it was a physical encounter or an intellectual tussle. He was domineering, filled with limitless energy, and rather set in his ways. He would have made a poor businessman but as a lawyer or politician he would have been a shining success. His salary was generally low and his large family was often close to poverty, but the coffers of his business friends were almost his for the asking. He cared little for the small amenities of life, was subject to occupational hazards of bronchitis, colds, and sore throats, and was a glutton for work.[25] He was an extrovert. He could hold men in the palm of his hand. He loved little children. And he had a way with women.

Stereotypes can be misleading, however, for one of the most important characteristics of Northern evangelists was a highly individualistic nature. Diversity, originality, and a certain inconsistency marked the man of God. Where one threw Satan at the feet of his hearers, another tossed tree stumps over the heads of his congregation. Where one tackled hecklers and wrestled in the shadows of a camp meeting, another pulled maidens to their knees on ballroom floors. The evangelists were most alike in being different.

There was a certain similarity in their dynamic natures, in their magnetic personalities. Many have commented on Finney's hypnotic eye, on his psychic influence over people, and others have made similar observations about Knapp, Maffitt, Cartwright, and Lyman Beecher. The evangelist was never weary of action. Having gained one objective he moved on to another, always driving forward with tremendous energy. Connected with this was a certain restlessness, a desire to be always on the go. We see it in

---

[25] "It is a well-known fact that there is a species of bronchitis, or affection of the lungs, peculiar to the ministers of the United States, arising from their excessive labors in their vocation." Marryat, *A Diary in America, 1837-1838*, III, 116. See also Combe, *Notes on the United States of North America*, I, 163; Cartwright, *Autobiography*, pp. 406-407.

Finney's letters as he responds enthusiastically to this invitation or that, as he moves on from place to place even on his honeymoon. We find it in Knapp's autobiography as he details his lengthy itineraries. Baker confessed to this restlessness every time he concluded a tour. This dynamic quality spurred them on in the face of hardship, disappointment, and defeat.

But if the evangelist was colorful, dynamic, magnetic, and restless he was also extremely introspective. There was something of John Bunyan in each of these men. Daniel Baker as a youth was subject to fits of depression. Into his diary he poured self-deprecating thoughts, gloomy observations, dire prophecies. "Resolved, That I am but too much subject to sinful passions," he once wrote to himself, "inconsistent with that meekness and gentleness positively enjoined by the meek and lowly Jesus; that I will endeavor to get the better of them, and keep them all under proper subjection." [26] Nathaniel Emmons engaged in similar exercises. "When I was young, I had many serious thoughts," he later recalled. "I was sensibly struck with a conviction of my great guilt and the awful thought of dying unprepared . . . and I had some lively apprehensions of the state of the damned." [27]

This self-analysis resulted in extreme pessimism that is reminiscent of Augustine's moody thoughts. George Duffield often recorded morose observations in his diary. In 1828 he wrote, "spoke with fluency—thoughts multiplied to my hand, but oh my heart! Not one kindly melting emotion either in prayer or in the sermon. I take shame to myself on this day's labour." [28] Often this gloomy disposition combined with a vivid imagination to produce hallucinations and fearful illusions in the minds of the evangelists. "Ofttimes, when alone," John Newland Maffitt wrote, "I have been alarmed, and thought I beheld some ghastly spectre threaten me with instant death, or imagined that the hour of general judgment was arrived." [29] Although none of them followed Luther's

---

[26] Quoted in Baker, *The Life and Labors of the Rev. Daniel Baker*, p. 43.

[27] Quoted in Sprague, *Annals of The American Pulpit*, I, 693-694.

[28] Duffield Diary, Nov. 16, 1828, quoted in Vander Velde, "The Diary of George Duffield," *Mississippi Valley Historical Review*, XXIV, No. 1 (1937), 27.

[29] Maffitt, *Tears of Contrition*, p. 139.

example and threw inkwells at the devil, many of them, it is apparent, would have liked to!

A further similarity exists in the dogmatic, uncompromising natures of the evangelists. They were all eminently sure of themselves, knew what they wanted, and knew that they were right. The sheer superiority of their attitude toward others is sometimes staggering. As Asahel Nettleton put it, "To all who oppose revivals, I would say, beware lest you be found fighting against God." [30] It must have been difficult, and somewhat terrifying, trying to argue with one who knew God was on his side, who held Satan at bay, and whose single gesture sent scores scurrying toward salvation. Jacob Knapp best revealed this egotism when he declared, "The destinies of multitudes, dead, living, and yet unborn, are linked with the influences I have exerted." [31]

Knapp's statement suggests another resemblance among these men. Exaggeration was not uncommon to them. Revivals were not just a success, they were a sweeping victory. Entire towns fall at their feet; whole families burst into tears in an instant; opponents are quashed, squelched, completely routed with a suddenness, the regularity of which is amazing. Figures of converts reach astronomical proportions. "The whole city seems on the eve of a great moral revolution," wrote one revivalist of little Albany in 1830." [32] Others echoed similar sentiments about New York, Philadelphia, Boston, Rochester, and Cincinnati. Crowds were not convinced, they were "smitten"; interest in religion was not aroused, there was a "stirring of dry bones," to use Finney's phrase. They lived and spoke and preached in terms of crisis and climax. If exaggeration is a trait of the American, it is even more applicable to the Northern evangelist.

If there were similarities in the personalities of the evangelists, there was also a uniformity in many of their beliefs. First of all, they had a kindred faith in Providence and its infinite power. To Albert Barnes, "there is over all things, and embracing all things,

---

[30] Nettleton, "Thoughts on Revivals," in *Remains of the Late Rev. Asahel Nettleton*, p. 399.

[31] Knapp, *Autobiography*, p. 188.

[32] S. W. Whelpley to Finney, Nov. 27, 1830 (Finney Papers).

a great plan . . . one presiding Intellect over all . . . a God who has his own purposes, and who makes those of his creatures subordinate to his own." All events were considered as the working of God's will. Barnes, Finney, and Beecher believed in "one comprehensive plan which embraces all people and all times." [33] As the Methodist James Finley put it, "The pious mind can not fail to see a Divine hand overruling and conducting the whole." [34]

While they agreed about Providence they also had parallel opinions about progress. They were one in their belief in the future, in their assumption of the greatness of the nineteenth century. Barnes asserted that his life had spanned years that were "among the most eventful that have occurred in the history of the world." [35] No other period was as great, no other age brought such improvements to man. Nor would this progress cease. The future would bring even greater benefits to mankind, even greater glory to God. "I believe in a future age, yet to be revealed," announced Horace Bushnell. The world, he asserted, was "an unhatched egg as yet," destined to improve all the time. [36] This progress was linked irrefutably in their minds with the spread of Protestantism, which may help explain the deep-rootedness of their anti-Catholic views.

In speaking of the future the evangelists also followed each other in their anticipation of a millennium, a period of great happiness when holiness would be triumphant. This concept was an important corollary of their search for salvation and was deeply embedded in religious tradition. Jonathan Edwards had believed the millennium was to start in America, and history since his day seemed to point in that direction. The importance of this hoped-for event in the thoughts and conversations of the evangelists cannot be overemphasized. It was an ever-present topic for their consideration. Lyman Beecher was a firm believer in its coming.

[33] Barnes, *Life at Threescore and Ten*, pp. 68, 80.
[34] Finley, *Autobiography*, p. 118.
[35] Barnes, *Life at Threescore and Ten*, p. 22. See also pp. 81, 90-91. For a similar view, see Magoon, *Republican Christianity*, pp. 7-8.
[36] Bushnell, *Work and Play*, pp. 39-40.

"I foresaw it from the first," he wrote. "I felt as if the conversion of the world to Christ were near." [37] Beecher, Duffield, and other revivalists talked as though they were about to march to the final victory of the Protestant church over the forces of darkness. References to "these latter days" crept into their speech. At times a revival was so successful they almost thought the hour was at hand. "Oh what does the Lord mean New York shall do?" wrote one devout during the 1830 revival. "Methinks the Millennium has already commenced and that this state is the starting point." [38] Daniel Baker had similar thoughts several years later in writing his sons of the need of ministers. "Only think, the Emperor of China giving encouragement to the introduction of the Christian religion into his dominions! The Sandwich Islands affair upon a large scale. Surely, the millennium must be at hand." [39]

Revivalists used the imminence of such an event to spur on their potential converts. They employed it as a warning, indicating that men in their actions could postpone its coming. Justin Edwards used it to preach temperance. "The millennium will never come so long as sober men continue the use of ardent spirits," he warned. [40] Manual education enthusiasts looked on their type of training as "a system of education that is to introduce the Millenium" and thought of themselves as hastening the event. "If you and I live 20 years longer, or half that," George W. Gale wrote Finney, "we shall see it." [41] Lyman Beecher used it to spur on his followers to the task of moral reform. "If we endure a little longer," he promised, "the resources of the millennial day will come to our aid. Many are the prophetic signs. . . . The last vial of the wrath of God is running." [42]

[37] Lyman Beecher, *Autobiography*, I, 70.
[38] H. B. Pierpont to Finney, Dec. 25, 1830 (Finney Papers).
[39] Daniel Baker to a son at Princeton, July 22, 1845, in Baker, *The Life and Labors of the Rev. Daniel Baker*, p. 328.
[40] Justin Edwards to "Relatives in Colchester," Jan. 2, 1830, quoted in Hallock, *Light and Love, a Sketch of the Life and Labors of the Rev. Justin Edwards*, p. 324.
[41] George W. Gale to Finney, Jan. 29, 1831 (Finney Papers).
[42] Beecher, *A Reformation of Morals Practicable and Indispensable*, p. 30.

Another idea evangelists held in common was a certain anti-intellectualism that stemmed partly from their training, partly from their suspicion of their more educated, more refined colleagues. Many of them spoke slightingly of the "Rabbis" among their profession who displayed a cultured mind and a polished pen. Although they were given and received a number of honorary degrees, the evangelists decried the awarding of such honors to men of God. Bushnell was reluctant to receive his when the honor came. Jacob Knapp remarked, "I consider the custom of conferring titles of distinction on ministers of the gospel to be wrong." Henry Ward Beecher echoed him in believing that a doctorate "is of about as much use as a butment to a church." [43] Westerners such as Cartwright and Finley were especially denunciatory of the "downy-faced D. D.'s" in the East. Finley, although he heartily approved of universal education, once wrote, "I have wondered if the great multiplication of books has not had a deleterious tendency, in diverting the mind from the Bible." [44]

An additional common denominator among evangelists was their great emphasis on emotion. They were primarily men of feeling. Theirs was a world of the heart. They spoke to the heart; they lived by the heart. Although their appeal was often made on rational grounds, their manner of delivery, their whole approach ensured them success among emotional people. All the techniques of the revival, the use of song, the clever use of prayer, the careful appeal to men's (and women's) hearts were based on an emotional foundation. One of their number, Maffitt, even compiled an *Oratorical Dictionary* (1835) to illustrate how words could produce the desired emotional effect. In this work he declared,

To avail ourselves of the full power of eloquence we must . . . respect and cherish the affections; we must deepen and verify them; we must cease to repress the intense aspirations of humanity after the great and the beautiful. . . . Truth must be planted in the hotbed of feeling if we would taste its richest fruits and please our senses with its flowery developments. . . . Man becomes like his God when he can by a word unchain the impulses

<hr />

[43] Knapp, *Autobiography*, p. 193; Henry Ward Beecher, "American Slavery," *Patriotic Addresses*, p. 190.
[44] Finley, *Autobiography*, p. 171.

of every deep, generous and rich feeling which ever throbbed in the bosom of humanity, and bring to earth the vast sweet thoughts of heaven.[45]

If we turn to the activities of the evangelists and their place in society we see once more that they were cast in the same mold. They were, first, the outstanding men in their profession. Second, they resembled each other in their antagonism toward opponents and in their opposition to other sects. Dogmatic as they were and egotistical as they appeared to be, they looked with disfavor upon conflicting points of view. Every other sect was a rival, almost as dangerous at times as the devil himself. Thus Finney crusaded against Universalists, and Beecher fired salvo after salvo into the Unitarian camp. George Duffield wrote about sects other than his own as though they were enemies in the field.

A reservoir of antagonism was tapped on many occasions. Edward N. Kirk played on orthodoxy's fear of Universalism. "The Universalist forces from Maine to Maryland have rallied," he announced, "and the Devil's ablest have proclaimed the glad tidings." Joshua Leavitt's New York *Evangelist* set up a constant volley against the liturgy and other features of the Episcopal Church. Orson Parker, bellicose Calvinist, ripped into his "Methodist brethren" who, he believed, "have thrown an immense amount of fog around the sinner's mind." [46] Some of his Methodist brethren, on the other hand, ripped into Orson Parker and others like him for proselytizing Calvinism, which "was an enemy that must be struck down wherever it showed its head." [47] Peter Cartwright, who took every opportunity to invade the pulpits of other denominations and debate their doctrines, spoke and acted like a military general, "invading" Calvinist strongholds and "taking possession" of Baptist meeting houses.[48]

Because of the personalities and views of the evangelists it was to be expected that they would engage in many disputes through-

---

[45] Maffitt, *The Oratorical Dictionary*, pp. xvii-xviii.

[46] Edward N. Kirk to Finney, June 27, 1832 (Finney Papers). For anti-Episcopalian strictures, see Waylen, *Ecclesiastical Reminiscences of the United States*, pp. 413-417. Orson Parker to Finney, Oct. 15, 1868 (Finney Papers).

[47] Waters, *Peter Cartwright*, p. 74.

[48] See Cartwright, *Autobiography*, pp. 56, 110, 331-332, 341-342, 357, 369, 393.

out their careers. Nettleton attacked Finney; Finney attacked Beecher; Beecher attacked the Lane students; Fairfield West attacked Bushnell; and the number of persons who were ranged against Jacob Knapp was legion. Albert Barnes was accused of heresy; Lyman Beecher was charged with similar theological crimes; Henry Ward was accused of more worldly ones. Conferences and general sessions were their battle ground, letters and articles a particular form of ambush. When these men were not preaching or praying they were engaging in forensic debate or plotting some new charge or countercharge. The air was electric with their fights. For a number of reasons Edward N. Kirk refused to work with Finney even at the height of the 1857 revival. "I did not request you to come to Boston to labor," he wrote Finney, "and am entirely unable to regard myself as responsible for the results of your labors. . . . I told you . . . I would not invite you to labor with me until you or I was changed. I have seen no reason to alter that decision. We may talk this over in heaven. In this world it would do no good." [49] Even the mild-mannered Bushnell engaged hotly with Finney on occasion. "You make out so heavy bill against me which I regret that I cannot now go over," he once wrote in reply to the Oberlin divine's strictures on his book. "You are totally out in your indictment and if I don't forget it when I get force to go over the ground I will show you that you are." [50]

In spite of their many disputes and their antagonism against each other these evangelists did manage occasionally to work together. There was a time when even Kirk invited Finney to help him lead a revival. "You must come and help me at my four days' meeting," he once wrote. "I have pulled on the old chord until I am expecting every day to hear it snap. You cannot tell how it oppresses me sometimes. I want your help. Do come." [51] Hardly a day passed that Finney did not receive requests for advice or help from men with whom he had formerly tilted lances, as well as from

[49] Edward N. Kirk to Finney, March 1, 1858 (Finney Papers).
[50] Horace Bushnell to Finney, July 23 (n.d.) (Finney Papers).
[51] Edward N. Kirk to Finney, April 15, 1830 (Finney Papers).

those within his own camp. "O tell me how I may thrust the two edged sword into the sinners inmost soul!" one minister wrote. "Do give me hints by which I may learn to preach law with effect." [52]

Often the revivalists worked as a team, overriding differences of doctrine or sect. "Maffitt and Knapp and Kirk will be left on the ground here," wrote Finney at the close of one of his revivals in Boston. "Knapp has begun to dy [sic]. Kirk is to be here in two weeks." [53] On other occasions they worked in succession, hitting a town in waves one after another. Herman Norton, the rabid anti-Catholic revivalist, made it a practice to follow in Finney's wake. He went to Reading after Finney had been there; he followed him to New York City and later went to Cincinnati after Finney moved to Oberlin. Kirk for a while followed Knapp's successful tour, visiting Baltimore, New Haven, and Boston after the Baptist had left. Co-operation was almost as strong in linking the evangelists as controversy separated them. In any case, paradoxical though it may seem, both a tendency toward dispute and a willingness to work together characterized the Northern evangelist.

Another common characteristic of these men, namely, their assumption of almost limitless prerogatives, has already been noted. Although they were ministers of the gospel, the revivalists held all topics within their sphere. No field was foreign to their touch, no subject too remote on which to pass judgment. They all defended ardently this right to speak authoritatively on any and all matters.

Every subject, whether of business or of morals, comes fairly within the province of the pulpit. It is our duty to commend that which is right; and to lift the voice of entreaty, and remonstrance, in regard to that which is wrong. It is one of the duties of our office. . . . We claim the right as a part of our high embassage, of discussing any subject, whoever it may affect, or whatever calling it may reach, with perfect freedom. [54]

A final affinity that links these men was their subjection to attack, often bordering on persecution, by the more worldly portion

---

[52] J. J. Shipherd to Finney, March 14, 1831 (Finney Papers).
[53] Finney to Henry Cowles, Dec. 23, 1841 (Cowles Papers).
[54] Albert Barnes, *The Immorality of the Traffic in Ardent Spirits*, pp. 3-4.

of the population. The public press ridiculed their meetings. The Camden papers poked fun at Finney; the Boston press blasted Beecher and Knapp; New York papers caricatured Leavitt. They were chased by mobs; anonymous letters threatened them; churches were closed to them. "Many slanderous reports have been circulated," complained Daniel Baker, "and I have been caught up in a tempest of persecution." [55] "I see an attack on you in the *Standard* of this week," Lewis Tappan warned Joshua Leavitt. "It is calculated to wound and perhaps irritate you. . . . The answer requires deliberation, caution, meekness, thoroughness, demolition." [56] Charges against the character of the evangelists were most numerous. Finney, Maffitt, Barnes, Lyman, and Henry Ward Beecher were accused of immorality. Even the quiet, retiring Nettleton was charged with "indiscreet conduct with women." [57] But the most bitterly persecuted was John Newland Maffitt, whose morals were assailed and whose reputation was shattered. The New York *Police Gazette* pounced upon him for his affair with a Brooklyn belle, chased him out of New York, followed him South, and made his last days unbearable. "O Ellen," he cried, walking the floor of his sister's room before his death, "they have broke my heart." [58]

The closing years of an active man's life are difficult ones to live. Those evangelists who were still surviving by 1870—Finney, Leavitt, Barnes, and Bushnell—approached the end with little left to do. All their lances were shattered; they were the rear guard of a routed age. Leavitt was back East awaiting the end after an abortive business venture in St. Louis. With little of his old fire he set to work on an article about Nathaniel S. S. Beman, their old cohort, "with especial reference to the New Lebanon convention." [59] Barnes was specializing in reminiscent sermons, left ludicrously high and dry as his Church healed up the doctrinal wounds

[55] Baker, *The Life and Labors of the Rev. Daniel Baker*, p. 96.
[56] Lewis Tappan to Joshua Leavitt, Oct. 17, 1843 (Lewis Tappan Papers).
[57] Birney, *The Life and Letters of Asahel Nettleton*, p. 79.
[58] Quoted in Redford, *Western Cavaliers*, p. 328.
[59] William Hayes Ward to Finney, Sept. 13, 1871 (Finney Papers).

he had opened so long before. Finney was kept busy preparing for a trip to California and reading letters from old admirers. There were also old quarrels to patch. He wrote Lewis Tappan, "I pray you to forgive whatever in your judgment may have been amiss in my treatment of you, at any period of my life," and the aging Tappan replied, excusing Finney for a letter he had written some thirty-seven years previously, "I can see now, that there were expressions in the letter peculiar to yourself." [60]

Finney even considered embarking on one last lecture tour in the 1870's. He still received urgent invitations to preach. In 1873 he took part in the ninth annual convention of the National Association for the Religious Amendment of the Constitution.[61] There was still some fire left in his spirit, but the flesh was weak. The end came quietly for him in California in August, 1875. Barnes had already died in 1870; Leavitt followed in 1873; and Bushnell held out until 1876. Then there was only Henry Ward, deeply enmeshed in the biggest trial of his life, and he was hardly the one to carry on the old tradition. With Finney's death, the last religious link with the 1830's was gone.

In spite of their failures, in spite of the fact that their philosophy, their methods, and their programs were rejected, in spite of the fact that after the Civil War theology and social reforms were no longer as closely allied as formerly, nevertheless the evangelists did leave a heritage for those who came after them. The Moodys and Sankeys adopted and modified the techniques employed by the Finneys and Beechers. Many of the postwar religious organizations built on the foundations laid by the moralistic social architects of the 1830's. The hard crust of Protestantism to which the evangelists contributed remained a potent force in American society. The tradition of dressing old, worn-out theology in modern clothes and applying it to modern situations was strengthened by the evangelists, who thus helped make possible the modern synthesis in the Protestant ethic. Finally, the Northern evangelists pushed their ideas into the main stream of American thought and made

---

[60] Lewis Tappan to Finney, March 4, 1872 (Finney Papers).
[61] See Phelps, *Church and State in the United States*, III, 587.

the nation more devout, more dogmatic, and more conservative. One cannot help but note the strength and continuance of such sentiments among pious Protestants as anti-Catholicism, temperance, ideas of church and state. While these movements had their rise and fall, there was nevertheless a certain timelessness about them. The opinions of the American evangelists concerning them remained steady through the years. The evangelists served not so much as originators as leaven, fermenting in every generation or so reminders of their pet peeves and prejudices. Thus, in spite of their apparent failure, the evangelists were more influential than their numbers would lead one to expect.

Indeed, an intangible measure of their influence can be seen in the strength of their hold on the American mind. The evangelistic quality of Bryan's campaign, the Biblical fervor of some of Wallace's supporters in the Progressive party, and the diversion of President Truman from the details of the Korean fighting to pray with Billy Graham, 1950 counterpart of Knapp, Beecher, and Finney, are but a few examples. Northern evangelists contributed something else to the shaping of American thought. In their assertion of a dualism, an either-or approach to life, they helped make philosophically acceptable the hard and fast concept of absolute good and evil which hampers so much of modern thinking. To use the East-West split as an example, the Protestant American, steeped in this evangelistic tradition, accepts the idea of good and evil in the interpretation of power politics and the struggle between capitalism and communism, totally accepting the one and totally rejecting the other.

What message, it may be asked, have these evangelists for our troubled times? Have they anything to offer to help solve the persistent problems of the present? Their world was not our world; their assumptions, methods, and conclusions are foreign to us. Nevertheless, although we may reject their leadership, we must remember that the nineteenth century had its fears and insecurities just as the mid-twentieth. There were two worlds then just as now. The great fear then centered about the after life and the unknown forces of evil. In the twentieth century we have merely transferred their fear of the supernatural and otherworldly to an apprehension of a foreign nation and its ideology which for modern Western man represents the personification of evil.

It is difficult to realize that the dread of damnation, of eternal punishment and all that it meant, was a fear far greater in the minds of the nineteenth-century devout, and more particularly the evangelist, than the uneasiness of twentieth-century man who faces utter annihilation at the hands of unleashed atomic energy. It may be argued that theirs was an imaginary threat while ours is a real and pressing one. Nevertheless, it is also patent that nineteenth-century man considered himself impotent in the face of his fear. There was, after all, even in the most liberal orthodox circles, little one could do by himself to be saved. We, however, acknowledge no such impotency. Dealing with natural phenomena, we still have it within our power to control and devise our destiny. The menace of a hydrogen bomb would probably seem slight to the emotional evangelist describing for his hearers the implications of hell fire and the loss of one's soul. Modern man has transferred the fears of religion and prejudice into those of science and reality. Modern man is better prepared to face these latter fears than his predecessors were the former.

There is another purpose the nineteenth-century Northern evangelists serve for our time. They broke away from established authority; they struck out in new directions; they had confidence in their position; and they dared to persevere in the face of opposition. It took courage to meet hostile crowds, to preach unpopular doctrines, to be out of step with the times, to serve an unknown master for little pay or thanks. And the evangelists were courageous men. We may reject their ends and their means, but the spirit inherent in their endeavor could be a lesson for our times when once again it takes courage to stand against the tide.

This handful of men, so diverse and yet so much alike, would be an anachronism in our own times. Yet in their own age they led lives that were fully lived and followed careers that were well spent. But they themselves should have their own epilogue. Harriet Beecher Stowe, in writing of her father's colorful career, observed, "It was an exuberant and glorious life while it lasted. The atmosphere of his household was replete with moral oxygen, full charged with intellectual electricity." Horace Bushnell, in a fragment of an autobiography written near the end of his life, declared, "My figure in this world has not been great, but I have had a great experience . . . it has been a great thing even for me to live." [62]

[62] Quoted in Hoyt, *The Pulpit and American Life*, p. 60; Cheney, *Life and Letters of Horace Bushnell*, p. 2.

BIBLIOGRAPHY

MANUSCRIPT COLLECTIONS

Albert Barnes Papers, Presbyterian Historical Society Library.
Clergymen Miscellaneous Letters, 1719-1873—Simon Gratz Collection, Library of Congress.
Henry Cowles Papers, Oberlin College Library.
Charles G. Finney Papers, Oberlin College Library.
Correspondence and Papers of Joshua Leavitt, Library of Congress.
Papers of Benjamin Tappan, Library of Congress.
Lewis Tappan Papers, Library of Congress.
Theodore Dwight Weld Papers, Library of Congress.

BIBLIOGRAPHICAL GUIDES AND REFERENCE WORKS

Allison, William H. Inventory of Unpublished Materials for American Religious History. Washington, D. C., 1910.
Bowerman, G. F. A Selected Bibliography of the Religious Denominations of the United States. New York, 1896.
Hastings, James, ed. Encyclopedia of Religion and Ethics. New York, 1912.
Jackson, Samuel Macauley, ed. The New Schaff-Herzog Encyclopedia of Religious Knowledge. Grand Rapids, Mich., 1950.
Johnson, S. M. A Bibliography of American Church History, 1820-1893. American Church History Series, Vol. XII, New York, pp. 441-513.
Mathews, Shailer, and Gerald B. Smith. A Dictionary of Religion and Ethics. New York, 1921.
Methodist Episcopal Church. General Conference Journal. New York. n.d.
Mode, Peter G. Source Book and Bibliographical Guide for American Church History. Menasha, Wis., 1920.
Presbyterian Church in the United States of America. Minutes of the General Assembly, 1835, 1837, 1838. Philadelphia, 1836, 1837, 1838.

SELECTED WORKS OF REPRESENTATIVE NORTHERN EVANGELISTS

Barnes, Albert. An Address, Delivered July 4, 1827, at the Presbyterian Church in Morristown. Morristown, N. J., 1827.
——— The Casting Down of Thrones, a Discourse on the Present State of Europe. Philadelphia, 1848.

—— The Causes of Intemperance in Cities and Large Towns. Philadelphia, 1834.

—— The Church and Slavery. Philadelphia, 1857.

—— The Conditions of Peace. Philadelphia, 1863.

—— The Connexion of Temperance with Republican Freedom. Philadelphia, 1835.

—— Essays on Intemperance. Morristown, 1828.

—— The Gospel Necessary to Our Country. Washington, 1852.

—— Home Missions. New York, 1849.

—— The Immorality of the Traffic in Ardent Spirits. Philadelphia, 1834.

—— An Inquiry into the Scriptural Views of Slavery. Philadelphia, 1846.

—— Lectures on the Evidence of Christianity in the Nineteenth Century. New York, 1868.

—— Life at Threescore. Philadelphia, 1858.

—— Life at Threescore and Ten. Philadelphia, 1869.

—— The Literature and Science of America. Utica, N. Y., 1836.

—— The Love of Country. Philadelphia, 1861.

—— Miscellaneous Essays and Reviews. 2 vols. New York, 1855.

—— Plea on Behalf of Western Colleges. Philadelphia and New York, 1846.

—— The Position of the Evangelical Party in the Episcopal Church. Philadelphia, 1844.

—— The Progress and Tendency of Science. Philadelphia, 1840.

—— The Rule of Christianity in Regard to Conformity to the World. Philadelphia, 1833.

—— The Throne of Iniquity, or, Sustaining Evil by Law. Harrisburg, Pa., 1852.

—— The Way of Salvation. Morristown, N. J., 1830.

Beecher, Edward. The Conflict of Ages. Boston, 1855.

—— Narrative of Riots at Alton in Connection with the Death of Rev. Elijah P. Lovejoy. Alton, Ill., 1838.

—— The Papal Conspiracy Exposed. Boston, 1855.

—— The Question at Issue. Boston, 1850.

Beecher, Edward, and Theron Baldwin. An Appeal in Behalf of the Illinois College, Recently Founded at Jacksonville, Illinois. New York, 1831.

Beecher, Edward, Jonathan Blanchard, and David Macdill. Secret Societies, a Discussion of Their Character and Claims. Cincinnati, 1867.

Beecher, Henry Ward. Freedom and War. Boston, 1863.

—— Lectures to Young Men. 2d ed. New York, 1856.

—— Patriotic Addresses. New York, 1887.

—— The Plymouth Collection of Hymns and Tunes. New York, 1855.

Beecher, Lyman. Autobiography, Correspondence, etc. of Lyman Beecher. Ed. by Charles Beecher. 2 vols. New York, 1864.
—— The Bible, a Code of Laws. Andover, Mass., 1818.
—— The Designs, Rights, and Duties of Local Churches. Andover, Mass., 1819.
—— Lectures on Political Atheism. London, n.d.
—— Letters of the Rev. Dr. Beecher and Rev. Mr. Nettleton on the "New Measures" in Conducting Revivals of Religion. New York, 1828.
—— The Means of National Prosperity. New York, 1820.
—— The Memory of Our Fathers. Boston, 1828.
—— The Nature, Occasions, Signs, Evils and Remedy of Intemperance. New York, 1827.
—— A Plea for the West. 2d ed. New York and Cincinnati, 1835.
—— A Reformation of Morals Practicable and Indispensable. 2d ed. Andover, Mass., 1814.
—— The Remedy for Duelling. New York, 1809.
—— Resources of the Adversary and Means of Their Destruction. Boston, 1827.
—— A Sermon, addressed to the Legislature of Connecticut, May 3, 1826. New Haven, Conn., 1826.
—— Views in Theology. New York, 1836.
—— Works. 3 vols. Boston, 1852-1853.
Bushnell, Horace. An Address before the Hartford County Agricultural Society. Hartford, 1847.
—— "The Age of Homespun" in Litchfield County Centennial Celebration, 1851. Hartford, 1851.
—— Barbarism, the First Danger. New York, 1847.
—— Building Eras in Religion. New York, 1881.
—— California, Its Characteristics and Prospects. New Haven, 1858.
—— The Census and Slavery. Hartford, 1860.
—— Christ in Theology. Hartford, 1851.
—— Common Schools. Hartford, 1853.
—— Crisis of the Church. Hartford, 1835.
—— A Discourse on the Moral Tendencies and Results of Human History. New York, 1843.
—— A Discourse on the Slavery Question. Hartford, 1839.
—— The Fathers of New England. New York, 1850.
—— Forgiveness and Law. New York, 1874.
—— God in Christ. Hartford, 1849.
     The Growth of Law. Hartford, 1843.
—— Moral Uses of Dark Things. New York, 1867.
—— Nature and the Supernatural. New York, 1858.

—— The Northern Iron. Hartford, 1854.

—— Politics under the Law of God. Hartford, 1844.

—— Popular Government by Divine Right. Hartford, 1864.

—— Prosperity Our Duty. Hartford, 1847.

—— Reverses Needed. Hartford, 1861.

—— Sermons for the New Life. New York, 1858.

—— Sermons on Living Subjects. New York, 1872.

—— Society and Religion, a Sermon for California. Hartford, 1856.

—— Speech for Connecticut. Hartford, 1851.

—— Spiritual Dislodgements. Hartford, 1857.

—— Twentieth Anniversary. Hartford, 1853.

—— The Vicarious Sacrifice. New York, 1866.

—— Views of Christian Nurture. 2d ed. Hartford, 1848.

—— Women's Suffrage, the Reform against Nature. New York, 1869.

—— Work and Play. New York, 1864.

Cartwright, Peter. Autobiography. New York, 1856.

—— Fifty Years as a Presiding Elder. Cincinnati and New York, 1871.

Colton, Calvin. Abolition a Sedition. Philadelphia, 1839.

—— Church and State in America. London, 1834.

—— History and Character of American Revivals of Religion. 2d ed.
London, 1832.

—— The Junius Tracts. New York, 1844.

—— The Last Seven Years of the Life of Henry Clay. New York, 1856.

—— A Lecture on the Railroad to the Pacific. New York, 1850.

—— Life of Henry Clay. New York, 1844.

—— The Life and Times of Henry Clay. New York, 1846.

—— Manual for Emigrants to America. London, 1832.

—— Political Abolition. New York, 1844.

—— Protestant Jesuitism. New York, 1836.

—— Public Economy for the United States. New York, 1848.

—— The Rights of Labor. 3d ed. New York, 1847.

—— A Voice from America to England. London, 1839.

Duffield, George. The American Patriot. Detroit, 1852.

—— The Death of Gen. William Henry Harrison. Detroit, 1841.

—— The Immorality of the Traffic in Ardent Spirits. Carlisle, Pa., 1834.

—— The Nation's Wail. Detroit, 1865.

—— The True Scholar. Detroit, 1845.

Edwards, Justin. Letter to the Friends of Temperance in Massachusetts.
Boston, 1836.

—— On the Traffic in Ardent Spirits. New York, n.d.

—— The Sabbath Manual. New York, n.d.

—— The Temperance Manual. New York, 1847.

Emmons, Nathaniel. A Discourse, Delivered Sept. 3, 1792 to the Society

for the Reformation of Morals in Franklin. Worcester, Mass., 1793.
—— Works. 6 vols. Boston, 1842.
Finley, James B. Autobiography of Rev. James B. Finley, or; Pioneer Life in the West. ed. by W. P. Strickland. Cincinnati, 1854.
—— History of the Wyandott Mission at Upper Sandusky, Ohio. Cincinnati, 1840.
—— Life among the Indians. Cincinnati and New York, 1857.
—— Memorials of Prison Life. Cincinnati, 1851.
—— Sketches of Western Methodism. ed. by W. P. Strickland. Cincinnati, 1857.
Finney, Charles G. An Autobiography. London, 1903.
—— The Character, Claims and Practical Workings of Freemasonry. Cincinnati, 1869.
—— A Fourth Voice from America. London, 1850.
—— How to Change Your Heart. New York, 1836.
—— Lectures on Revivals of Religion. 6th ed. New York, 1835.
—— Lectures on Systematic Theology. Oberlin, Boston, and New York, 1846.
—— Lectures to Professing Christians. New York, 1837.
—— Memoirs of Rev. Charles G. Finney. New York, 1876.
—— Reminiscences of C. G. Finney. MSS, Finney Papers, Oberlin College Library.
—— Revival Memories. MSS, Finney Papers, Oberlin College Library.
—— Sermons on Important Subjects. 3d ed. New York, 1836.
—— Sermons on the Way of Salvation. Oberlin, 1891.
—— Views of Sanctification. Oberlin, 1891.
Green, Beriah. An Address, Delivered at Whitesborough, N.Y., Sept. 5, 1833. Utica, N. Y., 1833.
—— The American Student. Whitesboro, N. Y., 1838.
—— The Basis of a Sound Reputation. Whitesboro, N. Y., 1837.
—— The Divine Significance of Work. Whitesboro, N. Y., 1842.
—— Faith and Works. Whitesboro, N. Y., 1841.
—— Sketches of the Life and Writings of James Gillespie Birney. Utica, N. Y., 1844.
—— Success. Utica, N. Y., 1843.
Kirk, Edward N. Christian Missions—A Work of Faith. Boston, 1865.
—— The Church and the College. Boston, 1851.
—— The Church Essential to the Republic. New York, 1848.
—— On the Traffic in Intoxicating Liquors. Albany, 1835.
—— Plea for the Poor. Boston, 1843.
—— Protestantism and Romanism. N.p., 1860.
—— Sermons in England and America. New York, 1840.
Knapp, Jacob. Autobiography of Elder Jacob Knapp. New York, 1868.

Leavitt, Joshua. The Monroe Doctrine. New York, 1863.

Maffitt, John N. Literary and Religious Sketches. New York, 1832.

—— The Oratorical Dictionary. Nashville, 1835.

—— Tears of Contrition. New London, Conn., 1821.

Nettleton, Asahel. Rev. Asahel Nettleton's Letter to Dr. Lyman Beecher, on Revivals. N.p., n.d.

—— Remains of the Late Rev. Asahel Nettleton. Ed by Bennet Tyler. Hartford, 1845.

—— Temperance and Revivals. Boston, n.d.

—— Village Hymns for Social Worship. New York, 1826.

Norton, Herman. Record of Facts concerning the Persecution at Madeira in 1843 and 1846. New York, 1849.

—— Signs of Danger and of Promise, Duties of American Protestants at the Present Crisis. New York, 1853.

—— The Sin and Remedy of Licentiousness. New York, 1835.

—— Startling Facts for American Protestants. New York, 1844.

Wayland, Francis. Address before the Rhode Island Society for the Encouragement of Domestic Industry. Providence, 1852.

—— The Affairs of Rhode Island. 2d ed. Providence, 1842.

—— Appeal to the Disciples of Christ. Boston, n.d.

—— The Dependence of Science upon Religion. Providence, 1835.

—— A Discourse on the Philosophy of Analogy. Boston, 1831.

—— Domestic Slavery considered as a Scriptural Institution. New York and Boston, 1845.

—— Dr. Wayland on the Moral and Religious Aspects of the Nebraska Bill. Rochester, 1854.

—— The Duties of an American Citizen. 2d ed. Boston, 1825.

—— The Duty of Obedience to the Civil Magistrate. Boston, 1847.

—— The Education Demanded by the People of the United States. Boston, 1855.

—— Elements of Intellectual Philosophy. Boston, 1854.

—— Elements of Moral Science. New York, 1835.

—— The Elements of Political Economy. New York, 1837.

—— Limitations of Human Responsibility. Boston, 1838.

—— The Moral Dignity of the Missionary Enterprise. Boston, 1824.

—— The Moral Law of Accumulation. Providence, 1837.

—— Occasional Discourses. Boston, 1833.

—— The Philosophy of Analogy. Providence, 1831.

—— Report to the Corporation of Brown University on the Changes in the System of Collegiate Education. Providence, 1850.

—— Thoughts on the Present Collegiate System in the United States. Boston, 1842.

—— University Sermons. Boston, 1849.

CONTROVERSIAL LITERATURE AND WORKS BY CONTEMPORARIES

Armstrong, George D. The Christian Doctrine of Slavery. New York, 1857.

Bacon, Leonard. Sermon at the Funeral of Rev. Lyman Beecher. New York, 1863.

Baird, Robert. The Progress and Prospects of Christianity in the United States. London, 1851.

Baird, Samuel J. A History of the New School and of the Questions Involved in the Disruption of the Presbyterian Church. Philadelphia, 1868.

Baker, Daniel. A Scriptural View of Baptism. Washington, 1827.

Bancroft, George. An Oration delivered on the Fourth of July, 1826. Northampton, Mass., 1826.

Belcher, Joseph. The Religious Denominations in the United States. Philadelphia, 1854.

Beman, Nathaniel S. S. The Influence of Ardent Spirits in the Production of the Cholera. Troy, 1832.

Birney, James G. American Churches the Bulwark of American Slavery. 2d American ed. Newburryport, 1842.

Bolles, John A. Review of "The Affairs of Rhode Island." Providence and Boston, 1842.

Bradley, Joshua. Accounts of Religious Revivals in Many parts of the United States from 1815 to 1818. Albany, 1819.

Burchard, Charles. A Statement of Facts in Relation to the Case of Rev. Jacob Knapp. New York, 1846.

"Candour." Theological Pretenders; or, an analysis of the Character and Conduct of the Rev. J. N. Maffitt. New York, 1830.

Cheeseman, Lewis. Differences between Old and New School Presbyterians. Rochester, 1848.

Cowles, Henry. Holiness of Christians in the Present Life. Oberlin, 1840.

Crocker, Zebulon. The Catastrophe of the Presbyterian Church in 1837. New Haven, 1838.

Cushing, Caleb. A Discourse on the Social Influences of Christianity. Andover, Mass., 1839.

Dix, John R. Pulpit Portraits; or, Pen Pictures of Distinguished American Divines. Boston, 1854.

Dorr, Thomas W. Report of the Trial of Thomas Wilson Dorr, for Treason against the State of Rhode Island. Boston, 1844.

Dwight, Timothy. Theology, Explained and Defended. 4 vols., 11th ed. New Haven, Conn., 1845.

Elsemore, Moses. An Impartial Account of the Life of the Rev. John N. Maffitt. New York, 1848.

Ely, Ezra Stiles. The Duty of Christian Freemen to Elect Christian Rulers. Philadelphia, 1828.

Fuller, Zelotes. The Tree of Liberty. Philadelphia, 1830.

Hibbard, Rufus F. Startling Disclosures Concerning the Death of John N. Maffitt. New York, 1856.

Hicks, Elias. Journal of the Life and Religious Labours of Elias Hicks. New York, 1832.

—— Letters of Elias Hicks. Philadelphia, 1834.

Hotchkin, James H. A History of the Purchase and Settlement of Western New York. New York, 1848.

Humphrey, Edward P. A Discourse on the Death of General Zachary Taylor. Louisville, 1850.

Humphrey, Heman. An Address Delivered at the Collegiate Institute in Amherst, Massachusetts. Boston, 1823.

—— A Parallel between Intemperance and the Slave Trade. New York, 1828.

Johnson, Richard M. "Report of the Committee of Post Offices and Post Roads of the United States House of Representatives," Reports of the Twenty-first Congress, First Session, No. 271. Washington, 1830.

Jones, Pomroy. Annals and Recollections of Oneida County. Rome, N. Y., 1851.

Junkin, George. The Vindication, containing a History of the Trial of the Rev. Albert Barnes. Philadelphia, 1836.

Kilbourne, Payne K. A Biographical History of the County of Litch-field, Connecticut. New York, 1851.

Lansing, Dirck C. Sermons on Important Subjects of Christian Doctrine and Duty. Auburn, N. Y., 1825.

McDowall, John R. Memoirs. New York, 1838.

McVickar, John. Outlines of Political Economy. New York, 1825.

Magoon, Elias L. Republican Christianity. Boston, 1849.

Mahan, Asa. Scripture Doctrines of Christian Perfection. Oberlin, 1839.

Martineau, Harriet. The Manifest Destiny of the American Union. New York, 1857.

—— The Martyr Age of the United States of America. Newcastle upon Tyne, 1840.

Mason, Erskine. An Evangelical Ministry, the Security of a Nation. New York, 1848.

—— A Pastor's Legacy. New York, 1853.

Mather, Cotton. Essays to Do Good. Boston, 1710.

"Moderatus." Review of . . . President Wayland's . . . Limitations of Human Responsibility. Providence, 1840.

Morgan, John. The Holiness Acceptable to God. Oberlin, 1846.

Nelson, David. The Cause and Cure of Infidelity. New York, 1841.

Nevin, John W.   The Anxious Bench.   Chambersburg, Pa., 1843.

Reese, David M.   The Humbugs of New York.   New York, 1838.

Rice, Roswell.   An Oration . . . on the Rev. John N. Maffitt.   Troy, 1874.

Robinson, John.   The Testimony and Practice of the Presbyterian Church in Reference to American Slavery.   Cincinnati, 1852.

Schaff, Philip.   America, a Sketch of the Political, Social, and Religious Character of the United States of North America.   New York, 1855.

Southard, Nathaniel.   Why Work for the Slave?   New York, 1838.

Stone, William L.   Matthias and His Impostures.   3d ed.   New York, 1835.

Tappan, Henry P.   The Life of the Rev. Herman Norton.   New York, 1853.

Tappan, Lewis.   Immediate Emancipation the Only Wise and Safe Mode. New York, 1861.

—— Reply to Charges Brought against the American and Foreign Anti-slavery Society.   London, 1852.

Taylor, Nathaniel W.   Concio ad Clerum.   New Haven, 1828.

Thome, James A.   Prayer for the Oppressed.   Boston, 1859.

Thompson, Joseph P.   The Faithful Preacher, a Discourse Commemorative of the Late Dirck C. Lansing.   New York, 1857.

Tyler, Bennet.   Memoir of the Life and Character of Rev. Asahel Nettleton.   Boston, 1844.

Vethake, Henry.   Principles of Political Economy.   Philadelphia, 1838.

Webster, Daniel.   Works of Daniel Webster.   Vol. vi.   Boston, 1851.

Weeks, William R.   The Pilgrim's Progress in the Nineteenth Century. New York, 1849.

Weld, Theodore D.   American Slavery as It Is.   New York, 1839.

—— A Statement of the Reasons which Induced the Students of Lane Seminary to Dissolve their Connections with That Institution.   Cincinnati, 1834.

—— The Bible against Slavery.   New York, 1837.

Whelpley, Samuel.   The Triangle.   New York, 1816.

Whipple, Charles K.   The Methodist Church and Slavery.   Boston, 1859.

—— The Relations of Anti-slavery to Religion.   New York, 1856.

Wilbur, Asa.   An Examination of the Comparative Statistical Results of the Labors of Elder Jacob Knapp in the State of Massachusetts.   Boston, 1855.

Williams, Thomas A.   A Discourse on the Official Character of Nathaniel Emmons.   Boston, 1851.

Wood, James.   Facts and Observations Concerning the Organization and State of the Churches in the Three Synods of Western New York and the Synod of Western Reserve.   Saratoga Springs, N. Y., 1837.

American and Foreign Anti-slavery Society. Annual Reports. Nos. 7-13. New York, 1847-1853.

American Anti-slavery Society. Annual Reports. Nos. 1-7. New York, 1834-1840.

American Tract Society. Annual Reports. Nos. 1-8. New York, 1826-1833.

—— Tracts, General Series. New York, n.d.

Anti-Masonic Scrap-book. Chicago, 1883.

A Brief View of the American Education Society. Andover, 1826.

Debate at the Lane Seminary. Boston, 1834.

Exposition of the Course of Conduct Pursued by the Rev. Jacob Knapp. Hamilton, N. Y., 1846.

Facts Involved in the Rhode Island Controversy. Boston, 1842.

Memoir and Select Remains of the late John R. McDowall. New York, 1838.

Minutes of the Philadelphia Convention of Ministers and Ruling Elders in the Presbyterian Church in the United States Called by the Minority of the General Assembly of 1836, May 11, 1837. Philadelphia, 1837.

National Kansas Aid Convention Proceedings. Buffalo, 1856.

Northwestern Christian Anti-slavery Convention at Chicago. Cleveland, 1859.

Presbyterian Church in the U.S.A., Presbytery of Philadelphia. A Report of the Debates in the Presbytery of Philadelphia. Philadelphia, 1831.

—— A True and Complete Narrative of all the Proceedings of the Philadelphia Presbytery, and of the Philadelphia Synod, in Relation to the Case of the Rev. Albert Barnes. Philadelphia, 1830.

Proceedings and Addresses of the Sabbath Convention. Chambersburg, Pa., 1848.

Proceedings of the New York Anti-secret Society Convention, 1870. N.p., 1870.

Read and Decide for Yourself. A Review of the Proceedings of the General Assembly of the Presbyterian Church in the United States, at their Session of 1837. N.p., n.d.

The Relation of the Pulpit to Slavery. Oneida County, N.Y., 1836.

Remarks on Barnes' Inquiry. Philadelphia, 1844.

Report of the Fourth Anniversary of the Ohio Anti-slavery Society, Held in Putnam, Muskingum County, Ohio, May 29, 1839. Cincinnati, 1839.

Right and Wrong in Massachusetts. Boston, 1839.

Trial of the Rev. Albert Barnes before the Synod of Philadelphia . . . on a Charge of Heresy. New York, 1836.

Trial of the Rev. Lyman Beecher, D.D., before the Presbytery of Cincinnati on the Charge of Heresy. New York, 1835.

The True History of the Late Division in the Anti-slavery Societies. Boston, 1841.

RELIGIOUS AND CONTEMPORARY PERIODICALS

Advent Herald
Advocate of Moral Reform
American Almanac and Repository of Useful Knowledge
American Annual Register
American National Preacher
American Quarterly Register
Biblical Repertory and Princeton Review
Christian Examiner
Christian Spectator
Christian Union
Congregationalist
Connecticut Evangelical Magazine
The Home Missionary
The Independent
McDowall's Journal
New York *Evangelist*
New York *Observer*
Oberlin Evangelist
Oberlin Quarterly Review
Presbyterian Quarterly
The Protestant
Religious Telescope
Spirit of the Pilgrims

REPORTS OF TRAVELERS

Buckingham, James. The Eastern and Western States of America. 2 vols. London, 1842.
Combe, George. Notes on the United States of North America. 2 vols. Philadelphia, 1841.
De Roos, Frederick F. Personal Narrative of Travels in the United States and Canada in 1826. 3d ed. London, 1827.
Fearon, Henry B. Sketches of America. 3d ed. London, 1819.
Grund, Francis J. The Americans, in their Moral, Social, and Political Relations. Boston, 1837.
Hall, Captain Basil. Travels in North America in the Years, 1827 and 1828. 3 vols. Edinburgh, 1829.
Lieber, Francis. Letters to a Gentleman in Germany. Philadelphia, 1834.
—— The Stranger in America. 2 vols. London, 1835.

Mackay, Alexander. The Western World; or, Travels in the United States in 1846-47. 3 vols., 4th ed. London, 1850.

Marryat, Captain. A Diary in America, 1837-1838. 3 vols. London, 1839.

Martineau, Harriet. Society in America. 2 vols., 4th ed. New York, 1837.

Tocqueville, Alexis de. Democracy in America. 2d American ed. New York, 1838.

Trollope, Mrs. Frances M. Domestic Manners of the Americans. 2 vols. London, 1832.

Sturge, Joseph. A Visit to the United States in 1841. Boston, 1842.

Waylen, Edward. Ecclesiastical Reminiscences of the United States. London, 1846.

Wyse, Francis. America, Its Realities and Resources. 3 vols. London, 1846.

SECONDARY SOURCES

Abbott, Lyman. Henry Ward Beecher. Boston and New York, 1903.

Adams, Alice D. The Neglected Period of Anti-slavery in America, 1808-1831. Boston and London, 1908.

Addison, Daniel D. The Clergy in American Life and Letters. New York and London, 1900.

Atkins, Gaius G., and Frederick L. Fagley. History of American Congregationalism. Boston and Chicago, 1942.

Bacon, Leonard. History of American Christianity. New York, 1897.

Bailey, John W. Knox College. Chicago, 1860.

Bailey, Sarah L. Historical Sketch of Andover. Boston, 1880.

Baker, William B. The Life and Labors of the Rev. Daniel Baker. Philadelphia, 1859.

Barnes, Gilbert H. The Antislavery Impulse. New York and London, 1933.

Barnes, Gilbert H., and Dwight L. Dumond. ed. Letters of Theodore Dwight Weld, Angelina Grimké Weld and Sarah Grimké, 1822-1844. 2 vols. New York and London, 1934.

Barrows, John H. Henry Ward Beecher. New York, 1893.

Bates, Ernest S. American Faith, Its Religious, Political and Economic Foundations. New York, 1940.

Beardsley, Frank G. A History of American Revivals. 2d ed. New York, 1912.

—— A Mighty Winner of Souls, Charles G. Finney. New York, 1937.

Bennett, William W. Narrative of the Great Revival which Prevailed in the Southern Armies during the late Civil War. Philadelphia, 1877.

Billington, Ray A. The Protestant Crusade, 1800-1860. New York, 1938.

Birney, George H. The Life and Letters of Asahel Nettleton, 1783-1844. MSS, Hartford Theological Seminary, 1943.

Blau, Joseph L. Cornerstones of Religious Freedom in America. Boston, 1949.

Bonar, Andrew A. Nettleton and His Labours. 2d ed. Edinburgh, 1860.

Brastow, Lewis O. Representative Modern Preachers. New York and London, 1904.

Bronner, Frederick L. "The Observance of the Sabbath in the United States," Harvard Summaries of PhD Theses, 1937. Cambridge, Mass., 1938.

Brown, Charles R. They Were Giants. New York, 1934.

Buckham, John W. Progressive Religious Thought in America. Boston, and New York, 1919.

Burgess, John W. The Middle Period, 1817-1858. New York, 1901.

Caswell, Alexis. A Sermon on the Christian Work of the Rev. Francis Wayland. Providence, 1868.

Chace, George I. The Virtues and Services of Francis Wayland. Providence, 1868.

Cheney, Mary A. Life and Letters of Horace Bushnell. New York, 1880.

Cochran, William C. Charles Grandison Finney. Philadelphia, 1907.

Cole, Arthur C. The Irrepressible Conflict, 1850-1865. New York, 1934.

Commager, Henry Steele. Theodore Parker. Boston, 1936.

Commons, John R. History of Labor in the United States. Vol. I. New York, 1918.

Cooke, George W. Unitarianism in America. Boston, 1902.

Craven, Avery. The Coming of the Civil War. New York, 1942.

Cross, Whitney R. The Burned-over District. Ithaca, N. Y., 1950.

Curti, Merle. The Growth of American Thought. New York, 1943.

Davenport, Frederick M. Primitive Traits in Religious Revivals. New York, 1917.

Davis, Emerson. The Half Century. Boston, 1851.

Dexter, Franklin B. Biographical Sketches of the Graduates of Yale College. Vols. V and VI. New York, 1911, New Haven, 1912.

Dorchester, Daniel. Christianity in the United States. New York and Cincinnati, 1888.

Dumond, Dwight L. Antislavery Origins of the Civil War in the United States. Ann Arbor, Mich., 1939.

—— ed. Letters of James Gillespie Birney, 1831-1857. 2 vols. New York, 1938.

Dunning, A. E. Congregationalists in America. New York, 1894.

Eggleston, Edward. The Circuit Rider. New York, 1874.

Elsbree, Oliver W. The Rise of the Missionary Spirit in America, 1790-1815. Williamsport, Pa., 1928.

Fairchild, James H. Oberlin: The Colony and the College, 1833-1883. Oberlin, 1883.

Fish, Carl R. The Rise of the Common Man. New York, 1927.

Fletcher, Robert S. A History of Oberlin College from Its Foundation through the Civil War. 2 vols. Oberlin, 1943.

Foster, Frank H. A Genetic History of the New England Theology. Chicago, 1907.

Fowler, Philemon H. Historical Sketch of Presbyterianism within the Bounds of the Synod of Central New York. Utica, N. Y., 1877.

Fox, Early L. The American Colonization Society, 1817-1840. Baltimore, 1919.

Gabriel, Ralph H. The Course of American Democratic Thought. New York, 1940.

Gillett, E. Hall. History of the Presbyterian Church in the United States of America. Rev. ed., 2 vols. Philadelphia, 1864.

Gladden, Washington. Pioneers of Religious Liberty in America. Boston, 1903.

Goodykoonz, Colin B. Home Missions on the American Frontier. Caldwell, Idaho, 1939.

Grant, Helen H. Peter Cartwright: Pioneer. New York, 1931.

Greenblatt, William. Some Social Aspects of the Panic of 1857. Master's Essay, 1948, Columbia University Library.

Greene, M. Louise. The Development of Religious Liberty in Connecticut. Boston and New York, 1905.

Hall, Thomas C. The Religious Background of American Culture. Boston, 1930.

Hallock, William A. Light and Love, a Sketch of the Life and Labors of the Rev. Justin Edwards. New York and Boston, 1855.

Harlow, Ralph V. Gerrit Smith, Philanthropist and Reformer. New York, 1939.

Hawley, Charles. The History of the First Presbyterian Church, Auburn, N.Y. Auburn, 1865.

Headley, Phineas C. Evangelists in the Church. Boston, 1875.

Hibben, Paxton. Henry Ward Beecher: An American Portrait. New York, 1927.

Hills, Aaron M. Life of Charles G. Finney. Cincinnati, 1902.

Hough, Franklin B.   A History of Jefferson County in the State of New York.   Albany, 1854.
Hoyt, Arthur S.   The Pulpit and American Life.   New York, 1921.
Howard, Joseph.   Life of Henry Ward Beecher.   Philadelphia, 1881.
Johnson, F. Ernest, ed.   Wellsprings of the American Spirit.   New York, 1948.
Johnson, Oliver.   William Lloyd Garrison and His Times.   Rev. ed. Boston, 1894.
Keller, Charles R.   The Second Great Awakening in Connecticut.   New Haven, 1942.
Krout, John A.   The Origins of Prohibition.   New York, 1925.
Lacy, Benjamin R. Jr.   Revivals in the Midst of the Years.   Richmond, Va., 1943.
Lauer, Paul E.   Church and State in New England.   Baltimore, 1892. Johns Hopkins University Studies in Historical and Political Science, 10th series.
Leonard, Delavan L.   A Century of Congregationalism in Ohio.   Oberlin, 1896.
Little, Henry S.   Home Missions Heroes.   New York, 1904.
Lloyd, Arthur Y.   The Slavery Controversy, 1831-1860.   Chapel Hill, N. C., 1939.
Loud, Grover C.   Evangelized America.   New York, 1928.
Ludlum, David M.   Social Ferment in Vermont, 1791-1850.   New York, 1939.
McCartney, Clarence E.   Sons of Thunder.   New York and Chicago, 1929.
McComas, Henry C.   The Psychology of Religious Sects.   New York, 1912.
McCorkle, William A.   In Memoriam, a Discourse on the Life and Character of the Late Rev. George Duffield.   Detroit, 1868.
McMaster, John B.   A History of the People of the United States.   Vol. V.   New York and London, 1900.
Macy, Jesse.   The Anti-slavery Crusade.   New Haven, 1919.
Maffitt, Emma M.   The Life and Services of John Newland Maffitt.   New York, 1906.
Malone, Dumas.   Saints in Action.   New York, 1939.
May, Henry F.   Protestant Churches and Industrial America.   New York, 1949.
Mead, Edwin D.   Horace Bushnell, the Citizen.   Boston, 1900.
Mead, Sidney E.   Nathaniel William Taylor, 1768-1858, a Connecticut Liberal.   Chicago, 1942.
Mears, David O.   Life of Edward Norris Kirk.   Boston, 1877.
Mecklin, John M.   The Story of American Dissent.   New York, 1934.

Miller, Basil. Charles G. Finney, He Prayed Down Revivals. Grand Rapids, Mich., 1940.

—— God's Great Soul Winners. Anderson, Ind., 1937.

Miller, Perry. Jonathan Edwards. New York, 1949.

Mode, Peter G. Frontier Spirit in American Christianity. New York, 1923.

Moore, E. A. Robert J. Breckenridge and the Slavery Aspect of the Presbyterian Schism of 1837. Chicago, 1932.

Mowry, Arthur M. The Dorr War. Providence, 1901.

Mueller, George. The Life of Trust. Boston, 1864.

Munger, Theodore T. Horace Bushnell, Preacher and Theologian. Boston and New York, 1899.

Murray, James O. Francis Wayland. Boston and New York, 1891.

Myers, Alexander J. W. Horace Bushnell and Religious Education. Boston, 1937.

Nevins, Alan. Ordeal of the Union. 2 vols. New York, 1948.

Nichols, L. Nelson. History of the Broadway Tabernacle of New York City. New Haven, 1940.

Nichols, Thomas L. Forty Years of American Life, 1821-1861. 2 vols. London, 1864.

Norwood, J. N. The Schism in the Methodist Episcopal Church, 1844. New York, 1923.

Park, Edwards A. Memoir of Nathaniel Emmons. Boston, 1861.

Perry, Ralph B. Puritanism and Democracy. New York, 1944.

Pierce, Edward L. Memoir and Letters of Charles Sumner. 7th ed. Boston, 1893.

Purcell, Richard J. Connecticut in Transition, 1775-1818. Washington, 1918.

Rammelkamp, Charles H. Illinois College, a Centennial History. New Haven, 1928.

Randall, James G. Civil War and Reconstruction. New York, 1937.

Redford, Albion H. Western Cavaliers. Nashville, Tenn., 1876.

Rhodes, James F. History of the United States from the Compromise of 1850. Vol. I. New York, 1893.

Rosenberry, Mrs. Lois K. Mathews. The Expansion of New England. Boston and New York, 1909.

Ross, Harvey L. Lincoln's First Years in Illinois. Elmira, N.Y., 1946.

Rourke, Constance M. Trumpets of Jubilee. New York, 1927.

Rowe, Henry K. The History of Religion in the United States. New York, 1924.

Schlesinger, Arthur M., Jr. The Age of Jackson. Boston, 1946.

Schneider, Herbert W. The Puritan Mind. New York, 1930.

Seitz, Don C. Uncommon Americans. Indianapolis, 1925.

Siebert, Wilbur H.   The Underground Railroad from Slavery to Freedom. New York, 1899.

Spicer, Carl L.   The Great Awakening of 1857 and 1858.   Ohio State University Abstracts of Dissertations, Summer Quarter, 1935.   Columbus, 1936.

Sprague, William B.   Annals of the American Pulpit.   New York, 1857-1869.

Stevenson, Richard T.   The Growth of the Nation, 1809 to 1837.   Philadelphia, 1905.

Stokes, Anson Phelps.   Church and State in the United States.   3 vols. New York, 1950.

Stowe, Charles E.   Life of Harriet Beecher Stowe.   Boston and New York, 1899.

Stowe, Charles E. and Lyman B.   Harriet Beecher Stowe.   London, 1911.

Stowe, Lyman B.   Saints, Sinners and Beechers.   Indianapolis, 1934.

Strickland, Arthur B.   The Great American Revival.   Cincinnati, 1934.

Swaney, Charles B.   Episcopal Methodism and Slavery.   Boston, 1926.

Sweet, William W.   The American Churches, an Interpretation.   New York, 1947.

—— Makers of Christianity.   New York, 1937.

—— Religion on the American Frontier.   4 vols.   Chicago, 1931-1946.

—— Revivalism in America, Its Origin, Growth and Decline.   New York, 1944.

Tappan, Lewis.   The Life of Arthur Tappan.   New York, 1870.

Tawney, R. H.   Religion and the Rise of Capitalism.   New York, 1926.

Thompson, Ernest T.   Changing Emphases in American Preaching. Philadelphia, 1943.

Thompson, Noyes L.   The History of the Plymouth Church.   New York and London, 1873.

Thompson, Robert E.   A History of the Presbyterian Church in the United States.   New York, 1895.

Trumbull, Henry C.   My Four Religious Teachers.   Philadelphia, 1903.

Turner, Frederick J.   The United States, 1830-1850.   New York, 1935.

Tyler, Alice F.   Freedom's Ferment.   Minneapolis, 1944.

Visser 'T Hooft, William.   The Background of the Social Gospel in America.   Haarlem, 1928.

Walker, Williston.   The Creeds and Platforms of Congregationalism. New York, 1893.

—— A History of the Congregational Churches in the United States. New York, 1894.

Ward, Susan H.   The History of the Broadway Tabernacle Church. New York, 1901.

Waters, Philip M.   Peter Cartwright.   New York and Cincinnati, 1910.

Wayland, Francis Jr. and H. P. A Memoir of the Life and Labors of Francis Wayland. 2 vols. New York, 1867.

Weber, Herman C. Evangelism, a Graphic Survey. New York, 1929.

Weber, Max. The Protestant Ethic and the Spirit of Capitalism. Talcott Parsons transl. New York and London, 1930.

Wells, John M. Southern Presbyterian Worthies. Richmond, Va., 1936.

White, Henry A. Southern Presbyterian Leaders. New York, 1911.

White, James C. Personal Reminiscences of Lyman Beecher. New York, 1882.

Winslow, Ola E. Jonathan Edwards. New York, 1940.

Wright, George F. Charles Grandison Finney. Boston and New York, 1891.

ARTICLES IN CURRENT PERIODICALS

Bosworth, Mrs. L. A. M. "A Stormy Epoch, 1825-1850," Papers of the Ohio Church History Society, VI (1895), pp. 1-22.

Brackett, William O. "The Rise and Development of the New School in the Presbyterian Church in the U.S.A. to the Reunion of 1869," Presbyterian Historical Society Journal, XIII, Nos. 3 and 4, (Sept. and Dec., 1928), pp. 117-140, 145-174.

Brewster, H. Pomeroy. "The Magic of a Voice; Rochester Revivals of Rev. Charles G. Finney," Rochester Historical Society Pub. Fund, Series iv (1925), pp. 273-290.

Brown, William A. "Changes in the Theology of American Presbyterianism," American Journal of Theology, X (July, 1906), pp. 387-411.

Bryson, Gladys. "The Emergence of the Social Sciences from Moral Philosophy," International Journal of Ethics, XLII, No. 3 (April, 1932), pp. 308-323.

Burroughs, Wilbur G. "Oberlin's Part in the Slavery Conflict," Ohio State Archaeological and Historical Publications, XX, Nos. 2 and 3 April-July, 1911), pp. 269-334.

Chambers, M. H. "Rev. Peter Cartwright, D.D.," Transactions of the Illinois State Historical Society for the Year 1902, pp. 47-56.

Cole, Charles C. Jr. "The Evangelist as Theological Disputant," Ohio State Archaeological and Historical Quarterly, LXII, No. 3 (July, 1953), pp. 219-233.

—— "Finney's Fight Against the Masons," ibid., LIX, No. 3 (July, 1950), pp. 270-286.

—— "The Free Church Movement in New York City," New York History, XXXIV, No. 3 (July, 1953), pp. 284-297.

—— "Horace Bushnell and the Slavery Question," New England Quarterly, XXIII, No. 1 (March, 1950), pp. 19-30.

—— "The New Lebanon Convention," *New York History*, XXXI, No. 4 (Oct., 1950), pp. 385-397.

Dike, Samuel W. "A Study of New England Revivals," *The American Journal of Sociology*, XV, No. 3 (Nov., 1909), pp. 361-378.

Fletcher, Robert S. "Bread and Doctrine at Oberlin," *Ohio State Archaeological and Historical Quarterly*, XLIX, No. 1 (March, 1940), pp. 58-67.

—— "The Government of the Oberlin Colony," *Mississippi Valley Historical Review*, XX, No. 2 (Sept., 1933), pp. 179-190.

—— "Oberlin and Co-education," *Ohio State Archaeological and Historical Quarterly*, XLVII, No. 1 (Jan., 1938), pp. 1-19.

Francis, Russell E. "The Religious Revival in 1858 in Philadelphia," *The Pennsylvania Magazine of History and Biography*, LXX, No. 1 (Jan., 1946), pp. 52-77.

Gaddis, Merril E. "Religious Ideas and Attitudes in the Early Frontier," *Church History*, II, No. 1 (March, 1933), pp. 152-170.

Holmes, Fenwicke L. "A Pulpit Personality—Lyman Beecher," *Hartford Seminary Record*, XIX, No. 2 (April, 1909), pp. 113-126.

Johnson, Charles A. "The Frontier Camp Meeting: Contemporary and Historical Appraisals, 1805-1840," *Mississippi Valley Historical Review*, XXXVII, No. 1 (June, 1950), pp. 91-110.

Kull, Irving S. "Presbyterian Attitudes toward Slavery," *Church History*, VII, No. 1 (March, 1938), pp. 101-114.

Lyons, Adelaide A. "Religious Defense of Slavery in the North," *Historical Papers, Trinity College Historical Society*, Series xiii (1919), pp. 5-34.

Lyons, John F. "The Attitude of Presbyterians in Ohio, Indiana and Illinois toward Slavery, 1825-1861," *Journal of the Presbyterian Historical Society*, XI, No. 2 (June, 1921), pp. 69-82.

McGiffert, Arthur C. Jr. "Charles Grandison Finney," *Christendom, an Ecumenical Review*, VII, No. 4 (Autumn, 1942), pp. 496-506.

Mathew, W. S. "Peter Cartwright and His Compeers," *Methodist Review*, CIX, (1926), pp. 674-683.

Mead, Sidney E. "Lyman Beecher and Connecticut Orthodoxy's Campaign against the Unitarians, 1819-1826," *Church History*, IX, No. 3 (Sept., 1940), pp. 218-234.

Nichols, Robert H. "The Plan of Union in New York," *Church History*, V, No. 1 (March, 1936), pp. 29-51.

Pratt, Henry E. "Peter Cartwright and the Cause of Education," *Illinois State Historical Society Journal* (Jan., 1936), pp. 271-278.

Price, Robert. "The Ohio Anti-slavery Convention of 1836," *Ohio State Archaeological and Historical Quarterly*, XLV, No. 2 (April, 1936), pp. 173-188.

Rammelkamp, Charles H.   "The Reverberations of the Slavery Conflict in
    a Pioneer College," *Mississippi Valley Historical Review*, XIV, No. 4
    (March, 1928), pp. 447-461.
Roelker, William G.   "Francis Wayland, a Neglected Pioneer of Higher
    Education," *Proceedings of the American Antiquarian Society*, LIII
    (1944), pp. 27-78.
—— "Francis Wayland . . . President of Brown University," *Rhode
    Island Historical Society Collections*, XXXII (1939), pp. 33-55.
Southall, Eugene P.   "Arthur Tappan and the Anti-slavery Movement,"
    Journal of Negro History, XV, No. 2 (April, 1930), pp. 169-197.
Stimson, Henry A.   "The New England Theology, Its Historical Place,"
    Bibliotheca Sacra, LXXIX, No. 3 (July, 1922), pp. 301-309.
Staiger, C. Bruce.   "Abolitionism and the Presbyterian Schism of 1837-
    1838," *Mississippi Valley Historical Review*, XXVI, No. 3 (Dec.,
    1949), pp. 391-414.
Swing, Albert T.   "President Finney and an Oberlin Theology," *Biblio-
    theca Sacra*, LVII, No. 227 (July, 1900), pp. 465-482.
Vander Velde, Lewis G.   "The Diary of George Duffield," *Mississippi
    Valley Historical Review*, XXIV, No. 1 (June, 1937), pp. 21-34.
—— "Notes on the Diary of George Duffield," *ibid.*, pp. 53-67.
Zorbaugh, Charles L.   "The Plan of Union in Ohio," *Church History*,
    VI, No. 2 (June, 1937), pp. 145-164.

INDEX